Contents

KU-372-798

ACKNOWLEDGEMENTS

There are literally hundreds of people who contributed and assisted with this book, and without whom it would never have happened. Sadly there are constraints which prevent me from naming them all. Thank you to everyone who was involved, giving of their advice, information and time. I am very grateful. I would especially like to thank the three people who really saw me through the various degrees of drama that went with the production of this book. They are Sean Fraser, my long-suffering editor; Annlerie van Rooyen from Struik Publishers, who was there (who is *always* there) to restore some sense, direction and calm during the dramas that so often seem to accompany the production of a book; and finally Lesley Hay-Whitton, also from Struik, who is there, at the end, to pick up all the pieces. Thank you, thank you, thank you!

I would also like to thank the other members of the Struik team who were involved in putting the book together, as well as all the provincial tourism authorities throughout the country, the smaller regional tourism organisations, and the numerous individuals within those organisations, the many tour operators, and the countless communities and individuals involved in running cultural tourism projects in the country.

I would especially like to thank Cindy and Brett Rossini, in whose house I lived while writing, Craig Daniels, in whose house I live whenever I am in Durban, Pat and Roger de la Harpe for their constant friendship and encouragement, Karen Key from Cape Talk radio for all her contacts in the Cape, Rob Earle from the Free State for his friendship and assistance over the years and for all his contacts, the boys from Amadiba Adventures in the Eastern Cape, Lee Botha for her good company – as always – during the Klein Karoo leg of the journey, Steve and Monica Hilton-Barber in Mpumalanga and the Northern Province, and all my friends and colleagues in KwaZulu-Natal who, during the past four years, have helped me out countless times with information, contacts and good humour.

And a big thank you, of course, to my wonderful and supportive family. I am really grateful to every one of you.

Sue Derwent
August 1999

4

INTRODUCTION

While it is true that many visitors come to South Africa to see wild animals, it is equally true that most people coming to the country are hoping to find out what South Africans, as people, are really like. There can be few people who have not heard of apartheid, and many visitors are intrigued by our history and past politics. After all, South Africa is perhaps as famous for her turbulent past as she is for her wild animals, beauty and hospitality. But politics is only one small aspect of any culture. Many people believe that just about everything that happens in a country can be considered a part of its culture.

In a country such as South Africa, where there are 11 different official languages and people from any number of ethnic and cultural backgrounds, you could spend the rest of your life trying to find the definitive South African cultural experience. This book is an attempt to provide some guidelines to tourists, both foreign and domestic, to tour guides, both foreign and domestic, and to South Africans in general, many of whom, like myself, are reassessing, pondering, and newly discovering what it means to be a South African.

A book like this could extend to many hundreds of pages, and could take years to write. In order to keep it reasonable, I have tried to highlight some of the places or experiences which I believe might best represent certain aspects of the diverse cultures you are likely to find here. Just about anything could become an enthralling cultural experience if you open your eyes and your mind. The most obvious things people look out for when learning about a culture, are religious and other spiritual practices, art and crafts, music, rituals and ceremonies, architecture and the clothes people wear. But culture is also about what people do every day. Speak to people whenever you can. Find out what they think, how they feel, what they laugh about, what makes them angry. Culture can also be about educating children, shopping for food, ethics, dancing, working the fields, transport, earning a living, love and marriage.

All these things reveal something about the people. Smell the smells, look at the colours, hear the sounds. Look at the way people build and decorate their homes, how they respond to their environment, the way they do their hair, what they smoke or drink. Listen to the languages they speak and how they greet each other; these are the real 'cultural' experiences. Buy a local newspaper, chat to the owner of a small corner café, stop at a trading store on a dusty road, catch a minibus taxi, go to movies, wander around an upmarket shopping mall, drive into the country and stay with a rural farmer. It is in these places that you will find real South Africans going about their everyday lives, and it is here, perhaps, that you will discover and be able to enjoy an authentic encounter with South African culture.

South African tourism is developing fast, and there were many exciting and interesting projects with a cultural emphasis that, at the time of writing, were still in the planning and development phases. I am sorry that we were unable to feature them all, and, as you will discover on your travels, there are many well-deserving and exciting projects not featured in this book. But perhaps we can leave these for adventurous tourists to discover at their own pace and in their own context. After all, it can be fun to discover things for yourself. In fact, often the most rewarding 'cultural' experiences are those you come across quite by chance, such as travelling to a rural area and being invited to a traditional Zulu wedding where there are no other tourists, simply because you happen to be at the right place at the right time.

While I am sure there are circumstances where my choice of projects will appear rather subjective, I have tried my best not to stereotype places or people. But I am the first to admit that I, like all South Africans and, indeed, all people the world over, am a product of my own culture.

Some people find it easy to chat to strangers, in which case 'cultural experiences' can be found aplenty. But, for others who may not like interacting personally with people they do not know all that well, I have also tried to offer opportunities to get to grips with South African culture in a less interactive way, such as museums, concerts, festivals, markets and ceremonies.

From the outset, you will realise that I am biased about South Africa. I have travelled to many countries around the world, and, while I acknowledge that every country has its own share and type of beauty and interesting people, I firmly believe that few countries are quite as extraordinary as South Africa. Nor are they populated by such diverse, complex and fascinating individuals as you will find here.

South Africans are famous for their cultural diversity. They are crazy, gentle, athletic, stubborn, artistic, pioneering, violent, friendly, talented, warm and hospitable. Their complexities and contradictions and those of the environment are endless. But, to me, this only makes it more interesting and the visit more worthwhile.

The prospect of learning something about South Africans, their history and their culture, (perhaps one and the same thing?) is a daunting one, even for South Africans. This, after all, is Africa. The climate can be unpredictable and the distances are often vast, and while South Africans in general are hospitable and friendly, many of the most interesting people can be quite difficult to access. The reasons for this are numerous. One reason is rooted in the policies of apartheid, where groups of people were forcibly separated along racial lines, leaving many individuals with little or no idea about the religions, beliefs, culture and history of their fellow countrymen. Another reason is that some of the most interesting people often live in deep rural areas that are physically difficult to reach. Some are semi-literate or speak only their local language, with perhaps a smattering of English. Others live in places that are quite dangerous for outsiders or people from another racial group and some people are, perhaps quite justifiably in the South African context, just a little wary of outsiders.

In a way, these are the reasons for writing a book of this nature. I hope it will assist visitors and supply opportunities for those who want to come into contact with 'real' South Africans from all walks of life by providing guidelines to visiting venues of cultural interest.

In the end, I hope the book may be useful, not just to interested foreign visitors and their tour guides, but also in encouraging South Africans of all races to venture out of their comfort (or discomfort) zones and start learning a bit more about each other and, perhaps, even themselves.

DISCOVERING SOUTH AFRICA

BACKGROUND

South Africa has a total population of approximately 44.6 million people living in nine provinces. Before the general election in 1994, no African language had official status in South Africa, but now there are 11 official languages spread across an enormously diverse nation.

When the first settlers arrived in South Africa, the area was inhabited in many parts by the San (Bushmen). Today, these people live mainly in the Kalahari and remote areas of Namibia, eking out a precarious living from the land. There is, however, much evidence of their passing in the extraordinary rock paintings to be found in many parts of the country.

The precise reasons for the migration of black people down through Africa to the southern regions are not known, but many groups left their land further north to seek new homes and pastures in relatively unexplored territories. Those who settled in what is today South Africa are descended from four major groups that are again subdivided into nine distinctive ethnic groups. The Sotho comprise the North Sotho, the South Sotho and the Tswana. The Nguni comprise the Zulu, Xhosa, Swazi and Ndebele. The Shangaan-Tsonga can be found in the Gazankulu and Mpumalanga areas, while the Venda people live largely in the Northern Province.

Although the different groups have many common characteristics and each has its own traditional home area, the black population has spread throughout the cities, towns and rural areas of South Africa. In many of the rural areas, traditional customs are still part of day-to-day life and the ancient cultures and lifestyles continue to be nurtured. But, particularly among urban black South Africans, many traditions have been eroded largely due to contact with a highly industrial society and many traditional customs, once integral to African culture, survive only as tourist attractions.

Today there are approximately 34.3 million black, 5.4 million white, 3.8 million coloured and 1.2 million Asian South Africans living in the country. Plagued by a history of blind categorisation, many South Africans are understandably sensitive about being described in racial terms, but this is slowly changing. Sometimes it is necessary to be able to give a physical description of someone and, for visitors who feel awkward or unsure, there are some terms you may safely use without offending anyone. 'African' or 'black' generally refers to the Nguni, Sotho or other groups of people whose ethnicity belongs to this continent. 'Indians' and 'Asians' describe people whose origins go back mainly to India and the Far East. Those

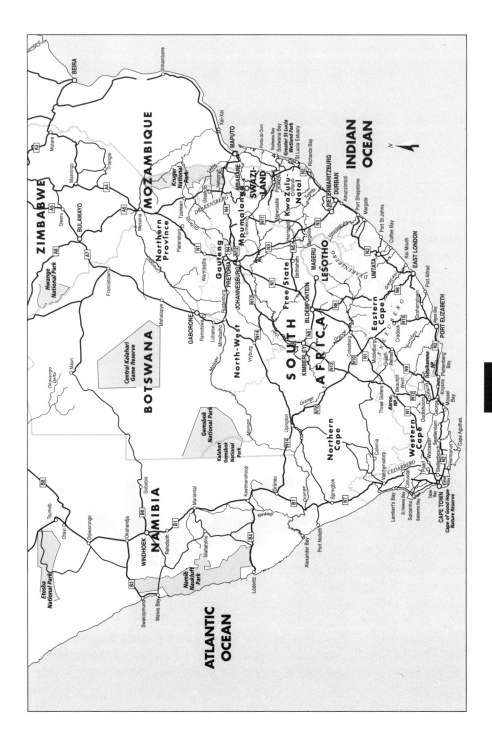

people with European origins are usually called 'whites', while 'coloured' is an accepted contemporary term for people of Indonesian, Malaysian or mixed origins. But, ultimately, almost all citizens would probably like to be known simply as 'South Africans'.

TRAVELLING IN SOUTH AFRICA

The best advice I ever had about travelling was 'expect nothing' – particularly if you are interested in people and their cultures. That way, everything will be new, everything will be an adventure and nothing will disappoint you. Pleasant experiences will be an additional bonus, and all the things you find difficult or unpleasant can be put down as part of your own personal experience of Africa.

Expectations reduce the joy of discovery which, after all, for many people, is what travel and learning about new cultures is all about. So, expect nothing and try to keep an open mind.

By all means, read and learn as much as you can about a country and its people before you visit, but remember too that things change; that is the nature of life, especially in Africa. If you are open to new experiences, you are far more likely to have a more authentic cultural experience than if you are blinkered by preconceived ideas.

There is a story of a European tourist who arrived in South Africa expecting to see all the vestiges of apartheid in place. Despite the fact that a new government had been in place for several years, she did not expect to see black and white South Africans socialising together. And, instead of appreciating that culture is always be in transition and that much progress has been made in the country, she was bitterly disappointed to discover that blacks and whites often mixed freely and generally got along rather well. Instead of delighting her, this ruined her entire holiday.

LANGUAGE

Since 1994, South Africa has had 11 official languages. Although Zulu is the language spoken as home language by the largest number of people, followed by Xhosa, and then Afrikaans – English is spoken, or at least understood, by the large majority of the population. Most people in urban areas speak English, but, in rural areas, this is not always the case. This means that, if you want to engage people in conversation, it might be an idea to take along a guide who can translate and interpret for you.

But try to learn a few words in an African language, even if it is just how to say 'hello', 'goodbye' and 'thank you'. It can be lots of fun, and the effort is always appreciated.

HIRING GUIDES

You may not want a guide with you every minute of every day, but there are circumstances where hiring a guide is advisable. If you are venturing into townships or rural areas – and I hope you do venture off the beaten track, because that is where you will often have the most astonishing cultural experiences – it is best to take someone with you who knows the local language and can help with directions. Many places are badly signposted if at all.

From a security point of view, it is essential to go with a guide into townships and certain off-the-beaten tracks areas. But it is also very rewarding to have someone with you who can explain exactly what is going on, why things are the way they are and what people are doing.

Within some sectors of the tourism industry, South Africa is still very much in its developmental stages. One sector is in the registering of guides. There are any number of really outstanding white guides registered with SATOUR. However, throughout the apartheid years, blacks were entirely excluded from tourism and this has resulted in a sad dearth of registered black tour guides. This is, however, changing, particularly since black tour guides are much in demand not only because of their access to certain localities and their command of local languages, but also because of their intimate understanding of their own culture.

For many blacks, though, it is still rather difficult to become registered. Often, a person may speak English well and have a fantastic way with tourists and wonderful stories to tell, but not have the finances to be trained, textbooks have not yet been translated into their language, or the syllabus requires them to learn vast amounts of irrelevant details. The tourism authorities are committed to dealing with these issues, but it will be some time before this is sorted out. In the meantime, do try to make use of the services of a registered

tour guide but be aware of the dynamics of the situation. In smaller centres or rural areas, it may be a good idea to ask at the local tourism information office for recommended local guides. The guides may not yet be qualified, but they will often be informative and interesting.

If you want to learn something about a particular culture, it is usually more interesting to go with someone from that background and locality.

Remember, too, that, by hiring guides, you are providing employment for people who may otherwise have no other possibilities of earning an income.

TIPPING AND DONATIONS

In formal situations such as restaurants, the standard international tipping guidelines apply in South Africa. Ten per cent of your bill is adequate but, if you have had exceptional service, you may want to add a little extra. However, in more informal situations, there is a great temptation to give money to poor people, especially children. Under no circumstances whatsoever should you give money directly to children. Rather ask your guide whether there is an institution in the area that is helping the people, or which may be able to put the money to good use, such as the local school or community development project.

SECURITY

South Africa has a high rate of unemployment and many people are poor. There is a high level of crime but, that aside, most South Africans are friendly and willing to help. It does not necessarily follow that, if people are poor, they are likely to steal: many of the poorest people are the most friendly and hospitable. But it does mean that, wherever you go, you should be aware that people may be desperate, and you should take reasonable precautions. Be sensible. If you are on the lookout for good cultural experiences, it is likely that, at some point, you will end up in poor areas, where the obvious rules apply. Do not carry wads of money, wear flashy expensive jewellery or leave valuables such as cameras, video cameras, and expensive equipment lying unattended. To even the most honest, hard-working but desperate person, your valuable possessions may prove a temptation too hard to resist. But, at the same time, don't be put off. Hundreds of thousands of people live happily and safely in this country, and most are friendly and delighted that outsiders will take the trouble to visit.

WHAT TO EXPECT

TOWNSHIPS

If you really want a sense of what South Africa is about, I would go so far as to say that a visit to a township is essential. I would strongly recommend, however, that you do not venture into any of the townships without someone who knows the area and the residents well. As one of the saddest legacies of apartheid, the townships are home to some of the country's most underprivileged citizens, who have seen some of the darkest years of their lives here, often in squalid conditions. Some of the townships, or at least sections

of townships, have never seen any serious violence, political or otherwise, and it is quite safe for you to visit, probably even without a guide. However, situations fluctuate, and it would be better to go with a tour group or a guide.

A list of recommended guides and tour operators can be obtained from the tourist offices in most of the major (and some of the smaller) urban centres.

SHEBEENS AND TAVERNS

The once illegal shebeens have become part of everyday life in South African townships. At one stage, black people were unable to drink in pubs or obtain liquor from regular outlets, which gave rise to South Africa's shebeen culture. Shebeens and taverns are run largely by township women (who, in traditional society, are the beer makers) and, when alcohol was outlawed in the townships, the women began to sell alcohol and often food from their homes.

Visitors are advised not to visit township shebeens and taverns unless accompanied by a professional tour operator or guide. Some shebeens and taverns are used to outsiders. However, like any place in the world where alcohol is consumed, there is always the possibility of a nasty incident. For this reason, it is not advisable to venture into townships after dark unless you are accompanied by a tour guide or a local.

CULTURAL VILLAGES

While I highly recommend a visit to a cultural village at the start of your visit, many people are highly critical of them.

Some people believe that their 'cultural' experience is diminished because it is not 'genuine' but rather orchestrated for the benefit of tourists.

This may be so but, in most cases, for tourists to access traditional rural African life can be extremely difficult indeed. Firstly, rural villages are dotted about in often inaccessible parts of the countryside. Where there are roads, they are often dirt roads and sometimes quite impassable in an ordinary vehicle. Secondly, many of the older and more traditional rural folk do not speak much English, and communication may therefore be extremely difficult.

Thirdly, travelling around in remote rural areas can be extremely dangerous if you are unaware of the political dynamics in certain areas. Finally, and perhaps most importantly, is the issue of the effects tourists have on rural indigenous cultures.

Many people believe that cultural villages do not reflect contemporary African culture and are, therefore, not 'authentic'. This may be true, but most of the so-called cultural villages will give you at least some historic background and an analysis of how practices are changing. This is most useful when travelling around rural areas. You will at least know what to look out for, and could be in a better position to understand what it is you are looking at. But cultural practices do change, and many people believe that one of the signs of a healthy culture is that it should be dynamic.

Unless you have time to travel into rural areas, it is unlikely that you will see many people in traditional dress unless you chance upon a ceremonial occasion. As a result, cultural villages allow visitors access to what may otherwise be inaccessible. Cultural villages also provide an extremely important function in that they are repositories of history, giving a living portrayal of activities, crafts and the way of life during a certain period in the history of a people that may otherwise be lost to modern society.

A third reason why some people disapprove of cultural villages is that they believe that they are exploitative, that employees are trotted out like performing monkeys for tourists and then herded away at night. But, while this may well have been the case in the past, these days there are many cultural villages where local people participate in the day-to-day management of the village even if it is a white-owned business concern. If you are uncomfortable about any of these issues, you may want to find out about the extent of local involvement in the management before you decide to visit a particular village, or how locals benefit from the existence of the village. Cultural villages may often be the only place of employment for the many unskilled rural people living in severely economically depressed rural areas. But in the end this should never be an excuse for a business to pay poor wages or exploit people.

MEETING THE PEOPLE

A good way to get to understand any culture is to spend time with the people. There is plenty of bed-and-breakfast accommodation throughout the country, but those in rural areas tend to be more personal. You may end up eating with the family, which is a wonderful way to hear the real inside stories about modern South Africa. Remember, though, that everyone has his or her prejudices or understanding of a situation, and these may not necessarily be based on fact, particularly when interpreting cultural practices of other people. Be sensitive to the situation. The country has undergone massive changes. Many white South Africans are still struggling to come to terms with the changes and, at the same time, there are many traditional black people who have had very limited exposuree to Western culture.

In South Africa, and in rural areas in particular, most forms of tourism experienced by rural people in the past have been of a fairly abusive nature. People were removed from their land with little or no compensation when many of the nature reserves were proclaimed. They have also been prosecuted for harvesting indigenous resources, such as marine life, trees and plants on which many of them rely for sustenance, while outsiders came in, trashed the place and then left behind mounds of litter. Try to be sensitive to other people's culture. While you may be on a quest for an 'authentic' cultural experience, you are impacting on the everyday lives of other people and your very presence in someone's home, or perhaps at a traditional ceremony, has consequences.

GAUTENG

About the province

In Sesotho, Gauteng means 'Place of Gold'. It is the commercial, financial and industrial heartland of the country. Home to 7.4 million people, it is the most densely populated of the provinces. Some 70% of South Africa's workforce is located here, producing 40% of the country's Gross Domestic Product. Soweto, famous in the liberation struggle, is close to Johannesburg, provincial capital and main point of entry for overseas visitors. Gauteng is home to Pretoria, South Africa's administrative capital and headquarters to most of the major mining, insurance, banking and financial institutions.

IN GAUTENG

- life seems so much faster than in other places in the country;
- gold is mined and money is made;
- houses are surrounded by walls and electrified fences;
- you will find Soweto.

This chapter

- **Johannesburg and Soweto:** One a financial powerhouse and the country's economic heartland, and the other the spiritual home of the resistance struggle.
- **Pretoria:** The administrative capital and seat of government.

JOHANNESBURG AND SOWETO

The Nguni name for Johannesburg is 'iGoli', appropriately derived from the word 'gold' because it was here, in 1886, that the news that gold had been discovered lead to the birth of what is today South Africa's largest, busiest and most cosmopolitan city. In less than a century, the dusty, frenzied mishmash of shacks, wagons, horses, buildings, diggings and gold-hungry men grew into the modern metropolis Johannesburg is today. But, although much as changed, much has stayed the same. The wagons and horses have long gone and some of the dust has settled, but it is still very much a place of buildings and frenzied activity based largely on the fortunes still sought by its people.

The southwestern township (known as Soweto), on the outskirts of Johannesburg, is the largest in Africa. It was also the seat of years of resistance against the apartheid government, where the youth and their parents took the struggle to the streets. The Soweto of today is vibrant, rich in cultural diversity and known throughout the world for the role it played in the downfall of the nationalist government.

Soweto and Johannesburg cannot exist without each other. Johannesburg is not only about money and Soweto is not only about riots. Both are about real people.

Most residents of Soweto are employed in Johannesburg's city centre and about 250 000 people commute by taxi and bus into the city everyday, while another 110 000 or so commute by rail.

Being a converging point for millions of people from diverse backgrounds, the greater Johannesburg area represents 'Africa at the crossroads'. It is a developing and transforming mix of Europe and Africa, Eastern and Western cultures, and there are endless opportunities for meeting people from all walks of life and getting to know how they feel about the land in which they all live.

TOWNSHIP TOURS

Soweto is possibly one of the best-known of all South Africa's townships, mainly because of the international media coverage it received during the student riots in 1976, when the youth protested against the poor facilities at 'black' schools, the inferior education they were receiving there, and the fact that Afrikaans was the language of instruction. This 'insurrection', in turn, led to massive repressions by the government – and violence broke out across the Witwatersrand.

Depending on your tour guide – it is always advisable to go with a guide – you will see either the stereotypical township squalor of an informal settlement and what many visitors imagine to represent the whole of Soweto, or you will see the wealthy splendour of the more affluent suburbs that few visitors – most white South Africans included – even know exist. A good guide will show you both sides,

and will take you to the main historical and political sites around the township.

Most township tours cover the tourist 'milk run' – the rather standard attractions to which tourists are inevitably taken. You will, however, find a few guides who will introduce you to the residents and offer a more intimate experience of township life – but this happens more often in township tours in other cities than in Soweto. There are also opportunities to stay overnight in some areas, but you will need to make prior arrangements with your tour guides.

Regina Mundi Church

This Catholic church is often considered the spiritual home of the freedom struggle because it was where political meetings, protest rallies and community gatherings were held during the apartheid era. It is the largest church in Soweto and the funeral services of many political victims were conducted from here, giving it great significance, not to only the people of Soweto, but also to those involved in the struggle throughout the country.

The tour around the church will show you the bullet holes in the ceiling and walls that were apparently fired by police from *inside* the church while trying to break up a meeting. There is also the broken altar railings behind which people crowded while trying to escape police and their dogs. In the church is a famous painting of a black Madonna that was donated to the church. There is also a small gallery, the Ma-Africa Art Gallery, and a shop where visitors can purchase local works of art (10% of the selling price goes to the church).

Hector Petersen Memorial Square

The Hector Petersen Memorial has been equated to the Vietnam Memorial in the USA, but, while it is not quite as elaborate, the sentiments it arouses in a number of visitors are often much the same. The memorial on the square consists of the small marble stone – bearing a brief inscription about Hector Petersen and the struggle for freedom – surrounded by large transport containers that act as a photographic gallery of events surrounding the 1976 riots. The photographs are powerful and heartbreaking. Hector Petersen, not yet a teenager, was the first child to be shot and killed by police at the start of the 1976 uprising. The students began a mass demonstration on 10 June 1976 and marched from Orlando High and Morris Isaacson schools towards Orlando West.

Nelson Mandela's Home

Said Nelson Mandela of his four-roomed Soweto house: 'For me, Number 8115 in Orlando West was the centrepoint of my world, the place marked with an X in my mental geography. It is the only home I ever knew as a man before I went to prison.' And it is this home to which he returned for 11 days after he was released from 27 years of incarceration.

Usually historic homes that have been converted into museums belong to people who are long since deceased; it is rather a strange sensation to be wandering around the home and looking at the possessions of people who, even though they now live elsewhere, are still alive. Nevertheless, it is fascinating to visit this tiny home, filled as it is with original furniture and other mementoes, including family photographs, certificates, letters and gifts given to Mandela and his former wife, Winnie.

A tour guide is on hand to relate the stories of police harassment, danger, bullet holes, bombs and ultimate triumph. Each room has a story to tell. On the bed in the tiny bedroom is the kaross (garment of skins) that caused controversy when Mandela wore it during his trial. There are also various pairs of boots and shoes – as if to symbolise the 'long walk to freedom', with a story behind each pair. The house is being 'upgraded' as a tourist venue, with a restaurant in the small back yard that may – or may not – detract from the authentic feel of the house.

Winnie Madikizela-Mandela's Home

Winnie Madikizela-Mandela was once known as the Mother of the Nation for all the work she did during the apartheid years and when her husband was incarcerated by the apartheid government. While still popular among a large sector of the population, she has been dogged by scandal and rumours. Many notorious events are purported to have taken place at her plush Soweto home. Visitors cannot enter the house, because she still owns it and is often in residence, but most tours drive past and will fill you in on the details.

Bishop Tutu's Home

Another drive-past visit is the former home of Archbishop Desmond Tutu, which is not open to the pubic. Bishop Tutu is perhaps best known for his outspoken views on human rights, his vigilant campaign against apartheid, and the work he has done to help the people of South Africa. A good guide will fill you in on the details of his many achievements and awards. Today, the Archbishop – once the head of the Anglican faith in South Africa – is most acclaimed as one of the country's Nobel Peace Prize winners and as Chairman of the Truth and Reconciliation Commission.

Freedom Square

It is at this spot in Kliptown that the African National Congress (ANC) adopted the Freedom Charter that set out the organisation's aims to establish justice in the country. Hundreds of volunteers had worked tirelessly, approaching groups throughout South Africa to assess and formulate the demand for a free and democratic South Africa. Their views were all incorporated into the Freedom Charter and, on 26 June 1955, the Congress of the People – which was attended by 2 884 delegates and 7 000 spectators – adopted the underlying principles of the African National Congress. Freedom Square has been declared a National Heritage Site, but there is, as yet, no commemorative plaque.

Avalon Cemetery

This cemetery is the historic resting place of famous political activists, including Helen Joseph, Joe Slovo and Lilian Ngoyi. If you are with a tour, the guides will usually give you time to wander around the gravestones.

Morris Isaacson High School

Many of the preparations for the 1976 demonstrations were made at this school, and students marched from here to the police station before they were confronted by troops at the start of the 1976 riots. Some of South Africa's prominent political leaders were educated here. The school has emerged from a history of sub-standard 'Bantu' education, and now stands proud in an area that today includes 261 primary schools, 64 secondary schools and 75 crèches. Generally, a tour will take you past the school, but, if you are interested in visiting to chat to the staff and pupils, you will need to make prior arrangements with your guide.

Chris Hani Baragwanath Hospital

'Baragwanath' is the largest hospital in the southern hemisphere – but is also the only one serving the hundreds of thousands of people of Soweto and surrounding communities. Named, in part, after Chris Hani, a popular leader during the liberation struggle who was assassinated by right-wing fanatics shortly before the 1994 democratic elections, Baragwanath was once a military hospital, but has grown into a massive general hospital with some of the most advanced medical facilities in the world. It is possible to tour the hospital, but prior arrangements need to be made with your tour guide.

Shebeens and Taverns

The busier, more popular or well-known tour operators tend to take visitors to shebeens or taverns that are used to the tourist trade (and charge accordingly). So, if you want a more authentic experience, you need to enquire beforehand to find out what you can expect on your tour.

MUSIC AND DANCE

There are 15 theatres and any number of clubs or music spots in and around Johannesburg. These venues cover the widest range of music, so be sure to consult the local press (such as *The Star*) or ask at tourist information centres.

There are far fewer venues for traditional dance performances, so your best bet is to visit a cultural village (*see* page 22) and Gold Reef City (*see* page 23), although, during peak holiday seasons (over Easter and Christmas), hotels may provide traditional dance exhibitions for their guests and a visit to a working mine may coincide with a performance by mine dancers (*see also* page 153).

Finally, while it may seem that many dances are laid on purely for tourists, the dances are quite authentic and the performances much the same as they would occur in the rural areas from which many of the dancers come.

The Market Theatre Complex

In 1975, a small group of dedicated actors scraped together enough money to save the run-down Edwardian market hall from demolition. Today, the old Indian produce market has become the biggest of the complex's theatres, and the surroundings have been transformed into a vibrant cultural showcase, where you can find fine art galleries, buy good food and browse in the busy flea market. The Market Theatre itself has played a significant role in the development of indigenous theatre and has provided an outstanding platform for many of the country's top playwrights and actors.

Kwaito

This local mix of Rhythm & Blues and American Hip-Hop is the most popular party music among young people in South Africa – and is fast attracting worldwide recognition. *Kwaito* – sometimes referred to as d'gong – has strong European, American and Jamaican reggae influences but, rolled together, it is uniquely South African. The electronically programmed backbeat – with dance beats chanted or sung – is combined with lyrics that incorporate street slang and local languages to give it a thoroughly local vibe. Some claim that the name *kwaito* is derived from the 'Amakwaitos', a group of gangsters, while others say it is ghetto music that takes its name from the Afrikaans slang word 'kwaai', meaning that 'the music is hot and the people are kicking.' Colourful, vibrant, trendy, controversial and fast, *kwaito* is considered a youth sound, and is guaranteed to have people dancing in seconds. Some of the big-name *kwaito* groups include Bongo Maffin, Skeem, Abashante, TKZee and Boom Shaka, and may be seen at venues such as La Frontiere in Hillbrow, Planet Hollygroove and Tandoor in Yeoville, Insomnia in Randburg, and Synergy in Orange Grove.

The Civic Theatre

Slightly more of a mainstream venue than the Market Theatre, the Civic hosts productions of ballet, children's theatre, drama and musicals. The complex incorporates three small venues and the main theatre, one of the most technically advanced in South Africa. A popular attraction is the backstage tour – where visitors may well bump into some of the performers or catch a glimpse of their rehearsals.

Kippies Jazz Club

Kippies Jazz Club – or 'Kippies', as it is affectionately known by locals – is named after the legendary saxophonist Kippie Morolong Moeketsi. Live Jazz in this intimate bar keeps the Johannesburg locals going until late into the night and is a great spot to meet a cosmopolitan crowd. It is managed by well-known South African musician Sipho 'Hotstix' Mabuse.

Witwatersrand National Botanical Garden Concerts

These wonderful open-air music concerts are held on alternate Sundays between May and August, with performances by a variety of musicians and choirs and an emphasis on popular, light classical and modern music. Johannesburg families take their picnic baskets and enjoy an afternoon out on the lawns during the balmy winter months.

Club 707i

This club, in Orlando West, Soweto, caters for the glamorous, black yuppie crowd, and makes a change from the mainstream clubbing that dominates the city. A good place to hear *kwaito* (*see* box on page 19).

Roxy Rhythm Bar

The 'Roxy' has become somewhat of a household name in the northern suburbs of Johannesburg, and is a showcase for good South African bands.

The Bassline

This lively venue in Melville – open seven days a week – boasts great live jazz bands, blues and drumming.

Da Flava

Da Flava in the city centre is the place to rub shoulders – literally, as it is very popular and always pumping – with the young black party crowd. The music here is largely *kwaito* and hip-hop.

MUSEUMS AND GALLERIES

There are a number of museums and galleries in Johannesburg. Once again, watch the local press for calendars of events, or ask at the publicity and tourist information centres (*see* page 31).

Newtown Cultural Precinct

The site of the Newtown Cultural Precinct, between Chinatown, the Oriental Plaza and Diagonal Street in the city centre, was built in the early 1900s as the Indian produce market. While some of the buildings have been demolished and new ones built, some of the original buildings were converted into the Market Theatre Complex. Today, the old produce market houses the Market Theatre Complex (*see* page 19) and the old fruit market is now MuseumAfrica (*see* below). Kippies Jazz Club (*see* page 20) was once the old Victorian public toilets. Although the area around the Newtown Cultural Precinct is part of an urban renewal plan, security still poses a problem at certain times of the day and night (particularly during weekends). This should not deter you from visiting this usually busy part of town, but do take care with your valuables and drive with your car doors locked at all times.

MuseumAfrica

The museum includes the Bensusan Museum of Photography, the Museum of South African Rock Art and the Geological Museum. The focus is on the people of southern Africa and their heritage – from the Stone Age to the present. There are some innovative and fun displays featuring the country's complex political, social and geographic histories. The Johannesburg section features models of Tswana and San (Bushmen) people, squatter camps and township shebeens.

The Museum of South African Rock Art

The San left us with a priceless and unique artistic heritage consisting of thousands of Stone Age paintings and engravings on the walls of caves, cliffs and overhangs throughout the country. Their art depicts not only the lives of the hunter-gatherer communities, but also offers some insight into the spiritual world of the San. The museum boasts some unique original paintings and engravings, and a replica of a rock cliff on which are explained many aspects of rock art.

Bensusan Museum of Photography

The development of photographic technology during this century is indeed fascinating, and is a subject covered by the Bensusan Museum, which is more than just a collection of old cameras – although those are here too. Make a point of seeing the amazing special effects demonstrating the intriguing properties of light, shadow and colour in 'Alhazen's Light House'.

The Geological Museum

Display cases are crammed with rocks, fossils, gems and minerals, some of which are fluorescent and glow in their cases. There is also an interesting exhibit covering South Africa's geological formations and a display of the history of gold and prospecting in South Africa.

The Bernard Price Institute's (BPI) Museum of Palaeontology

This small museum is the only one in South Africa dedicated entirely to fossils. On view are some of the most important fossils of prehistoric reptiles, mammals and dinosaurs discovered in southern Africa. A special feature includes a fossil preparation laboratory where visitors can watch a technician preparing fossils for identification and research.

The Bleloch
Museum of Minerals

The Bleloch Museum has a collection of more than 50 000 mineral and rock specimens that reflect southern Africa's mineral wealth. There are also fascinating displays of crystallography, South African stratigraphy and economic and physical geology.

The Johannesburg
Art Gallery

Among the many treasures that are housed in the Johannesburg Art Gallery, situated in the middle of the busy city centre, are works by Picasso, Rodin, El Greco, Henry Moore and Van Gogh. The valuable prints collection contains work by Rembrandt, Whistler and Toulouse-Lautrec. South African, African and traditional art are well represented. Look out for the work of Walter Battiss, Willie Bester, Karel Nel, Gerard Sekoto and Jackson Hlungwani (see also page 47). There is an active education facility and the guided walks conducted around the gallery are most interesting.

The Everard Read
Gallery

Everard Read is well known for its regular exhibits of contemporary art. It also sells paintings and sculpture by leading South African and overseas artists.

The Soweto
Art Gallery

The gallery supports works by local artists and includes works by Benjamin Macala and Duke Ellington Ketye.

The Goodman Gallery

The work on view is generally by contemporary South African artists.

The Gertrude Posel
Gallery

This well-known gallery, situated at the University of the Witwatersrand, has permanent collections which include The Standard Bank Collection of African Art. The focus here is on traditional Southern, Central and West African art.

CULTURAL VILLAGES

The Sibaya

'Sibaya' is the Zulu word for 'cattle kraal', and this cultural village in Johannesburg provides a historical view of Zulu people, including some background on Shaka, the warrior king, and his rise to power. There are explanations of the dress, housing and traditions of the Zulu people from the early days to the present, and on offer are traditional food and beer – and the opportunity to learn some Zulu dance steps (which is not as easy as it looks).

MONEY
AND MINING

Much of the fast-paced lifestyle of Johannesburg has developed as a result of the discovery of gold in the area over a 100 years ago. Money continues to play an important part in the character of the city, which has become well known on the world's financial, industrial and commercial circuits. It is also has a reputation as the place to do business in Africa.

Johannesburg Stock Exchange

As the financial capital, a visit to the Johannesburg Stock exchange may give you some idea as to what makes the people of Johannesburg tick. In South Africa, Diagonal Street means the Stock Exchange and it seems quite appropriate that you tour this money marketplace where investors buy and sell shares. It is fascinating to watch the bustling activity on the trading floor on a busy day when hundreds of thousands of shares are traded – and where fortunes are made and lost in a matter of seconds.

Diamond Cutting

The Erikson Diamond Centre and Jewel City Mynhardts are two places where you can take an educational tour through the diamond-cutting process. The Diamond Centre outlines the history of diamonds in South Africa, and you can watch the manufacture, design and settings of the gems and also see a video about the stone that has played such an integral role in the economy of the country. You may also purchase gold and diamond jewellery at reasonable wholesale prices.

Gold Reef City

This historical theme park is on the site of Crown Mines in the west of Johannesburg, which – until it ceased production in 1975 – was the world's richest gold mine. There are tours down into the underground mine, a chance to see gold being poured, as well as a most impressive coin press – apparently one of oldest in the world.

Gold Reef City tells the story of gold and the people of bygone times who first mined it. It has become one of Johannesburg's main tourist attractions – and some may find it rather commercial in character – but it continues to draw thousands of visitors a year. Apart from the reconstructed town, with its tin-roofed houses and shops and old-world setting, this is a good place to see traditional dancing from all around the country, including the miners' gumboot dancing (see also page 153). There is usually also a *marimba* band playing.

The Gold Claims

When gold was first discovered on what became known as the Main Reef on the farm Langlaagte in 1886, people raced to the area in the greatest gold rush of all time. George Harrison, who had discovered the outcrop of gold-bearing reef, went off to Pretoria to report his claim and, within days, the then Transvaal Republic was inundated with a population of speculators and workers. About 600 stands were surveyed on the ground that became known as Johannesburg, and were sold by public auction in 1886. The first stand on offer was where Pritchard and Diagonal streets meet today. Although there is nothing to mark the spot, a commemorative plaque is apparently being planned.

ARCHAEOLOGY

Melville Koppies

Melville Koppies (hills), today surrounded by Johannesburg's residential areas, were used by various African peoples for thousands of years – long before white settlers arrived. Stone Age sites date from the time of the hunter-gatherers. Iron Age farmers and miners left behind ruins of stone-walled villages and ancient smelting furnaces. There are two smelting sites to visit and a number of trails and hikes through the hills. The Melville Koppies site is generally not open to the public, but can be visited by prior arrangement with the Delta Environmental Centre (see page 32).

Sterkfontein Caves

Sterkfontein Caves are one of South Africa's most valuable palaeontological sites and could shortly be declared a World Heritage Site by the United Nations Educational, Scientific and Cultural Organisation (UNESCO). The caves became known throughout the world when, in 1947, Robert Broom discovered the skull of *Australopithecus africanus*, a hominid that lived in Africa between three and one million years ago. The skull became known as Mrs Ples and confirmed Sterkfontein's status as a treasure trove for palaeontologists. More than 600 hominid fossils have since been discovered in the caves.

Tours into the caves are in some places physically arduous, but the thrill of knowing the secrets to understanding human ancestry that lurks in the depths of limestone and dolomite makes it all worthwhile. There are also wonderful stalactites and stalagmites to be seen. The caves have not yet been developed for tourism – which, for now, may be a pleasant advantage as they remain largely untouched and have not been too commercialised.

The Robert Broom Museum

The Robert Broom Museum, or Sterkfontein Caves Museum, is dedicated to the palaeontology, geology and archaeology of the world-famous caves, and provides comprehensive and up-to-date displays on human evolution. The museum also runs guided tours of the fossil-rich caves where Mrs Ples was found.

The Sterkfontein Caves Museum

See The Robert Broom Museum above.

Wonder Caves

Wonder Caves are only a 30-minute drive from Johannesburg and not far from the Sterkfontein Caves. The caves, which have been dated at 2.2 billion years, boast spectacular rock formations. Like Sterkfontein, Wonder Caves have not been developed for the tourist market – there are few facilities – although guided tours are offered every day of the week.

PRETORIA

About 26% of the population of the country lives within a 200-kilometre radius of Pretoria. The city has long been an administrative centre of the country – even in the days of the Voortrekkers who left the Cape and trekked across the country in protest against British regulations, finally arriving in the region during the 1850s. Pretoria, known as the 'Jacaranda City' because of the masses of beautiful jacaranda trees that burst into flower during spring, developed around Church Square and has spread out from there. It was here, in

Pretoria, at the Union Buildings, that Nelson Mandela was inaugurated as the country's first democratically elected president on 10 May 1994.

MUSIC AND DANCE

State Theatre

The State Theatre is regarded by many as the centrepiece of culture in Gauteng, not only because of the variety and quality of productions performed there, but also because of the theatre building itself. It is indeed massive, and is equipped with some of the most modern lighting and sound equipment around. There is a 1 300-seat opera house and 88 dressing rooms, and no expense was spared in fitting out the immense foyers in grand style. A full calendar of opera, ballet, drama, choral and symphony concerts are staged throughout the year. In the dark years of apartheid, it came to symbolise the Nationalist government and Afrikanerdom, and was considered to be rather conservative in its approach to the performing arts. Today, however, it is much more open to alternative and experimental theatre.

Live Music

There are a number of venues in Pretoria where you can hear South African musicians perform. However, because the venues seem to change hands often – and, with it, the programme – be sure to check the local newspapers, or ask at the Pretoria Tourism Information Centre (see page 32). A few of the better-known and most popular 'live' venues are:

- Bootleggers, which offers a variety of live music;
- CrossRds Blues Bar, which is known for its good live jazz (and, sometimes, blues);
- Camel Tavern, whose music is best described as 'live and loud'.
- Upstairs at Morgan's is most popular for its parties (hosted by DJs), but may occasionally feature good live bands.

MUSEUMS AND GALLERIES

Tswaing Crater Museum

'Tswaing' means 'place of salt' in the Tswana language, and it is still known by many as 'the Pretoria Saltpan'. The main feature of the Tswaing site is the 220 000-year-old meteorite impact crater, one of the youngest and best-preserved small, bowl-shaped meteorite impact craters in the world. Because of its unique variety of ecosystems and its international and historical importance, the site – about 40 kilometres north of the city – is currently being developed as a protected site in consultation with representatives of some of the more than a million people who inhabit the surrounding settlements.

It is thought the site was first used by humans over 800 years ago when the early Tswana-speaking people, the Moloko, arrived and began mining the salt, which is still saleable. For most of the 20th century, soda-ash from the site has been used to provide alkali used in the mines.

There are both guided and self-guided excursions to the crater and surroundings.

These include a visit to displays – either at the museum or on site – depicting aspects of the crater, the culture of the people of the area, and other aspects of Tswaing's natural and cultural history, seeing Tswaing's indigenous cattle (similar to Nguni cattle) and walking the Crater Trail. The latter can take a couple of hours and is the only walking trail in a meteorite impact crater in the country. Other popular attractions include the excellent bird-watching opportunities and a floral paradise of about 420 species.

Pretoria Art Museum

Pretoria Art Museum has an outstanding collection of some of South Africa's great artists, amongst them Walter Battiss, Anton van Wouw and Pierneef, and is in the process of acquiring new works by exciting contemporary artists. In order to encourage a greater appreciation of South African fine art, the museum stages regular exhibitions, lectures and guided tours. Tapestries, sculptures, graphics, photographs and ceramics are among the museum's collection of more than 3 000 pieces.

Transvaal Museum

A large elephant from Maputaland (lying between the Maputa River and Swaziland) dominates the entrance to the Transvaal Museum in Pretoria; outside in the garden stands the gigantic skeleton of a whale.

The museum tells visitors the story of the evolution of the country and its flora and fauna, starting with the development of the tiny organisms that were to evolve into reptiles. Among the popular displays are the exhibits on ancestral fish, such as sharks – reconstructions based on fossil tooth finds – and reptiles, including a showcase on dinosaurs.

The displays on the development of humankind include fossils, life-sized reconstructions and models of ape-men – and an impressive gorilla. Alongside is an exhibit on whales (including dolphins) found in the southern oceans. Finally, there is a good collection of birds arranged according to *Roberts' Birds of Southern Africa*, with an audio-visual showing the birds and recordings of their calls.

Pioneer Open-air Museum

This small museum gives a delightful depiction of Voortrekker farm life in the early part of the century. Although it is used predominantly for educational purposes by school groups, it is also open to other visitors. There is a humble farmhouse of the type used by the earliest of white settlers in the Pretoria district, and the furnishings, household items and farming implements give visitors an idea of the tenacity and resourcefulness of the early pioneers. There are regular demonstrations of many of the now almost forgotten domestic skills and, if you visit on the appropriate day, you will be greeted with the aromas of freshly baked farm bread – baked in an original outdoor clay-and-fire oven – and the strong bitter coffee that is ground on the premises. Butter is churned, soap is boiled and jam is cooked.

The little farmhouse was built in 1840 and is the typical thatched white-washed cottage of its day, with walls constructed from a mixture of earth, the soil from ant heaps and dung, with the dung-smeared floors polished with river stones. There is also an old watermill, threshing floors and stables, and live farm animals roam about the yard.

CULTURAL VILLAGES

Some of the region's well-known cultural villages are within easy reach of Johannesburg and Pretoria, even though many are actually in Mpumalanga and the Northern Province rather than in Gauteng. These cultural villages offer some insight into the lives of the Ndebele, siPedi, Sesotho, Tswana and other groups living in the central and northern parts of the country.

The Ndebele originate from two major groups: the Ndzundza, who make up approximately 90% of the Ndebele, and the Manala. The Ndzundza, more commonly known today as the Southern Ndebele, have settled in the Highveld to the northeast of Pretoria, while the Manala – or Northern Ndebele – have, as a result of their close association, become integrated with the Northern Sotho people.

The Southern Ndebele have been the subject of much interest and research for a number of decades, mainly because of their artistic nature which has found expression and developed into an art culture of remarkable ingenuity and vitality. They are, perhaps, most famous for their beadwork and the large painted murals that cover the walls of their traditional mud dwellings. The striking dress of Ndebele women cannot be mistaken for that of any other indigenous group within southern Africa. As with many of Africa's indigenous peoples, Western civilisation has had tremendous impact on the Ndebele lifestyle, distinctive clothing and unmistakable style of decorative visual art.

There is, however, a good chance that the Ndebele's artistic skills will not disappear altogether as the rural women, with their typical creative dexterity, are adapting many of their traditional skills towards more commercial applications to help them earn an income. There are numerous cultural villages in the northern provinces of the country where a visitor can still experience some of the historic aspects of this fascinating culture, but, even with the onslaught on their traditional culture, many of the customs still exist beyond these cultural villages – as a drive through the rural countryside will reveal.

Kgodwana Cultural Village and Siyabuswa Village

In recent years, Ndebele home-building has seen the introduction of rectangular buildings and corrugated iron sheeting – rather than the traditional building methods and materials such as thatching grass on round homesteads of the past. The reasons for these changes are explained at Kgodwana. Visitors may wander around – with or without a guide – and see demonstrations of early construction methods, and watch Ndebele people go about their daily lives.

As with most of the Ndebele cultural villages, there is a strong emphasis on the arts and craftwork and here it is still possible to see women weaving. This craft is fast becoming a dying art among the Ndebele, who no longer use domestic articles such as woven storage containers or sleeping mats as widely as they used to. The women also painstakingly thread beads to make items such as the *nyoga* – the woven beaded train worn by a bride at her wedding – and the unusual *linga koba*, or 'long tears', consisting of two narrow strips of woven beading worn hanging down on each side of the head. Look out for the beaded dolls or *uphophi* (derived from the Afrikaans word, 'pop', for doll) that were once presented to young women as fertility charms. Nowadays, much of the symbolic value of many of these items has been lost to commercialisation, and they have become increasingly representational.

But this only serves as testimony to the creative abilities of the rural Ndebele women to adapt their skills and to cross the threshold of the world in which they live in order to find ways of generating an income that will help them and their families survive.

The Kgodwana cultural village is a commercial enterprise, so you may want to visit Siyabuswa near Weltevreden. Because Siyabuswa is the real village where some of Kgodwana's Ndebele actually live, the staff at Kgodwana can make the necessary arrangements – but they will need to be informed in advance. Siyabuswa is also the royal homestead of King Mayitjha and is constructed in the typical style of the Ndebele. Visitors are able to walk around the outside of the homestead, but guests are not allowed to wander around on their own. The nearby Catholic church was painted by Francina Ndimande, a famous Ndebele mural artist, and her family. The village is the home of Francina and a number of other well-known artists and, for a truly authentic experience, you may be able to visit them in their homes.

Mapoche Ndebele Village

This small village is a part of the Tswaing Crater Museum (*see* page 25). Unless you already have some background to Ndebele traditions and culture, it is advisable to take a guided tour, but there is no need to book because people live here permanently. This is your opportunity to meet the chief, and the craftworkers who produce traditional beadwork and clothing.

MONUMENTS

The Democracy Wall

The commemorative Democracy Wall was commissioned for the Kutlawang Democracy Centre in Pretoria and has become a symbol of South Africa's human creativity and the reconstruction of the country. Walls have, throughout history, been symbols of protection and division and, in this context, the Democracy Wall includes all the elements of what walls have been and continue to be to South Africans. At the same time, it is an acknowledgement that African building styles are a form of architecture and not simply the 'uncivilised dwellings' they were perceived to be by many Westerners in the past.

Sculptor Neels Coetzee, working in collaboration with others, has symbolically combined the natural elements of earth, water and air with features of both ancient and contemporary walls. Featured in the wall are cement *dolosse* (that were invented by a South African engineer and are used as stabilisers in harbours throughout the world), granite boulders, semicircular structures reminiscent of rural corrugated-iron water tanks, porcelain electric insulators, as well as organic materials such as wooden fencing. A visit to the limestone quarry on Robben Island also served to inspire the artist to commemorate the island's significance in the wall. Indigenous plants have already taken root on the site. A blackboard – known as the Early Settler Blackboard – has been established, with space for passers-by to make their mark on the wall.

Union Buildings

The Union Buildings – designed by Sir Herbert Baker, whose distinctive style can be seen in hundreds of buildings around the country – have served as the seat of government since Pretoria became South Africa's administrative capital in 1910. Baker chose a site above the city with sweeping views over a natural amphitheatre, and used local sandstone, indigenous stinkwood panelling, and tiles from Vereeniging. Many consider the Union Buildings to be the crowning work of all Baker's achievements in Africa, and it was here that Nelson Mandela was inaugurated as president on 10 May 1994.

The buildings are closed to the public, but the formal terraced gardens are open. They are spectacular in spring when the flowers are in bloom, when they are probably the most photographed location in the city. This was also the venue of the presidential inauguration and the performance of the famed Three Tenors (Carreras, Domingo and Pavarotti) who sang here in celebration of South Africa's freedom.

Voortrekker Monument and Museum

Much has been said and written about this great monolith. To some, it is a cherished memorial to Afrikanerdom, while to others it represents everything negative about the country's turbulent history. The original purpose of the monument was to commemorate the Great Trek of the late 1830s. The Voortrekkers, the name given to those who participated in the Great Trek, were mostly white farmers who left the Cape to escape the increasing English influences. They trekked across the country from the relative safety of the coastal areas into an interior, which at the time was dominated by black Africans. During the 1940s, when the Afrikaner-dominated National Party gained control of the country and started institutionalising racial segregation, the monument became an icon of oppression to many.

The massive granite cenotaph, on raised ground with beautiful views all around, symbolizes the final resting place of Piet Retief – his actual grave is in KwaZulu-Natal (*see* page 170) – and other Voortrekkers who died during the Great Trek. Perhaps the most impressive feature is the Hall of Heroes, with its ripple-patterned floor and great domed ceiling. Inside is a frieze –

apparently the largest marble frieze in the world – featuring highlights of the Great Trek, including the massacre of Retief and the ensuing Battle of Blood River (*see* page 178). Outside is a bronze statue of a Voortrekker woman and her children, and encircling the monument is a wall of 64 covered ox-wagons cast in terrazzo.

The museum contains Voortrekker memorabilia, including guns, an ox-wagon, farming tools and cooking utensils. There is also a magnificent set of tapestries embroidered by nine needlewomen who took eight years to complete the piece.

At precisely midday on 16 December every year, a shaft of light penetrates the dome and falls directly on the symbolic depiction of Piet Retief's grave. The monument was apparently built in such a way that this happens only once a year, and is a truly remarkable phenomenon.

PLACES TO STAY

The Ring-Wagon Inn
(Die Ring Ossewaherberg)

Overlooking the Hartbeespoort Dam, just outside Pretoria, lies an unusual inn high up in the Daspoort hills. The 'inn' consists of the largest private collection of renovated ox-wagons in the country, representing the period between 1840 and 1940, and guests may actually overnight in the wagons, six of which have been converted into 'chalets'. While these ox-wagon chalets are somewhat more up-market than the originals may have been (they have en-suite bathrooms), it gives some idea what it was like for the Voortrekkers who trekked across the African bushveld in these wagons. Backpackers are accommodated in a converted double-decker bus.

GAUTENG
GENERAL
Tourism Johannesburg, Village Walk Shopping Centre, Maude Street, Sandown 2196; tel: (011) 784-1355, fax: (011) 883-4035
Gauteng Tourism Agency, tel: (011) 355-8040/8049
Johannesburg Metropolitan Tourism, tel: (011) 33-7665

JOHANNESBURG
TOWNSHIP TOURS
To visit the **Regina Mundi Church**, the **Morris Isaacson High School** and the **Chris Hani Baragwanath Hospital**, consult a tour operator rather than trying to arrange a visit on your own.
Imbizo Tours, PO Box 25031, Ferreirasdorp 2048; cell: 083 700 9098, tel: (011) 787-0914 (a/h); fax: (011) 781-1564
Moratiwa Tours, PO Box 31881, Braamfontein 2017; tel: (011) 869-6629
Jimmy's Face to Face, Budget House, 130 Main Street, Johannesburg 2000; tel: (011) 331-6109, fax: (011) 331-5388

MUSIC AND DANCE
The Market Theatre Complex, corner Bree and Wolhuter streets, Newtown, Johannesburg, 2001; PO Box 8656, Johannesburg 2000; tel: (011) 836-1648, fax: (011) 492-1235, e-mail: publicity@market.theatre.co.za
The Civic Theatre, Loveday Street, Braamfontein 2001; PO Box 31900, Braamfontein 2017; tel: (011) 403-3408, fax: (011) 403-3412
Kippies Jazz Club (see Market Theatre Complex above), tel: (011) 833-3316
Witwatersrand National Botanical Garden Concerts, end of Malcolm Road, Roodepoort; tel: (011) 958-1750

Club 707i, Orlando West, Soweto; tel: (011) 936-1591
Roxy Rhythm Bar, 20 Main Road, Melville 2092; tel: (011) 726-6019
The Bassline, 7 Seventh Street, Melville 2092; tel: (011) 482-6915
Da Flava, 22 Claim Street, Johannesburg 2001; tel: (011) 333-1961

MUSEUMS AND GALLERIES
Newtown Cultural Precinct, Bree Street, Newtown 2001; tel: (011) 838-4563
MuseumAfrica, Bree Street, Newtown 2001; tel: (011) 833-5624, fax: (011) 833-5636
Museum of South African Rock Art, Bree Street, Newtown 2001; tel: (011) 833 5624, fax: (011) 833-5636
Bensusan Museum of Photography, Bree Street, Newtown 2001; tel: (011) 833-5624, fax: (011) 833-4536
The Geology Museum, Bree Street, Newtown 2001; tel: (011) 833 5624, fax: (011) 833-4536
The Bernard Price Institute's (BPI) Museum of Palaeontology, Van Riet Lowe Building, East Campus, University of the Witwatersrand, Johannesburg 2001; tel: (011) 716-2727, fax: (011) 403-1423
Johannesburg Art Gallery, Klein Street, Joubert Park; PO Box 23561, Joubert Park 2044; tel: (011) 725-3130, fax: (011) 720-6000
Everard Read Gallery, 6 Jellico Avenue, Rosebank 2196; tel: (011) 788-4805, fax: (011) 788-5914
Soweto Art Gallery, Victory House, corner Commissioner and Harrison streets, Johannesburg 2001; tel: (011) 836-0252, fax: (011) 836-0252
Goodman Gallery, 163 Jan Smuts Avenue, Parkwood 2193; tel: (011) 788-1113
Gertrude Posel Gallery, Senate House, Main Campus, University of the Witwatersrand, Johannesburg 2001; tel: (011) 716-8032, fax: (011) 716-8030

GAUTENG DIRECTORY

CULTURAL VILLAGES

The Sibaya, Hugo's Place, Main Road, Kyalami 1684; PO Box 545, Rivonia 2128; tel: (011) 468-1196, fax: (011) 468-2657

MONEY AND MINING

Johannesburg Stock Exchange, (17) Diagonal Street, Johannesburg 2001; tel: (011) 377-2200

Jewel City Mynhardts, 240 Commissioner Street, Johannesburg, 2023; tel: (011) 334-2693

Cullinan and Diamond Mine Tours, Grace Masanga, P O Box 429, Cullinan, 1000; tel: (012) 734-0260

Gold Reef City Tours, Number 14 Shaft, Northern Park Way, Ormonde, 2159; tel: (011) 496-1600

ARCHAEOLOGY

Melville Koppies, contact Delta Environment Centre, Private Bag X6, Parkview 2122; tel: (011) 888-4831, fax: (011) 888-4106

Sterkfontein Caves and **Robert Broom Museum**, Kromdraai Road, Krugersdorp North 1741; tel: (011) 956-6342

Wonder Caves, tel: (011) 957-0106

PRETORIA
GENERAL

Pretoria Tourism Information Centre, Tourist Rendezvous Centre, corner Vermeulen and Prinsloo streets, Pretoria; PO Box 440, Pretoria 0001; tel: (012) 308-8900, fax: (012) 308-8891

MUSIC AND DANCE

State Theatre, corner Prinsloo and Pretorius streets, Pretoria; tel: (012) 322-1655, fax: (012) 322-3913

Bootleggers, 60 Glenwood Road, Lynnwood Glen 0081; tel: (012) 47-2025

CrossRds Blues Bar, The Tramshed, Van der Walt Street, Pretoria; tel: (012) 322-3263

Camel Tavern, Hilda Street, Hatfield 0083; tel: (012) 342-6655

Upstairs at Morgan's, 1st Floor, Burnett Centre, Burnett Street, Hatfield 0083; tel: (012) 362-6610

CULTURAL VILLAGES

Kgodwana Cultural Village, Private Bag X4030, Kwamhlanga 1022; tel: (013) 92-0894, fax: (013) 93-3138

Mapoche Ndebele Village, tel: (012) 341-1320, fax: (012) 341-6146

MUSEUMS AND GALLERIES

Tswaing Crater and Museum, PO Box 295, Soshanguve 0164; tel: (012) 790-2302, cell: 082 458 4862

Pretoria Art Museum, PO Box 40925, Arcadia 0007; tel: (012) 344-1807

The Transvaal Museum, 432 Paul Kruger Street, Pretoria 0001; tel: (012) 322-7632, fax: (012) 322-7939

Pioneer Open-air Museum, PO Box 28088, Sunnyside 0132; Church Street, Silverton 0184; tel: (012) 803-6086, fax: (012) 803-5639

MONUMENTS

Democracy Wall, corner Prinsloo and Visagie streets, Pretoria.

Union Buildings, Zeederberg Street, Pretoria.

Voortrekker Monument and Museum, PO Box 1595, Pretoria 0001; tel: (012) 326-6770

PLACES TO STAY

Ring-Wagon Inn, PO Box 178, Hartbeespoort 0216; tel: (012) 259-1506, fax: (012) 259-0200

32

MPUMALANGA

About the province

Mpumalanga is the Swazi and Zulu word for 'the place where the sun rises'. Parts of the province are dramatically beautiful with magnificent mountains, waterfalls and forests, but Mpumalanga is probably best known as Big Game Country. It borders the Kruger National Park (see page 52) and there are dozens of privately owned game reserves, nature reserves and sanctuaries teeming with wildlife. There are many legends (and evidence) of the earliest inhabitants of southern Africa, the small, mystical San (Bushmen), as well as the Ndebele, Pedi, Swazi, and Shangane people, all of whom have settled in the area today known as the province of Mpumalanga. There are also tales of big-game hunters in the Lowveld, fortune-seekers panning for gold in mountain streams, and colourful pioneers who helped settle the wilderness.

IN MPUMALANGA

- Jock of the Bushveld, a tough little Staffordshire bull terrier, became famous and was immortalised in Percy Fitz-Patrick's book of the same name;
- gold diggers came in their swarms to seek their fortunes;
- crocodiles may still be found in rivers outside game reserves.

This chapter

- **Nelspruit** The provincial capital.
- **Lydenburg**
- **Ohrigstad**
- **Pilgrim's Rest**
- **Waterval-boven and Waterval-onder**
- **Sabie**
- **Hazyview**
- **Barberton**
- **Lowveld Excursions**
- **Botshabelo**

NELSPRUIT

Nelspruit is the capital of the province of Mpumalanga and is a typical, fast-growing, rapidly urbanising town in the centre of a major agricultural region, growing tropical and subtropical fruits.

The town itself may not have too many 'cultural' events to attract the tourist, but this is where the majority of Mpumalanga's residents go to shop or conduct business and, from this perspective, it can be interesting to visit.

TOWNSHIP TOURS

There are few opportunities to tour one of Nelspruit's townships, but it can be done, although there are no 'official' tours as yet. The best way to arrange a township tour is to speak to the Nelspruit Tourist Information Office in advance (see page 44), and they will organise one of the black tour operators to assist you. The tour operator may take you to visit a township, meet some of the locals and possibly have a meal with family and friends. There are also opportunities to stay in the area after dark and to have a drink at a local shebeen or tavern.

MARKEтS

A number of markets sell virtually any-thing, from locally made art and crafts to a wide range of fresh farm products. Flea markets are held at the Promenade Centre and at Hall's Gateway. Hall's farm-stalls can be found throughout the province and are well known for their fresh farm products, such as fruit juice, dried fruit, jams and pickles.

The roads of the town are also lined with traders selling a colourful mix of avocados, paw-paws and bananas and there are a number of curio stalls on the way in and out of the town. These vendors sell items such as handmade rugs, carvings, bead-work, basketry and leather goods.

Riverside
Government Complex

In the new Riverside Government Complex, local rural crafters have been working on a 40-metre-long, three-metre-high embroidered and beaded mural that will cover the interior walls of the main centre building. This project involves 60 women – 30 Swazi and 30 Ndebele – who are telling the story of Mpumalanga from about 1 million BC right up until 1999, through documenting the political, social and mythological history of the region in the form of embroidery and beadwork. This is a magnificent and beau-tiful piece of work and really needs to be seen to be fully appreciated.

Nelspruit Civic Centre

Another place in Nelspruit to see the work of local artists is the permanent collection of South African art at the gallery in the Nelspruit Civic Centre. The gallery has its own section within the Civic Centre, and is well known for its collection of indigenous art. There is a permanent display of estab-lished artists, and a number of changing exhibitions that include a variety of fine arts, from painting to sculpture.

тᴏURS
AND EXCURSIᴏNS

Nelspruit Historical Trail

The Nelspruit Historical Trail winds through the town from the Promenade Centre to the Civic Centre and takes about an hour on foot. The trail looks at various aspects of Nelspruit's past, and in the library gardens is an original ox-wagon that has been restored.

LYDENBURG

In the late part of the 19th century, the town of Lydenburg was the capital of one of the old Boer republics, De Republiek Lydenburg, which later joined forces with the South African Republic (ZAR). But Lydenburg's history stretches back far fur-ther than a mere 100 or so years – there is evidence of volcanic activity in the form of the Mtololo Volcanic Pipes that date back 2 000 million years. Although the site is not really geared toward the tourist, it is indeed possible to see the volcanic pipes, which are located at the end of Voortrekker Street in Lydenburg.

MUSEUMS AND GALLERIES

Lydenburg Museum

The Lydenburg Museum has its own distillery and offers visitors the chance to taste mampoer, an alcoholic drink similar to brandy or schnapps that was made by the Voortrekkers (see page 29). Other exhibits include Stone Age artefacts that date back 1.5 million years. The museum also celebrates the arrival of the Pedi people and the Voortrekkers to the area, tells the story of six wars and depicts the Lydenburg of today.

A visit to the Lydenburg Museum not only gives visitors a rare glimpse into local history and indigenous culture, but also the opportunity to see one of the most remarkable archaeological finds ever to have been unearthed in Africa, the Lydenburg Heads. In 1957, Ludwig von Bering was just a young boy when he first discovered pieces of the now famous Lydenburg Heads in the hills that dotted his father's farm. He later developed a keen interest in archaeology and, between 1962 and 1966, he frequently went back to the site, collecting pottery shards that were later found to be pieces of seven clay heads. This, however, was only discovered when Bering attended the University of Cape Town as a medical student and became a member of the archaeological club. He had discovered and collected not just pottery shards, but also iron and ostrich-egg-shell beads, copper bands and pieces of bone. The heads were carbon-dated to AD 490 and are thought to have been sculpted by early Iron Age people. Similar pieces of clay heads were later found in the Sabie region. Although the purposes of the heads are obscure and one can only speculate what they may have been used for, it is thought that they were probably employed in a common cultural ritual, perhaps relating to initiation ceremonies. It is also thought that the heads probably represented certain African religious concepts and would, in all likelihood, have been hidden or destroyed during a burial. Copies of the two large heads and five smaller ones are on display at the museum.

OHRIGSTAD

HISTORICAL AND ARCHAEOLOGICAL SITES

Echo Caves

Echo Caves have not been as well developed for tourism as, for example, the Sudwala (see page 39) or Cango Caves (see page 110) – and this may indeed be part of their charm. The caves are rather lovely and the guides – some of whom are working part time to complete the practical year of their diploma in nature conservation – are both knowledgeable and enthusiastic. Many do not receive salaries (the caves are privately owned) but rely on the tips they receive from tourists, so, if they do a good job, feel free to tip generously. The caves served, at various stages of their history, as refuge for people fleeing from wars or from Boers and within

3

the caves are burial sites. There are also 'musical' stalactites, which people would beat with sticks, sounding a warning to the cave inhabitants of approaching danger. The paths in the caves are rather muddy and the lighting is not great, but the caves (and the tour guides) have a charm of their own.

The Museum of Man

Just down the dirt road from Echo Caves is a smaller cave in the side of the mountain, which has been turned into The Museum of Man. There are enormous sculptures and a few San artefacts, but because the museum is an open-air exhibition – and there is usually no one on guard at night – many of the pieces have been stolen from here and some of the sculptures have fallen into disrepair.

PILGRIM'S REST

In 1873, gold was discovered in the hills around what is today known as Pilgrim's Rest. The ensuing gold rush led to the establishment of a mining village perhaps best known for its fine wood-and-iron architecture, much of which is preserved today. The little boom town has been maintained and is considered to be of special importance because it depicts early gold-mining techniques and represents some of the socio-economic conditions that prevailed in the region at the time. However, delightful as it is, Pilgrim's Rest is rather a tourist trap. Busloads of tour groups arrive – usually over lunch

time – and on weekends the village fills with souvenir hunters. Still, it is worth a visit as it is the only village in the country to have been declared a national monument in its entirety.

The village snuggles in a deep green valley, and wood-and-iron miners' houses stretch along for about two kilometres on either side of the road. In all, there are six museums, a Victorian hotel, galleries, coffee shops and restaurants visited by thousands of people every year. But, in many ways, this is perhaps not unlike the old days when the town of Pilgrim's Rest was the centre of the madness of the gold rush. In its heyday, about 1 400 diggers lived here, along with storekeepers, hoteliers, prostitutes, bankers, transport riders and the other usual desperadoes and dreamers one would expect to find in places like this.

MUSEUMS AND GALLERIES

The Diggings Site Museum

Soon after alluvial gold was first discovered in Pilgrim's Rest, hopeful diggers rushed to the little valley to peg their claims. The Diggings Site Museum reveals the life and times of those often foolhardy, but adventurous, men and women who came in search of their fortune.

The site relates the history of life on the diggings, from the original tent dwellings to the more durable dwellings of wattle and daub, and reflects how prosperous storekeepers and businessmen began to establish the mining town by erecting structures of timber and corrugated iron. There are also displays of the various mineral extraction methods.

Alanglade House Museum

This beautiful colonial home served as the official residence to the Pilgrim's Rest mine manager. Surrounded by mountains and shady forest, Alanglade is situated just a few kilometres out of town and was occupied by a number of mine managers until 1972 when mining activities at Pilgrim's Rest ceased. The house is today furnished with objects from the early 20th century, reflecting a 'modern' Edwardian approach. The design of the house is simple, yet harmonious and was inspired by the work of the famous South African architect, Sir Herbert Baker.

Prospectors' Trail Network

This two-day trail extends from Pilgrim's Rest and follows a route along which you will see a number of old diggings, cocopan paths, historical railway paths, old mines, rivers and streams – all remnants of a bygone era. There is sufficient time to enjoy the surroundings as well as to stop at the various shops, museums and even Pilgrim's Rest's famous little pub. The trail is a great way to get a real feel for the place and certainly beats the more usual tour-bus experience. The trail starts either at Pilgrim's Rest or at Morgenson and is a relatively easy walk, following a circular route, and covering about 20 kilometres over the course of two days.

Joubert's Bridge

Look out for this sturdy little five-arch bridge spanning the Blyde River and marking the northern end of the village. The structure was erected in 1896 and named after the Republic's mining commissioner, JS Joubert.

Pilgrim's Rest and Sabie News

An interesting little building in the village once housed the offices of the *Pilgrim's Rest and Sabie News* and today boasts a number of exhibits relating to the turn of the century. On display are a few interesting old printing presses, typewriters and even some early newspapers. The Old Print Shop next door sells books – and the inevitable souvenirs.

Dredzen Shop Museum

By the late 1930s, there were sixteen general dealers in the village of Pilgrim's Rest – apart from the butcheries, bakeries and blacksmith shops. The Dredzen Shop Museum is representative of the typical general dealer store at Pilgrim's Rest between 1930 and 1950, a period that saw Pilgrim's Rest at its busiest.

HISTORICAL AND ARCHAEOLOGICAL SITES

Pilgrim's Rest Cemetery

Of the 320 known graves in the historic Pilgrim's Rest Cemetery, only 163 are marked with headstones. The different nationalities of the people who lie buried here reflect not only the cosmopolitan character typical of the Pilgrim's Rest gold-fields, but also life on the diggings, with accidents and disease the main cause of death. The oldest marked grave is that of Bazett Jervis Blenkins who died when he was crushed by a large boulder on his claim on 12 June 1874. There are also a number of children's graves, as many children died from drowning, snake bites, pneumonia and dysentery.

WATERVAL-BOVEN AND WATERVAL-ONDER

These historic little villages are so named because one is situated above (boven is the Dutch word for 'above') a really beautiful waterfall and the other below (onder) the Elands River Falls. An old steam train runs between the two villages every Sunday, stopping off at the waterfall and various other spots along the way.

Nzasm Tunnel

One of Waterval-Boven's main tourist sites is a historic tunnel constructed by the Nederlandsch Zuid-Afrikaansche Spoorweg Maatschappij (NZASM) at the request of President Paul Kruger. The tunnel was to serve the once-famous Eastern Line that was to run from Kruger's South African Republic to the sea at what was then known as Lourenço Marques (now Maputo), capital of Mozambique). Kruger was determined to have his own corridor to a port and, because of complications

encountered on the section of the line that ascended from the Lowveld up the Drakensberg escarpment, it was decided to build a line up the slopes of the Elandsberg, between Waterval-Onder and Waterval-Boven. Special locomotives were needed to hoist the coaches up such a steep incline – 208 metres over seven kilometres with a gradient of 1:20 in some places. A four-kilometre railway was constructed along this spectacularly scenic route, parts of which may still be seen near the eastern end of the tunnel where there is a lovely picnic spot overlooking the magnificent 228-metre Elands River Falls. The tunnel itself is 400 metres long and was finally completed in 1883 – and then abandoned in 1908 when a new line was constructed. Guides – the best are those who have been trained by the Mpumalanga Tourism office – are available to walk visitors through the tunnel. A short distance from the tunnel is another national monument, a sturdy five-arch bridge made of dressed stone. The bridge once carried the Eastern Line right across the precipitous gorge of the Dwaalheuwel Spruit.

Krugerhof

When the British forces approached Pretoria during the Anglo-Boer War in 1900, the government of the South African Republic moved to Machadadorp, but the area's climate aggravated President Kruger's ill health, so he relocated to Waterval-Boven – and the other members of the executive committee were forced to travel every day by train to discuss state affairs with him. Krugerhof became the residence of President Paul Kruger, and the little house still stands today. It is a pretty little home and there are plans to develop it further for the tourist market.

SABIE

Sabie Forestry Museum

The village of Sabie – the name is derived from the Shangaan *uluSaba*, meaning 'fearful' – in the foothills of the Drakensberg was established in 1895, and is surrounded by some of the largest manmade forests in the country. Nearby is the largest saw-mill in South Africa, so a visit to the Sabie Forestry Museum will give you some insight into the lives of the people who settled in the area following their dreams of a fortune in gold or timber. Part of the museum covers the development of forestry in South Africa, but the more interesting sections are the many fascinating exhibits depicting the countless uses and wonderful properties of wood. Interactive displays in the museum include a demonstration of the musical qualities of wood and another showing a 'talking tree' that tells the story of the evolution of the tree.

HAZYVIEW

CULTURAL VILLAGES

Shangane

Shangane village is situated near Hazyview, midway between the Blyde River Canyon and the Kruger National Park. As the name suggests, it deals mainly with the culture and tradition of the Shangaan. The village has been blessed by the local elders. Daytime tours depart from the bustling African market – which forms the centre of the village where local craftspeople work and trade – and wind through the fields to the home of a Shangaan family. Visitors are invited to experience the family culture and learn about their way of life. The midday tours are slightly longer, and visitors are able to see the famous Shangaan dancing, drink *byala* (homebrewed beer) and share a traditional meal with the family.

But, if you really want the full treatment, it is best to attend the evening festival which, although it may be put on purely for the benefit of the tourists, is entertainment at its traditional best. As the sun begins to set behind the mountains and the countryside gently settles for the night, the drums start up and a torch-lit procession arrives at the homestead of Chief Shoshangana. The choirs sing, the people dance and storytellers tell the story of the Shangaan people. It really does send shivers up your spine. But the evening is far from at an end – the chief's family serves a feast and the festivities continue long into the starry night.

HISTORICAL AND ARCHAEOLOGICAL SITES

Sudwala Caves and Cultural Village

Although the whole of the Sudwala complex, which consists of the famous Sudwala Caves, the Dinosaur Park and the Sudwala Kraal complex, has been specifically developed with the tourist market in mind, it has been done well; the kraal particularly retains the feel of Africa to a large extent. The caves are some of the oldest in the world, and it is possible for visitors to venture deep down into the bowels of the earth and see the wonderful crystal chambers and numerous formations of stalagmites and stalactites. Stone Age man once made his home in these caves, which were also used later during the battles between the Swazi and various other groups residing in the area during the 19th century. Tours of the caves, which include walking through great columns of dripstone formations, with names such as 'Screaming Monster', 'the Rocket Silo' and 'the Weeping Madonna', last about an hour and a half.

The kraal consists of a number of exquisitely crafted traditional African homesteads, which can be visited during the daily scheduled tours. The focus is on the Nguni people – Zulu, Swazi and Ndebele – and it is fascinating to compare the styles of building and customs of each group, which hail from the same cultural or linguistic background. At the entrance to the village is an *isivivane*, or stone cairn, upon which inhabitants traditionally throw a rock in order to ensure a safe journey.

MEETING THE PEOPLE

River Bend
Cottage

The Bucklands of River Bend Cottage have a lovely bungalow attached to their house that overlooks the forests, where they offer great bed-and-breakfast accommodation. The couple are very active in the local community, and, since they have lived in the area for some time, they are able to fill visitors in on what life is like in the Lowveld.

An added advantage is that the Bucklands grow their own coffee, and spend many of their evenings roasting and grinding the beans on the premises. The coffee is quite outstanding and makes a really wonderful gift to take home. Their home is not far from the tar road between Hazyview and Sabie.

BARBERTON

The town of Barberton developed after the discovery of gold in the area in 1884, but, by 1888, the boom was over and there was a mass exodus of disappointed fortune-seekers. Today the town is still small, but there are many reminders of the early days of the gold rush.

MUSEUMS AND GALLERIES

A number of Barberton's beautiful old houses have been converted into museums that evoke those long-gone mining times. Belhaven, which is one of the town's most elegant old buildings, is furnished in the style of a wealthy Edwardian family home. Fernlea House and Stopforth House are both now also museums.

In town, look out for the statue of Jock, the famous little Staffordshire terrier who was made famous in a book by Percy FitzPatrick, *Jock of the Bushveld*.

LOWVELD EXCURSIONS

ARt AND CRAFtS

Mpumalanga seems filled with small roadside craft shops, artists' studios and galleries. The Department of Arts and Culture has been working closely with black artists and crafters to set up formal centres from which their work can be sold. But this does not mean that the work is more expensive. In most cases, quite the contrary. The province has a large rural community, people who have few formal qualifications and even fewer chances of employment. To work as an artist and crafter offers women in particular an opportunity to earn their own living and, in some cases, to do so from home, which means that they can still take care of their families. Five centres have so far been established: two are up and running, while the others, although operational, are still in developmental stages. These centres are assisted by staff from the Department of Arts and Culture as part of their commitment to assisting the poorer sectors of the Mpumalanga community while, at the same time, enhancing cultural tourism experiences. Supporting local artists is one of the ways in which these traditional craft forms are kept alive. In most circumstances, craft here is sold wholesale and all the money goes directly to the crafter or artist. Many crafters work on the premises, while others work at their rural homes, from where the work is collected and transported to the centre to be sold.

Many of the products you are likely to find at these centres are replicas of the items once made traditionally by the people in the area – such as dancing sticks and leather aprons – while other products may be modern functional items made using traditional crafting methods.

Matsulu

One of the biggest of the craft centres is Matsulu – an enormous, beautifully thatched Swazi dome – along the N4 on the way to the Kruger National Park's Malelane entrance gate. While the centre is a place to find some excellent indigenous craftwork, there is also a fine art gallery, where local up-and-coming young artists are encouraged to show their work. This is an ideal opportunity both to peruse, as well as perhaps purchase, some authentic South African art. Matsulu has also just opened a small restaurant and, as part of a project to encourage young artists, a number of locals were given the task of designing and building a chair, all of which are now in use and on display at the restaurant. The restaurant also serves variations of traditional food.

Manzana

The Manzana craft centre (the name means 'healing water' – a reference to the nearby healing spa at Badplaas) is not as 'upmarket' as Matsulu, but it has been developed along the same principles. It also consists of a large thatched Swazi dome and boasts both a craft centre and gallery. Manzana is perhaps geared more for the domestic tourist rather than the foreign tourist, but the work is of the same good quality.

Makuleke

The Maluleke people were forcibly removed from their traditional land in 1969 during the apartheid years. This piece of land was finally returned to the Maluleke in May 1998 after their land claim was settled in their favour. The land – which lies between the Limpopo and Luvuvhu rivers in the Pafuri Triangle near the Kruger National Park's Punda Maria gate – will be co-managed by the South African National Parks Board for the next 50 years, in order to develop it as a conservation area.

There are plans afoot for lodges, craft centres and other wildlife- and tourism-related initiatives on this land, all of which will eventually benefit the local people as well as conservation and tourism.

MONUMENTS AND MEMORIALS

The Machel Memorial

Although this small memorial site situated near Mbuzini Village on the Mozambique border is far from just about anywhere else, it is a place of great significance for both the South Africans and Mozambicans living in this area. Near this site the late Mozambican president Samora Machel died when his aeroplane crashed into the hills. Despite the remoteness of the area, there are plans afoot to develop the region for cultural tourism, and the South African and Mozambican governments have decided to construct a memorial to the late president whose widow, Graça, is now married to former South African president Nelson Mandela. The residents of Mbuzini near to the site of the crash were subjected to heavy military operations during the apartheid years, and it is believed that the electric fence erected along the border killed even more people in the late 1980s and early 1990s than the Berlin Wall. The villagers made enormous sacrifices in order to help refugees who were fleeing the civil war that ravaged Mozambique, which had been sponsored by the South African military.

Further information regarding the development of this memorial site and the surrounding area can be obtained from the Mpumalanga Department of Sport, Recreation, Arts and Culture (*see* page 44).

BOTHSHABELO

Botshabelo is a historical town, museum and nature reserve not far from Middelburg. The Botshabelo Mission Station was founded in 1858 by two missionaries from the Berlin Missionary Society. The name Botshabelo means 'place of shelter, refuge or sanctuary' and it was to this station that many Pedi converts flocked during the persecution of Christians by Chief Sekwati. A fort was erected to protect the refugees and a larger church replaced the original pioneer-style church when that became inadequate. The community was self-sufficient, making its own bricks and cultivating its own food, and it had its own postal service, print shop, bakery and mill. There was also a book bindery, blacksmith shop and school. By 1873 there were 1 315 inhabitants at the mission.

CULTURAL VILLAGES

South Ndebele
Open-Air Museum

The Ndebele people are generally divided into the North and South Ndebele, while the South Ndebele are in turn divided into the Manala, Ndzundza and Mnwaduba groups. The South Ndebele Open-Air Museum at Botshabelo was constructed according to their architectural development, from the earliest hut constructions through to the rondavel-type homestead and the more modern rectangular- and square-shaped houses of today. The most prominent characteristic of the culture is the vibrantly painted houses and bright traditional dress. Typically, the houses are painted in the dry winter months or when there is a special occasion such as an initiation or a wedding ceremony. A tour around the village takes visitors inside many of the beautiful houses to see the interesting interiors.

Apart from the interesting architecture of both the Mission Station and the Open-Air Museum, there is also a curio shop and restaurant and it is indeed a treat to wander around the natural bushveld of the surrounding reserve.

41

MPUMALANGA
GENERAL
Mpumalanga Tourism Authority, PO Box 679, Nelspruit 1200; tel: (013) 752-7001, fax: (013) 759-5441

Department of Sport, Recreation, Arts and Culture, PO Box 1243, Nelspruit 1200; tel: (013) 752-7951, fax: (013) 755-1150

NELSPRUIT
GENERAL
Nelspruit Publicity Association, PO Box 5018, Nelspruit 1200; tel: (013) 755-1988, fax: (013) 755-1350

TOWNSHIP TOURS
See Nelspruit Publicity Association above

MARKETS
Riverside Government Complex (See Department of Sport, Recreation, Arts and Culture above)
Nelspruit Civic Centre, Nel Street, Nelspruit 1200; tel: (013) 759-9111

TOURS AND EXCURSIONS
See Nelspruit Publicity Association above

LYDENBURG
GENERAL
Lydenburg Information Office, PO Box 61, Lydenburg 1120; tel: (013) 235-2121, fax: (013) 235-1108

MUSEUMS AND GALLERIES
Lydenburg Museum, PO Box 61, Lydenburg 1120; tel: (013) 235-2130 ext 260

OHRIGSTAD
GENERAL
Ohrigstad Tourism Information, PO Box 34, Ohrigstad 1122; tel: (013) 238-0015

HISTORICAL AND ARCHAEOLOGICAL SITES
Echo Caves see Ohrigstad Tourism Information on this page
The Museum of Man see Ohrigstad Tourism Information on this page

PILGRIM'S REST
GENERAL
Pilgrim's Rest Information Centre, Private Bag X519, Pilgrim's Rest 1290; tel: (013) 768-1060, fax: (013) 768-1113

MUSEUMS AND GALLERIES
The Diggings Site Museum See Pilgrim's Rest Information Centre above
Alanglade House Museum See Pilgrim's Rest Information Centre above
Prospectors' Trail Network, Private Bag X503, Sabie 1260; tel: (013) 764-1058, fax: (013) 764-2071
Joubert's Bridge see Pilgrim's Rest Information Centre above
Pilgrim's Rest and Sabie News See Pilgrim's Rest Information Centre above
Dredzen Shop Museum See Pilgrim's Rest Information Centre above

HISTORICAL AND ARCHAEOLOGICAL SITES
Pilgrim's Rest Cemetery See Pilgrim's Rest Information Centre above

WATERVAL-BOVEN AND WATERVAL-ONDER
Waterval-Boven Info Bar PO Box 488, Waterval-Boven 1195, tel/fax: (013) 257-0150

Nzasm Tunnel *see* Waterval-Boven Info Bar on page 44

Krugerhof, contact the Barberton Museum, Private Bag X1626 1300; tel: (013) 712-4208

SABIE
GENERAL

Sabie Tourist Information PO Box 81, Sabie 1260; tel: (013) 764-3492

MUSEUMS AND GALLERIES

Sabie Forestry Museum, Private Bag X503, Sabie 1260, tel: (013) 764-1058

HAZYVIEW
GENERAL

Hazyview Information Centre, PO Box 81, Hazyview 1242; tel/fax: (013) 737-7414

White River Publicity Association, PO Box 2387, White River 1240; tel/fax: (013) 751-5312

CULTURAL VILLAGES

Shangane, PO Box 2500, Hazyview 1242; tel: (013) 737-7000, fax: (013) 737-7007

HISTORICAL AND ARCHAEOLOGICAL SITES

Sudwala Caves and Cultural Village, PO Box 30, Schagen 1207; tel: (013) 733-3073, fax: (013) 733-3077, e-mail sudwala@m-web.co.za

MEETING THE PEOPLE

River Bend Cottage, contact Tim and Kim Buckland, PO Box 160, Hazyview 1242; tel: (013) 737-8169, fax: (013) 737-8379

BARBERTON
GENERAL

Barberton Publicity Association, PO Box 33, Barberton 1300; tel: (013) 712-2121, fax: (013) 712-5120

MUSEUMS AND GALLERIES

See Barberton Publicity Association above

LOWVELD EXCURSIONS
ARTS AND CRAFTS

Matsulu *See* Mpumalanga Tourism Authority and Department of Sport, Recreation, Arts and Culture on page 44

Manzana *See* Mpumalanga Tourism Authority and Department of Sport, Recreation, Arts and Culture on page 44

Makuleke Village, contact National Parks Board, PO Box 787, Pretoria 0001; tel: (012) 343-1991, fax: (012) 343-0905

MONUMENTS AND MEMORIALS

The Machel Memorial
See Mpumalanga Tourism Authority and Department of Sport, Recreation, Arts and Culture on page 44

BOTSHABELO
GENERAL

Botshabelo, PO Box 14, Middelburg 1050; tel: (013) 243-5020, fax: (013) 263-1329

CULTURAL VILLAGES

South Ndebele Open-Air Museum *See* Botshabelo above

4

NORTHERN PROVINCE

About the province

The Northern Province is an area of deep and ancient African traditions. Situated in the far northern corner of the country, it is the province through which one must pass en route to Zimbabwe. It shares its eastern and western borders with Mozambique and Botswana respectively. The Northern Province largely comprises the areas previously known as the independent homelands of Lebowa, Gazankulu and Venda. The province, with its population of approximately 5.6 million people, has a high rate of unemployment and is possibly the poorest in the country.

Many people are still firmly entrenched in their ancient traditions, and the area thus provides a fascinating look at the very heart of Africa. The BaPedi settled mainly in the eastern areas, while other people include the maShangaan, Basotho, Tswana, Venda and Ndebele peoples. The early Voortrekkers and missionaries brought with them a strong European influence which has contributed to the development of the province as we know it today.

NORTHERN PROVINCE

- is where you will find the baobab, the mystical 'upside down' tree of Africa;
- is the home of the Ndebele, perhaps the most artistically creative people in the country;
- is the seat of Modjadji, the legendary Rain Queen;
- has some of the most fascinating archaeological sites in the country.

This chapter

- **The Northern region:** Soutpansberg, Elim, Louis Trichardt, Schroda and Schoemansdal.
- **The Kruger National Park:** The archaeological and historical heritage of the world-renowned game reserve.
- **The central and southern region:** The province's capital, Pietersburg, and Potgietersrus and Tzaneen.

THE NORTHERN REGION

The northern region is disscected by the Tropic of Capricorn to the south, the Limpopo River to the north, the Magalakwin River to the west and the Kruger National Park/Mozambique border to the east. It is a region of great mystery and beauty. The people you are most likely to encounter are diverse and include such groups as the Venda, Shangaan, Sotho and Afrikaner.

SOUTPANSBERG

The name Soutpansberg comes from the large salt pan at the base of the northwestern slopes of the mountain range. This region has a fascinating history that stretches back millions of years. The salt pans have been exploited from Stone Age times and many archaeological sites in the vicinity date back to the Stone and Iron ages. The region also boasts some fine examples of ancient rock art.

The Soutpansberg geological system is some 1.7 million years old, and remnants of the vast forests that covered the area have been unearthed in the area's coal beds. What are thought to be dinosaur footprints may be seen near Pontdrif on the border with Botswana, and there is also evidence of early human existence. Early Stone Age tools such as characteristically robust hand axes, choppers and cleavers have been found at a number of important archaeological sites. The sites at the Luvuvhu-Limpopo floodplains, for instance, date back at least 100 000 years.

ARCHAEOLOGY & HISTORY

The Old Rock

In the bed of the Sand River that runs through the Messina Nature Reserve is the world's oldest datable rock. It is a 3.852-million-year-old granite gneiss intruded by younger dolerite. Also in the Sand River gorge is Medike, a site where a series of fascinating San rock art – murals and etchings – can be viewed.

ARTS AND CRAFTS

The people of the Northern Province are generally highly regarded as artists and crafters, and many of them – especially the wood carvers and sculptors – have received international acclaim for their work. Some of these renowned artists still live in their rural homesteads and visitors may see them working under the shady trees that often serve as their studio. However, it is often rather difficult to find the artists in these remote rural areas. Unless you have an adventurous spirit, are in no rush, don't mind driving around on dirt roads and getting lost now and then, it is advisable to employ a guide. You also need to remember that there are no telephones or easy communications in these remote areas. So, even with a guide, you could arrive only to discover that the artists are not home. Fortunately, there is usually a friend or relative at the homesteads – and often finished and unfinished works to be seen.

Jackson Hlungwani

Jackson Hlungawani has become famous across the world, not only because of his magnificent carvings, but also because he is such a fascinating personality. He has been described as a 'wild eccentric', 'prophet', 'leader' and 'healer'. His sculptures are massive wooden pieces of strong religious images often mixed with mystical African overtones. He once established a unique stone sanctuary built on a renovated Stone Age site, which he called New Jerusalem. It became a community gathering spot where he preached and sculpted. Many of his massive wooden works of art were kept there in a 'sculpture garden'. The original New Jerusalem no longer exists, but the Stone Age site still overlooks the village of Mbokhota.

He is apparently considering 'resurrecting' New Jerusalem as The Church for Man, and has already started sculpting a massive tree trunk that will become the focal point of 'Kanana' (The Church for Women). In the meanwhile, even though he is no longer a young man, Hlungwani is still a productive and busy artist and can be be visited at his home. But don't be too disappointed if you don't find him there... he lives according to his own rules.

Johannes Maswangani

The sculptures of Johannes Maswangani are crafted out of painted wood and are often of a political nature, with some Christian overtones.

Maria Mabasa

Maria Mabasa is another of the region's world-acclaimed artists. She uses whole trees as the basis of her pieces, and also works with painted clay. She has represented South Africa internationally and can also be visited at her rural home.

Philip Rikhotso

Philip Rikhotso is famous for his painted wood sculptures depicting African folklore. His mythological works often feature radios or speakers.

SACRED SITES

There are a number of sites in the Northern Province that are of great religious or spiritual significance to the local people. Many of the sites may not be visited by outsiders at all, while others are open to the public, either on your own or with a guide. Much mystery and secrecy surrounds sacred sites, and information about them is not easily given to curious outsiders, so, wherever possible, you should use a local guide who can explain the importance of the venue. Visitors are urged to respect the spiritual importance of these places and, while it is quite acceptable to show some interest, do not push for information or access to areas that have special significance.

Bulai (Dingola) Execution Rocks

Some 20 kilometres west of Messina, on the way to Pontdrif are the Bulai (or Dingola) Execution Rocks where the Musina chiefs had their prisoners executed. Minor criminals were executed at Small Bulai near the side of the road, while the hardened criminals were executed at the large rock on the south side of the road.

Machema Ruins

These ruins are on a private farm on the Mopane Road near Waterpoort. The ruins are smaller but similar to the world-famous ruins of Great Zimbabwe in southern Zimbabwe, and date back to much the same time. As a result, many people believe that there must be a connection between the two cultures. The Machema Ruins are of great ancestral significance to local black people living in the area.

The Sacred Forest

Like many other groups and clans in the country, the Venda people of the Northern Province have their own sacred forests, and these are often the burial sites of chiefs.

The part of the Thathe Vondo Forest that lies between Thohoyandou and Makhado is a sacred site for the Tshivase people and is said to be protected by white lions. Nobody is permitted to walk in the area, and the forests are thought to be haunted – in fact, the belief is so strong that few locals dare to venture there.

Visits are by permission only and, because the Venda people believe that hikers may disturb the ancestral spirits, you may only travel through the sacred forest by car.

Lake Fundudzi

According to Venda legend, the sacred lake Fundudzi in the Thathe Vondo Forest is where the white crocodile lives. It is an old venue for ritual sacrifice and, because it was originally settled by powerful medicine men, is enveloped in superstition. No one washes or swims in the lake because it is believed to be the home of the god of fertility, a sacred python who made his home in the lake. According to legend, when the wife of the god realised that her husband was a python, she ran away, and brought on the start of a terrible drought.

To this day, offerings are still made every year by the local people to secure good rains for the region, and the famous 'Python' or Fertility Dance (also known as the *Domba*) is performed by bare-breasted young girls in a slow, rhythmic line to the throb of drums.

Outsiders are permitted to attend these ceremonies, and arrangements may be made through the offices of Venda Tourism (*see* page 61).

Phiphidi Falls and Guvhukuvhu Pool

Near Nzhelele, between Thohoyandou and Makhado, are the sacred Phiphidi Falls and the enchanted Guvhukuvhe Pool. The locals consider the falls and the pool below to be the home of the Zwidutwane, the water spirits. People often leave offerings of food, flowers or jars – and sometimes coins – on the rocks around the pools here and, if you visit, it is imperative that you do not disturb the jars or pick flowers at this sacred site.

Lwamomdo Hill

On the road between Louis Trichardt and Thohoyandou is a pretty mountain on which, it is said, live a troupe of sacred baboons who are revered by the Venda people. They believe that the baboons saved them from their Swazi attackers. In fact, the baboons act as a early warning system to the people who have a homestead high on the mountain. Whenever the baboons are disturbed, they go tearing up the mountain, making a great noise – in this way alerting the chief and his people.

ELIM

The small village of Elim played a pioneering role in the development of the Soutpansberg area. In 1870, a group of Swiss missionaries came to the Elim area on a reconnaissance trip, and were followed by Paul Berthoud and Ernest Creux who established a mission station at Valdezia in 1875 and then another at the farm Waterval in 1878. These two missionaries covered the area – usually on foot because horses were susceptible to sickness – from Elim to Pietersburg and the Mozambique coast. Within a year of settling here, they established the first post office in the area.

Dr George Liengme came to Elim in 1897 where he set up a primitive hospital in the old mill buildings, but President Paul Kruger was so impressed with Liengme's reputation as a miracle doctor that he gave his permission for a new hospital to be built. Work on the new buildings began in 1899 but was hampered by the outbreak of the Anglo-Boer War in the same year. The Elim hospital was, however, finally completed in 1900, and served the people within a 300-kilometre radius (including part of Southern Rhodesia, now Zimbabwe).

Prior arrangements can be made to visit the historic Elim Hospital and museum that commemorates the work of the Swiss missionaries and doctors in South Africa.

ARTS AND CRAFTS

Tsonga Textiles

Tsonga Textiles began as a self-help community project for women in the area around Elim, where they were taught to print and paint fabrics and produce curios. Although the project has now been taken over as a private enterprise, it is still possible to visit the successful workshop and watch the women painting cloths with beautiful African themes.

Twanani Textiles and Batik

Also near Elim is the workshop of Twanani Textiles and Batik, where visitors can watch local women produce beautifully decorated textiles, most of them in the batik design.

Mashamba Pottery

It takes quite some ingenuity to reach the two homesteads that comprise the Mashamba Pottery. After taking the Mashamba turnoff about 20 kilometres out of Elim, drive down some dusty (or muddy, depending on the season) roads through a number of small settlements, and you will pass through the drift to Mashamba Post Office. Although there are potters stationed at the post office, continue around the bend to the next village, take a small turn-off – and you will be confronted by piles and piles of pots lining either side of the road. It may seem strange that the two families have chosen to position their business so far from the main routes, but they do good business here – and, besides, their source of clay is in the nearby riverbed just across the road from their homesteads.

The pottery is very reasonably priced and ranges from massive pots of waist height to small bowls, jugs and crude cups. The potters produce and fire most of their work on the premises and are only too happy to show you around. The striking red-earth pots, plates and bowls – some decorative, some utilitarian – are piled all around the outsides of the homesteads and in the road outside, and a friendly· rivalry exists between the women from each family. But be warned: the potters can be quite persistent and are masters of making you feel guilty if you buy something from one side of the road and not the other.

SCHRODA

What is thought to be the earliest trading site in the southern African interior has been excavated at Schroda, part of the Venetia-Limpopo Nature Reserve and dated to somewhere between AD 800 and AD 950. It would appear that the inhabitants of Schroda traded with Arabs from further north, and archaeological data suggest that Schroda was the capital of a small chiefdom with a pottery tradition known as Zhizo. Hippopotamus and elephant ivory, skins from various animals – including crocodile – and, more than likely, rhinoceros horn, were exchanged by the inhabitants of Schroda for porcelain and glass beads, as well as cloth.

Schroda – and, along with it, the Zhizo pottery tradition – was replaced by what is called the Leopard's Kopje-A culture in about AD 950. A new trade capital was situated at K2, a few kilometres west of Schroda in what is now the Limpopo National Park.

The archaeological sites at K2 have produced more ivory and glass beads than any other contemporary settlements. The Leopard's Kopje-A culture slowly evolved into the Leopard's Kopje-B culture; at this point new capital was chosen at Mapungubwe Hill, approximately a kilometre from K2.

Mapungubwe

Mapungubwe (which translates as 'Hill of the Jackal') is one of the richest archaeological sites in the whole of Africa. It is located on the southern bank of the Limpopo River, west of Messina, and was an early Shona/Venda capital. Researchers claim that it was the first capital of the ancient kingdom of Great Zimbabwe as it reflects many of the features found in the later capitals of the Great Zimbabwe tradition. Among the most important cultural treasures found at Mapungubwe are some of the oldest gold objects found in southern Africa.

Archaeological excavations in the 1930s uncovered a royal cemetery of 23 graves, three of which held golden rhinos and jewellery. Also discovered were carved wooden and ivory items.

Some of the artefacts that were found at Mapungubwe have been declared national treasures and are presently housed at the University of Pretoria, while the bulk of the artefacts can be viewed at Pretoria's Cultural History Museum.

SCHOEMANSDAL

Schoemansdal Museum

The Schoemansdal Museum, some 15 kilometres west of the small town of Vivo, commemorates South Africa's pioneering history. The original town, known as Zoutpansbergdorp, consisted of a collection of wattle-and-daub structures used primarily as a base for hunting operations. At some point, it was decided that Zoutpansbergdorp needed a more permanent status and surveyors were sent to establish the town layout. The new location was about 500 metres north of the old town and the inhabitants systematically moved to their new location of Schoemansdal. For 19 years, early Schoemansdal was the most important trading centre in the area, with thousands of tons of game skins, horns, whips, wood and salt being exported to growing centres of Mozambique, Natal and the Cape Colony. The community used 10 455 kilograms of gunpowder and about 1 800 kg of lead annually – and approximately 91 000 kilograms of ivory was exported from Schoemansdal.

In 1867 Schoemansdal was abandoned, mainly due to war with the surrounding black peoples and the unhealthy living conditions, and the pioneers moved back to an area south of Pietersburg called Marabastad (now also known as Eerstegoud). The open-air museum houses such items of interest as the remains of the town's original structures – including shops and a water furrow system. In 1988, the 150th anniversary of the Great Trek, a monument was erected in Schoemansdal 'in honour of the courageous Voortrekkers', while the grave of Voortrekker leader Hendrik Potgieter is in the cemetery at the museum.

THE KRUGER NATIONAL PARK

The Kruger National Park, best known for the wildlife it shelters, also has approximately 250 known archaeological or historical sites. As yet, very few of these sites have been developed for tourists, although there are plans to do so in the future. To date, 78 have been marked for future development as tourist destinations and a few important sites are already open to the public. Two examples are Thulamela Hill in the far north of the Park, and the Masorini

Ruins near the Phalaborwa gate to the Park, both of which are expected to be declared national monuments.

The Kruger National Park museum and library houses a collection of cultural material and photographs representing the conservation and development of the Park itself, and also documents some of the many archaeological sites in the Park.

Thulamela

Thulamela (meaning Place of Giving Birth) is situated on Thulamela Hill near Pafuri in the far northern section of the Kruger National Park. The stone-walled hilltop site near the confluence of the Limpopo and Luvuvhu rivers is surrounded by baobab trees, and the ruins are probably the remains of a late Iron Age settlement.

While searching through the middens in the area, researchers unearthed gold beads, charcoal, ostrich-shell beads, perforated ornamental cowry shells, clay spindle whorls, ivory and metal rings – perhaps further evidence of links with traders from the East African coast. Radiocarbon dating indicates this site to have been inhabited from the 15th to mid-17th century. With sponsorship from the Gold Fields Foundation, the Thulamela Project was launched in July 1993, with the intended purpose of restoring the site into a museum. The reconstructed settlement was officially opened as a cultural museum on Heritage Day, 14 September 1996.

Prior to the change of government in 1994, the Venda, Tsonga and Shangaan descendants of Thulamela's original inhabitants had little say over the research and tourism initiatives conducted here, but today the local people are integrally involved in the development of the site and money from educational tours goes back to the community.

Visits to Thulamela can be arranged through a number of private tour operators or through the Kruger authorities who start their tour with a leisurely game-drive to Thulamela heritage site aboard an open eight-seater vehicle. The route passes the historical Crook's Corner, through the fever tree forests, Baobab Hill and stops for refreshments at the Pafuri picnic spot. The drive takes approximately six to seven hours, so you should set aside an entire day. The tours takes place daily, depending on the number of bookings and depart from the Punda Maria gate. Bookings and payments can be made at Punda Maria.

Masorini Ruins

Masorini is about 15 kilometres from the Phalaborwa gate of the Kruger Park, along the road to the Letaba restcamp. Research has revealed that the site was inhabited by a group of people belonging to the baPhalaborwa clan who made a living by manufacturing and selling iron artefacts.

When it was decided to restore the village of Masorini in 1973, there were only stone walls, grinding stones, potsherds, the remains of foundries dating back to the 19th century, and some implements from the Stone Age. When excavation work eventually began, however, it revealed hut floors and other remains that provided information about the inhabitants: the way in which iron was worked, the nature of their commerce and their socio-domestic activities. Although restoration is not

51

Art in the Kruger Park

These days there is more reason to visit the world-famous Kruger National Park than just for game-viewing. There are the unique archaeological and rock art sites (see page 52) and, even more interesting, is the opportunity to interact with local people – through their art. The social ecology unit in the Kruger National Park has set itself the task of facilitating and supporting the artists and crafters within the communities living adjacent to the Park, thereby contributing towards their economic empowerment. One notable initiative is the Skukuza Arts and Crafts Alliance, initiated in 1994 with individual woodcarvers who were previously selling their artefacts along the roads leading to the southern part of the Park. These woodcarvers were organised into an alliance and, in 1997, an outlet was built for them at Numbi gate, which is easily accessible to visitors staying at the southern camps of the Kruger, such as Skukuza, Berg-en-Dal, Biyamiti, Malelane, and Pretoriuskop. The carvers were taught to improve their skills in quality control, diversification, business management, and sales and marketing. Their products range from grass mats to carved animals, pottery bowls and basketry. A similar venture is due to be established at the Phalaborwa gate.

complete, Masorini has a number of reconstructed dwellings that blend harmoniously with the boulders on the slope of the hill. At the foot of the hill is a parking area, toilets, barbecue (braai) facilities and a thatch-roofed veranda with tables and chairs. There is also a visitors' hut that provides information – artefacts, photographs and illustrations – on the prehistory of the Kruger National Park and Masorini.

A guided visit to Masorini can be arranged through the Kruger authorities. Visitors to the village are shown the excavated remains of a smelting furnace (the smelting process is demonstrated using a reconstructed replica of the furnace). The breathtaking view from the top of the hill extends to to Shikhumba Hill where, according to legend, the Chief once lived.

The grave of João Albasini

The grave of João Albasini lies near the picnic site at Albasini Dam. At the same time that the white pioneers arrived in the Soutpansberg area, João Albasini, a Portuguese-born Italian, established himself at Delagoa Bay and set about hunting and trading skins and ivory. Legend has it that he lived in the manner of a medieval lord, gathering around him people from local communities who had fallen into disfavour with their chiefs, and – with 2 000 warriors among his followers – he eventually became known as the White Chief of the Magwamba group of the Shangaan.

Albasini was appointed by the Transvaal government as superintendent of the local peoples and became the Portuguese Vice Consul, and later, Justice of the Peace for the area. After his death in 1888, he was buried on his farm. A number of his relatives still live in the area, and his memory is honoured by the Shangaan people every year.

Kgopolwe and Phalaborwa Iron Age Sites

The sites at Kgopolwe and Phalaborwa (just outside the Kruger) are thought to be the oldest South African sites of the Iron Age. The first settlements sprang up as long ago as AD 800. At the Sealene site, there are remnants of walls from the royal residences of about 24 baPhalaborwa chiefs.

The ruins and the royal graves also found here are considered sacred and spiritual ancestral sites. The nearby site at Kgopolwe was apparently the second royal residence. It was only occupied during times of trouble, when the chief would move between homes in order to confuse people as to his whereabouts.

THE CENTRAL & SOUTHERN REGION

Today the provincial capital, the town of Pietersburg was founded in 1840 and was well known for its trade in ivory and game. However, following heated resistance from local Nguni people, and the ravages of malaria, the Voortrekkers were forced to abandon the town and it was only later re-established and named Pietersburg.

Potgietersrus was named after well-loved Voortrekker leader Pieter Potgieter, whose grave lies beneath a pile of stones in the grounds of the municipal buildings. Old wagon-wheel tracks that date back to the Great Trek – and the subsequent commemorations of this historic event in 1938 and 1988 – may still be seen in the town.

The town of Tzaneen is best known for its subtropical agriculture and winter vegetables, and most of the surrounding areas are, in one way or another, related to these activities. Despite the large tracts of land under cultivation, it is a beautiful area of rolling wooded hills, rivers and waterfalls.

PIETERSBURG

ARCHAEOLOGY & HISTORY

Stone Age Inhabitants

The most important middle Stone Age sites in the Northern Province can be found at Chuniespoort (south of Pietersburg) and the Limpopo River Valley, especially at the Mashakatini Pans in the Madimbo corridor and the floodplains north of the Luvuvhu River in the Kruger National Park.

San (Bushmen) hunter-gatherers and Khoikhoi pastoralists lived here in the late Stone Age, and San art – depicting elephant, giraffe and kudu, but not the eland shown in paintings in other regions of the country – may still be seen in parts of the Northern Province. The most important archaeological sites dating back to the late Stone Age can be found in the Limpopo National Park, Venetia-Limpopo Nature Reserve, Madikwe, Goro Nature Reserve, the

Lesheba Wilderness area, Leek, Aintree, Thombo-la-ndou and the Blouberg area.

One of the most remarkable features of the Soutpansberg, however, is the legacy of the early Iron Age communities that occupied the area from about AD 330. These people were able to smelt and forge iron, and owned domesticated cattle and sheep or goats. The earliest Iron Age site is at Silverleaves in the New Agatha Valley near Tzaneen and dates to AD 200, while the most important Early Iron Age sites in the Soutpansberg area are at Klein Afrika, or Plaas Marius, just north of the tunnels in Wyllie's Poort. There are also sites to be seen at Schoemansdal Environmental Education Centre in the Happy Rest Nature Reserve.

The Limpopo National Park and surroundings are rich in the cultural remains of the late Iron Age and many of the most important sites from this time can be found here.

CULTURAL VILLAGES

Bakone Malapa Open-air Museum

This village is situated about nine kilometres out of Pietersburg on the Chuniespoort Road, and offers visitors some insight into the background and history of the Bakone people, a sub-group of the Northern Sotho. While the open-air museum covers the historic aspects of the Bakone, it is also looks at the transformations taking place within the culture and lifestyle of these people as they attempt to adapt to modern contemporary influences. The village , which has been 'blessed' by the Bakone elders, has been reconstructed in the style

53

used by the Northern Sotho approximately 250 years ago but, at the time of construction, no existing homes of this nature could be found on which to base the living museum. The few homesteads in the village were finally reconstructed with the assistance of elderly Matlala men and women who could remember living in similar homes as children.

Two *lapas* (homesteads) contain exhibits that explain much of the Bakone's history. There are also demonstrations of traditional fire making, maize grinding and beer brewing. Handcraft demonstrations include pottery, wood carving, basketry and beadwork and a craft shop sells reasonably priced crafts made mainly by the locals.

Although the entire museum is a reconstruction, it is sited on an area of great archaeological significance. For thousands of years, people – among them Stone Age inhabitants, such as the San, Northern Ndebele and Tsonga-Shangaan people – have chosen to make their homes here and numerous artefacts have been excavated.

Tours are conducted at set times throughout the day, and most of the guides are excellent storytellers who can fill you in on all the cultural aspects of this age-old civilisation. The guides will also inform you of the intricacies of the rites and rituals that are performed at ceremonial occasions.

Tsonga Kraal
Open-air Museum

The origins of the Tsonga-Shangaan people are obscure, although it is believed that they came from the Mozambique coastline. Unlike most southern African people, the Tsonga are keen fishermen, which could be attributed to their ancestral links with the Mozambican coast. This cultural village to the southeast of Tzaneen is not a 'living' kraal in the sense that staff go home to their own villages after a day's work at the 'museum'.

On the programme at the Tsonga Kraal are demonstrations of how the original inhabitants extracted salt from the region's many salt pans, and of iron ore extraction and smelting. With their links to the Nguni people, who migrated southwards from central and eastern Africa bringing with them much livestock, it is inevitable that there would be goats and chickens wandering around the village.

There are also some fine specimens of Nguni cattle, and the cultural significance of these cattle is explained in the course of the tours. Some excellent performances of traditional dancing may also be seen at the village.

Nyani Cultural
Village

The only way you can visit the Nyani Cultural Village is if you are a guest at The Coach House, an up-market, five star-lodge on the hills outside Tzaneen. Sam Nkuna is a manager at The Coach House and organises tours to his village where you can experience the life of ordinary Shangaans under the leadership of Chief Kapama. There is also the opportunity to sleep over in the village, but you need to arrange this with Sam beforehand so that he can organise it for you.

PLACES OF WORSHIP

Zion City Moria

There are some 2 000 'indigenous' African churches in South Africa, most of them combining Christianity with elements of traditional African belief. Moria, located between Pietersburg and Haenertsburg, is headquarters to the largest of these churches, the Zionist Christian Church. On a Sunday, travelling anywhere in South Africa, you will inevitably see people from the Zionist Church dressed in their distinctive white and blue 'uniforms' and carrying staffs as they make their way to church. Every Easter, more than a million pilgrims flock to Moria to celebrate. People come in buses and taxis from throughout the country and camp out in the area to pray and worship. It is a truly African experience and, even though the sheer numbers of people can be daunting, it is quite safe and well worth a visit. If you happen to be in the area at the time and don't feel up to going on your own, ask at the tourist information office if they can arrange for someone to accompany you.

MONUMENTS

Concentration Camp Cemetery

At one point during the Anglo-Boer War, more than 4 000 Boer women and children were interned by the British in one of the infamous concentration camps close to Pietersburg. In the Concentration Camp Cemetery lie the graves of those who died of disease and starvation during this time.

MUSEUMS AND GALLERIES

African Roots Gallery

This small gallery, situated in the grounds of a private home, houses a wonderful collection of work by both black and white local artists. The gallery owner has a wealth of information regarding the local artists, and is one of the few people who can arrange tours out into the deep rural areas where you can visit the artists at work in their rural homesteads.

See also pages 47 and 48.

Eloff Gallery

The Eloff Gallery at the Palm Centre in Pietersburg contains original South African art and includes work by local Venda artists. On display are crafts, pottery and wooden sculptures.

Pietersburg Museum

Before setting off to visit the far distant corners of the province, visit the Pietersburg Museum and its adjoining art museum for a comprehensive overview of the cultural heritage of both Pietersburg and the rest of the province. The art museum has an extensive collection of more than 700 pieces representing work by regional and national artists.

The Hugh Exton Photographic Museum

This is a one-of-a-kind museum with more than 23 000 glass negatives taken by photographer Hugh Exton that capture the first 50 years of Pietersburg.

5

POTGIETERSRUS

Arend Dieperink Museum

This cultural history museum is situated in Voortrekker Road in nearby Potgietersrus and portrays the history of the town and how it was settled. An exhibit explains the archaeological diggings (and dinosaur fossils) at Makapansgat (see below), and there is also a variety of historical artefacts, a replica of a typical bosveldhuis, or bush house, as well as a collection of guns and rifles. In the quaint little yard is a threshing machine, boiler, ox-wagons, horse carts and a still used to make mampoer, a traditional alcoholic drink made from fruit.

Makapansgat

The renowned Makapansgat Cave, some 19 kilometres north of Potgietersrus, and the neighbouring archaeological sites are famous throughout the world. Nowhere else on earth is there such an extended and complete record of hominid occupation, and, as the Bernard Price Institute of the University of the Witwatersrand (see page 21) is still conducting research at the site, it may only be visited by appointment – and in the company of a guide.

There are a number of sites in the Makapansgat Valley, the oldest of which are the limeworks, dating to between 3.32 million to 1.6 million years ago. This site has yielded thousands of fossil bones, many of which were of the ape-man, Australopithecus africanus. There is also the Cave of Hearths, Hyena Cave, Buffalo Cave – in which the remains of the extinct buffalo Bos makapania was found along with hundreds of other animal deposits – Rainbow Cave (artefacts date back to between 100 000 and 50 000 years ago), Ficus Cave, Peppercorn Cave and the Historic Cave (which is also known as Makapansgat).

After the attack on the Voortrekkers at Moorddrift in 1854, Chief Makapane and his people retreated to the great caves and made them their stronghold. Although many of them managed to survive through the siege by living on the cave water and their stores of grain, some 1 500 people or (quite possibly) more perished from thirst and starvation during the gruesome struggle. Piet Potgieter was fatally shot during the attack and, when the Boers finally stormed the cave, they found it to be a place of the dead, permeated by an overwhelming stench of putrefaction. Only a few of Makapane's people had managed to escape. After that, the great caverns were avoided.

Visits to Makapansgat Valley can be arranged through the Arend Dieperink Museum in Potgietersrus (see page 62).

HOME-STAYS

Kings Walden

Kings Walden is worth visiting for the view and gardens alone. The old homestead is surrounded by a magnificent rambling garden laced with an endless network of little paths. It is situated on a magnificent ridge overlooking the rolling hills of Africa down into the Lowveld, and has been in the Hilton-Barber family for a few generations. Kings Walden was recently converted into a charming guesthouse, and the Hilton-Barbers are enchanting storytellers, who can fill you in on all the happenings of the area.

THE LANDSCAPE

The Big Baobab

There are a number of African legends surrounding these imposing and unusual trees, many of which have lived for as long as a staggering 2 000 years. Some folktales tell of God planting the tree upside down, while others claim that the blossoms are haunted by the spirits of Africa. Some people also believe that infertility can be cured by imbibing a concoction made from the pods.

One of the largest baobabs in the country can be found outside Leydsdorp east of Tzaneen. It is so large that, during the gold-rush years, it was converted into a pub (some specimens are so enormous that humans have set up temporary homes in the hollowed trunks). Mysteriously, the baobabs can continue to thrive even after the inner pulp has been burnt away.

The older trees have their own unique eco-systems that provide sustenance and shelter for a myriad creatures. Apart from the usual insects and birds that make use of the trees, elephants browse on the leaves and strip the bark, baboons eat the fruit, fruit bats and bushbabies pollinate the flowers and even humans have found an endless number of uses for the tree. For instance, over the centuries, the fibrous bark and spongy wood has been harvested for making rope, matting and baskets, and, more recently, paper and even cloth. The seeds are ground and roasted to make a beverage that tastes a little like coffee, and the pollen has apparently been used to make glue.

TZANEEN

Tzaneen Museum

The Tzaneen Museum is crammed full of artefacts of the local Tsonga and North Sotho peoples: pottery, basketry, beadwork, weapons, sacred drums and numerous other items of ethnological importance. It may be a small museum (only three rooms), but do plan on spending a few hours there. Nothing is labelled (visitors are guided around), and this encourages a more participative dialogue.

Most of the displays form part of a private collection belonging to the curator and he has assembled the world's largest collection of pole-carvings from the region. He has also managed to secure the royal drums of the late Rain Queen as well as a number of other utensils that are normally burnt after the death of a Rain Queen (see box on page 60). It is most unusual to be able to see these ancestral drums and hear the stories surrounding them.

Another unique exhibit is the sculptural depictions of Tsonga legends that stand under the trees in the yard. Some 20 legends have thus far been recorded, and 90 carved figures have been completed by well-known local sculptors. A staff member narrates the tales, thus preserving not only the oral tradition of the Tsongas, but also making the museum a popular visit for

Modjadji, the Rain Queen

East of Tzaneen, in the vicinity of Duiwelskloof, lives the legendary Rain Queen, Modjadji, whose reputation has instilled fear and respect throughout the peoples of southern Africa for centuries. The Lobedu ('Loh-beh-doo') are an off-shoot of the Karanga of Zimbabwe, best known for the unique stone wall structures they erected around their settlements. It is said that, when the Lobedu fled southwards, their rulers brought with them a legacy of rain-making magic. The group was originally ruled by men, but the last four rulers – dating back into the last century – have all been formidable women who hold the legendary rain-making powers and who are believed to be immortal. So powerful did the people believe the Rain Queen's magic to be, that it was enough to prevent attack during the terrible wars that once wracked southern Africa. The Rain Queens were never seen by ordinary mortals but, although much mystery and ancient ritual continue to surround the dynasty, the reigning queen – enthroned during the early 1980s – is much more accessible than her predecessors.

both children and adults. There is also a fine collection of woodcarvings by local artists – some of world-class status – and the collection records carvings covering a period of 100 years. The museum's pottery collection, on the other hand, covers a period of nearly 2 000 years and, again, includes rarely seen items belonging to the late Rain Queen.

The Cycad Forest

It is unlikely that you will get the opportunity to see Modjadji, the Rain Queen (see box above), or to observe any of the rituals surrounding the rain-making cere-monies, but you can visit the magnificent cycad forests that grow above the royal enclosure. The cycads are living fossils, and are survivors of a primeval plant group, the *Cycadales*, which was the dominant type of vegetation approximately 300 million years ago. The small nature reserve has the largest concentration of these ancient species of plants that have given rise to a great many mysteries and legends. Even in the mid-day African heat, the forests have an evocative atmosphere. The plants are sacred to the Lobedu people and have enjoyed the protection of Queen Modjadji for generations.

NORTHERN PROVINCE
GENERAL
Northern Province Tourism Board, PO Box 2814, Pietersburg 0700; tel: (015) 295-2829, fax: (015) 291-2654

ARCHAEOLOGY AND HISTORY
Face Africa Tours, contact Chris Olivier, tel/fax: (015) 517-7031, cell: 082 969 3270
See also Northern Province Tourism Board above

THE NORTHERN REGION
GENERAL
Venda Tourism, PO Box 9, Sibasa 0970; tel: (0159) 82-4900

SOUTPANSBERG
GENERAL
Soutpansberg Marketing and Tourism Association, PO Box 980, Louis Trichardt 0920; tel/fax: (015) 516-0040

ELIM AND LOUIS TRICHARDT
Elim Hospital and Museum (*see also* Northern Province Tourism Board above), tel: (015) 556-3418.
Tsonga Textiles, PO Box 1062, Louis Trichardt 0920; tel/fax: (015) 556-3214

SCHOEMANSDAL
Schoemansdal Museum, Private Bag X2410, Louis Trichardt, 0920; tel: (015) 516-3254
Schoemansdal Environmental Education Centre, Happy Rest Nature Reserve, Louis Trichardt; P O Box 737, Louis Trichardt, 0920; tel: (015) 516-0040

THE KRUGER NATIONAL PARK
National Parks Board, PO Box 787, Pretoria 0001; tel: (012) 343-1991, fax: (012) 343-0905
Kruger National Park (Social Ecology Unit), PO Box 787, Pretoria, 0001; tel (013) 735-5611, fax: (013) 735-6873
Department of Environmental Affairs, PO Box 217, Pietersburg 0700; tel: (015) 295-9300, fax: (015) 295-5819
Phalaborwa Association for Tourism, PO Box 1408, Phalaborwa 1390; tel: (015) 781-2758

THE CENTRAL AND SOUTHERN REGION
GENERAL
Tzaneen Tourism Centre, 23 Danie Joubert Street, Tzaneen 0850; tel: (015) 307-1294, fax: (015) 307-1271
Pietersburg Marketing Company, PO Box 11, Pietersburg 0700; tel: (015) 290-2010, fax: (015) 290-2009
(*See also* Northern Province Tourism Board on this page)

PIETERSBURG CULTURAL VILLAGES
Bakone Malapa Open-air Museum, Chuniespoort Road, Pietersburg 0699; PO Box 111, Pietersburg 0700; tel: (015) 295-2867
Tsonga Kraal Open-air Museum, Private Bag X502, Letsitele 0885; tel: (015) 386-8727
Nyani Cultural Village, contact The Coach House below
The Coach House, contact Sam Nkuna, PO Box 544, Tzaneen 0850; tel: (015) 307-3641

PLACES OF WORSHIP

Zion City Moria, contact Pietersburg Marketing Company above or Northern Province Tourism Board on page 62

MUSEUMS AND GALLERIES

African Roots Gallery, contact Doug Walker, tel/fax: (015) 297-0113, cell: 083 459 6799
Eloff Gallery, 34 Palm Centre, Pietersburg 0699; tel: (015) 297-0911
Pietersburg Art Museum, PO Box 111, Pietersburg 0700; tel: (0152) 290-2000, fax: (0152) 290-2131
Pietersburg Museum, PO Box 111, Pietersburg, 0700; tel: (015) 290-2182/3
Hugh Exton Photographic Museum, Pietersburg Civic Centre, Landdros Marais Street, Pietersburg 0699; PO Box 111, Pietersburg 0700; tel: (015) 290-2010

POTGIETERSRUS

Arend Dieperink Museum, PO Box 34, Potgietersrus 0600; tel: (015) 491-2244
Makapansgat, contact Arend Dieperink Museum above

HOME-STAYS

Kings Walden, PO Box 31, Tzaneen 0850; tel: (015) 307-3262

THE LANDSCAPE

The Baobab Pub, Contact Tzaneen Tourism Centre or Northern Province Tourism Board on page 61

TZANEEN

Tzaneen Museum, PO Box 700, Tzaneen 0850; tel: (015) 307-2425, fax: (015) 307-1713

NORTH WEST

About the province

It was in the North West Province that the famous Taung skull, the skull of a young australopithecine child, was discovered in 1924 – a skull that provided many answers to some of the puzzling questions around the origins of modern *homo sapiens*. For some people, this alone makes the province a fascinating place to visit and sets the scene for its long and far-reaching history. Many millions of years after the death of the Taung child the Nguni migrants, having travelled down from central and eastern Africa, began to arrive in what is now known as the North West Province. Still later, the Voortrekker settlers arrived, having trekked up in their ox-wagons from the Cape colony. All these hardy settlers have had a strong influence on this sometimes rough and rugged province.

IN THE NORTH WEST

- many people believe humanity may have originated;
- writer Herman Charles Bosman based his delightful stories about rural Afrikaners earlier this century;
- Sun City and the Palace of the Lost City offer an alternative look at local culture;
- visitors should probably be wary of *mampoer* and *witblits*.

This chapter

- **Mafikeng** The provincial capital
- **Groot Marico**
- **Madikwe**
- **The Pilanesberg**
- **Klerksdorp**
- **Potchefstroom**
- **Taung**
- **Vryburg**
- **Rustenburg**

6

MAFIKENG

Mafikeng, or 'place of boulders', is North West Province's capital city, perched right on the border of Botswana. The origins of the city go back to the time of the Difaqane, Shaka's reign of terror when thousands of black people were scattered throughout southern Africa (*see also* page 163). Mafikeng was later the focus of the world when it was besieged for seven months by Boer forces during the Anglo-Boer War, and today many historical sites places of interest in and around the city are closely related to this historic event.

Mafikeng is also the home of the famous Boy Scout movement established by Colonel Robert Baden-Powell, who was in charge of the British Garrison during the siege of Mafikeng. In 1972, which saw the beginning of the 'Bantustan era' of the apartheid government, Mafikeng became the seat of the Tswana Territorial Administration, but it has since been re-incorporated into South Africa.

MUSEUMS AND GALLERIES

The Molema House

Born in about February 1891, Dr Seetsele Modiri Molema was a political and medical activist who was an active member of the ANC. He was arrested in the Defiance Campaign in 1952, which was followed by a banning order in 1953. Dr Molema was educated at Healdtown and Lovedale College before departing to Glasgow in 1919 in order to qualify as a medical doctor. His mission was to train as many nurses as possible so that they, in turn, could help his people. Molema wrote a number of ethnographic and historic books – among them *The Bantu: Past and Present, Chief Moroka* and *Montshiwa 1815–1896 – Baroleng Chief and Patriot*. He died on 13 August 1965.

The Molema House was, however, also once the home of Sol Plaatjie, the celebrated black journalist and founding member of the ANC who wrote a well-known account about the Siege of Mafikeng from his own – rather than from a white colonial – perspective. The Molema House commemorating Dr Molema and Sol Plaatjie was built in 1920 and is called Maratiwa, which means 'Feel at home, you are most welcome'. The home is situated in the suburb of Monthiswa.

Sol Plaatjie's House

After the Siege, Sol Plaatjie moved from Maratiwa and built a house, which he named Seweding, where he lived with his family until 1910 when they moved to Kimberley. The house no longer exists, but the line of pepper trees planted by Plaatjie – as well as his well and cattle kraal – can still be seen.

See also page 78 as well as 'Sol Plaatjie's Newspaper Office' below.

Sol Plaatjie's Newspaper Office

This is the site of Sol Plaatjie's office, where the first Setswana protest newspaper called *Koranta ea Bechuana* was published and printed between 1902 and 1910. The newspaper was edited by Sol Plaatjie and financed by Silas Molema and later by Spencer Minchin. The Plaatjie family left for Kimberley in 1910 and, in 1912, Sol became the first Secretary General of the South African Native Congress, which in 1923 became the African National Congress (ANC).

Mafikeng Museum

The foundation stone of the old town hall was laid on the 26 June 1902 and the building completed in 1903. It was officially opened in 1904. The architecture of the grand old hall is elaborately colonial, with impressive pressed steel ceilings. A museum was created in 1975, using the small municipal collection of Siege material and, since 1988, displays have been developed to incorporate the history and cultures of other peoples in this area. There is also an excellent reference library attached to the museum, which is open to the public.

54

PLACES OF WORSHIP

St John the Evangelist Anglican Church

This church is the pride of Mafikeng, commemorating as it does, the famous Siege of Mafikeng that took place between 1899 and 1900. Designed by Sir Herbert Baker (who also designed the Union Buildings in Pretoria and many other notable structures throughout the country), the foundation stone was laid on the same day as that of the Town Hall – the date of King Edward VII's coronation. The church is constructed from brick from Lobatsie and red sandstone from the Motopo Hills in Zimbabwe.

HISTORICAL AND ARCHAEOLOGICAL SITES

Kanon Kopjie (Canon Koppie)

This historical site was first occupied by Stone Age people about 8 000 years ago. These early inhabitants hunted animals at the nearby Molopo River and, because of its geographical vantage point, the area has a long history of occupation. During the Bechuanaland War of 1882–1884, the Goshenites shelled the black town of Mahikeng (from which the name of the modern town is derived) from this spot. In 1885, the Warren Expedition – sent to Mahikeng to restore stolen land to the Baralong – built the stone walls, as well as Warren's Fort just north of the river. During the Siege, Kanon Kopjie was further fortified and occupied by the British who survived a determined Boer attack on

31 October 1899. An interesting curiosity is that the fort was linked to the Siege headquarters in town by telephone – even in those days.

Mafikeng Cemetery

The municipal cemetery contains military and civilian Siege and Anglo-Boer War graves – one of which is that of nine-year-old Frankie Brown who was the youngest member of the Siege cadets. A row of military crosses placed close together indicates the mass burial of the British killed in the Game Tree Attack, which took place on 26 December in 1899. The largest grave in the cemetery is that of Captain Andrew Beauchamp-Proctor, who was the most highly decorated South African airman of the First World War. A small section of the cemetery, near the road, contains the graves of the Irish Sisters of Mercy who lived at St Joseph's chapel between 1899 and 1970.

The Mafikeng Anglo-Boer War Concentration Camp

During the Siege of Mafikeng, a refugee camp was established for Boer families seeking safety, and after the Siege the camp was moved westwards along the Molopo River. Following the British 'scorched earth' policy – a response to the Boer guerrilla warfare – farms were burnt and the families, together with their servants' families, were forcibly moved into the camp. In 1900, this became known as a concentration camp, the first in South Africa, and the worst, until a visit by Emily Hobhouse in April 1901. The superintendent

65

Herman Charles Bosman

It was probably largely due to the fables of Herman Charles Bosman, one of South Africa's most acclaimed English short story writers, that anyone has even heard of Groot Marico. And, for anyone with an interest in rural Afrikaans culture, Bosman's tales of Groot Marico and its wonderfully eccentric inhabitants are essential reading. Groot Marico was one of the earliest places settled by the Voortrekkers in what was then the Transvaal. It was once an insular, conservative Afrikaner stronghold, but in recent years it has done much to open up and encourage tourists. Today, there is even a Herman Charles Bosman Literary Society that keeps alive the spirit of Bosman, and it is worth checking at the tourism information office to see whether there is a meeting of the society because they often have live readings of his work. These evenings are plenty of fun. The society organises events that draw hundreds of enthusiastic Bosman aficionados to the Marico district every year. There are plans to restore the little farm school at which Herman Charles Bosman taught in 1926.

Many famous (or notorious) people, such as Mzilikazi and his Matabele followers, David Livingstone, and characters from South Africa's past, settled – or at least tried to settle – in Groot Marico, and many of these people and events are immortalised in Herman Charles Bosman's delightful stories. Bosman perfectly described the place in *Marico Revisited*: 'There is no other place I know that is so heavy with atmosphere, so strangely and darkly impregnated with that stuff of life that bears the authentic stamp of South Africa.' So, if you are looking for a real South African experience, Groot Marico should definitely be on your list.

of the camp was eventually dismissed in August of that year for gross negligence.

Concentration Camp Cemeteries

Two concentration camp cemeteries can be visited. One, in an area known as Mazezuru and the larger of the two, contains the graves of Boer wives and children whose husbands had refused to surrender to the British. There are 825 marked graves but, during the 1949 restoration, the remains of three or four bodies were found in many of the shallow graves, and it is believed that many of these were of African children. In addition, 33 burgers who had been killed nearby during the Siege of Mafikeng, were reburied here in a mass grave. During restoration a single stone was taken from each grave and placed into a pile that was cemented together to form a cairn.

The smaller cemetery is in Magogoe and is the final resting place of women and children whose husbands had surrendered to the British. Again, remains of bodies believed to be those of African women and their children were found in many of the graves. There are 220 marked graves in this cemetery.

The Ruins of the Old Mfengu Settlement

The Mfengu, of Xhosa origin, had been part of Rhodes's Pioneer Column en route to the north and settled here in 1890. During the Siege, the Mfengu contingent helped to defend Mafikeng and ended up sustaining casualties equal to those of the British. In 1962, under the Group Areas Act of 1950, Makweteng – the name of the Mfengu settlement – was destroyed and the residents forcibly removed to the new Montshioa Township. The ruins of the original settlement can, however, still be visited here.

MONUMENTS

The Kgotla of the Barolong Boora Tshidi

This monument honours the approximately 400 Barolong people who died in the defence of Mafikeng during the Siege – more than double the number of British casualties. The site is the meeting place, or Kgotla of Chief Montshioa and has been in continuous use since the 1850s. Surmounting the monument is the Barolong totem of the *Tholo*, or kudu, and lower down, the word Mahikeng (meaning Place of the Rocks – the original name of the town) is inscribed.

GROOT MARICO

The meaning of the name 'Groot Marico' remains unclear, but it is thought that the word 'Marico' could have come from the Hurutse word *mari* (meaning 'blood'), the Tswana word for 'besieged place' (*madikwe*), and *madiso* (meaning 'pasture') or *malekwe* (meaning 'changeable').

TOURS AND EXCURSIONS

Mampoer Tours

Schoemanati, near Schoemansdrift, is a medal-winning distiller of *mampoer*, a traditional home-made concoction of fruit notorious for its mind-blowing alcoholic content. Apart from the tasting sessions, there are also talks on the history of *mampoer* production and broad selection of *mampoer*, *witblits* (another potent, 'traditional' alcoholic beverage), brandies and liqueurs. The distillery can only be visited by appointment.

At the Marico Valley *mampoer* distillery there are even more *mampoers* and liqueurs for visitors to try, so be sure to pace yourself. In true *platteland* style, the proprietors are both friendly and welcoming – and they also cater for traditional farm weddings, so you may be in luck and spot a bride and groom from the Afrikaans-speaking community.

At Syfer Gat, which is another champion *mampoer* distillery, they have not only *mampoer* and liqueur to taste, but also *witblits* and aged brandy – but you need to make an appointment to visit.

For something a little different, try the peach-flavoured *mampoer* and *soet blits* liqueurs that are distilled on the premises of the Klerksdorp Museum.

67

Tobacco Tours

Mampoer somehow often seems to be associated with tobacco – perhaps because in the old days (and even still today), in these old farming districts, many of the colourful characters still enjoy a good twist of tobacco with their shot of *witblitz* or *mampoer*. The tobacco tours take you to meet hardy tobacco farmers, learn something about how to produce the perfect tobacco leaf and usually allow you to eat more than your fill of traditional South African food along the way. The tours usually start with a large brunch with a local Afrikaans-speaking couple before heading off to see some of the local scenic spots and finally to more refreshments at the tobacco farm. *Mampoer* usually features somewhere along these trips ...

HISTORICAL AND ARCHAEOLOGICAL SITES

Gaditshwene Iron Age Ruins

The Tswana culture is highlighted by the enormous Iron Age settlement of the Bahurutshe people at Kaditshwene. This site was visited in 1820 by explorer John Campbell and is the largest settlement of its kind south of the Limpopo River. In its heyday – when Campbell visited in 1820 – it was apparently the same size as Cape Town at the time. Approximately between 16 000 and 20 000 Bahurutshe lived in this 'village', and were famous for their skills as miners and smelters of iron and copper, as well as extremely skilled stone masons. The Bahurutshe possessed

substantial quantities of copper and brass beads and kept huge herds of cattle.

Gaditshwene is situated on one of the highest hills in the area and each hut was surrounded by a neat stone wall. The interiors of these huts were apparently decorated with clay sculptures and paintings, and recent excavations indicate that the Batswana grouping – to whom the Bahuruthshe belong – may have occupied the area as long as 1000 years ago. This, however, is not substantiated by oral tradition – although carbon dating suggests that Gaditshwene was already in existence during the 17th century.

The settlement was eventually destroyed and its people massacred in gruesome attacks, first by the MmaNthatise and then later by Mzilikazi and his Ndebele. These attacks were common during the time now known as the Difaqane – a chain reaction of attack, defeat, destruction and migration – following the wars of Shaka's Zulu warriors.

Today, however, all that is left are the ruins of the village, and the site has not been touched since that time, neither has it been developed for tourism, although there are plans afoot to do so.

Aside from Gaditshwene, there are literally hundreds of Iron Age ruins in the district, which can be visited with the aid of a guide from the tourism office. It is not really feasible, at this stage, to try to find these spots on your own because, even though they are enveloped in a wonderful atmosphere and are indeed quite fascinating, some are difficult to find and many are somewhat overgrown.

The Spirit of Mampoer

Mampoer is an extraordinarily powerful alcoholic beverage, which was originally made from brewing indigenous fruit but these days made from many different fruits, such as peaches and apricots. *Mampoer* features in many hilarious incidents in some of Herman Charles Bosman's fables (*see* box on page 66). A number of *mampoer* tours operate in the Groot Marico district (*see* page 67), during which you can see the age-old distilling process and experience the taste of this rather powerful brew.

Some tours also include visits to old farm houses in the district where bread is still baked in an outside oven and the farmers' wives serve homemade *gemmerbier* (ginger beer) and *melktert* (milk tart), both traditional fare famous in South Africa. There are also opportunities to see whip-plaiting demonstrations: during the days of the Voortrekkers, these long leather whips were an essential part of the ox-wagon trail, and it takes rather astonishing skills to crack the whips.

CULTURAL VILLAGES

Kortkloof Tswana Village

The short 14-kilometre drive from Groot Marico to the Kortkloof village is quite enchanting. The village, the home of a number of Tswana-speaking people, is entirely authentic. Many people like the idea of meeting African people in a setting that has not been contrived for tourists, but however tempting this might be, it is best to arrange a tour to the village through the Groot Marico Tourist Information office (*see* page 75). This way, you can be sure that people are expecting you and will be in a position to offer you traditional food, and a tour of the various homesteads: there is a delightful variety of tin shacks, traditional homes, mud houses and a mixture of stone and corrugated iron homesteads. If you are lucky, there will also be a demonstration of traditional dancing.

There is not much in the way of African crafts or curios at this village but, in some ways, this makes a pleasant change. There are, however, homesteads in the surrounding rural districts where families are still making and baking traditional clay pots and you should ask your tour guides to help you find them.

Mapoch Ndebele Village

The Mapoch village does not belong to any authority or governing body, but rather to the residents who live there and, like Kortkloof, it is an authentic traditional village. Originally inhabited by the followers of Nyabela who lived on the farm Hartebeesfontein until 1953, the first village disappeared due to urbanisation and what little evidence there was left of the village was collected by concerned individuals. The new settlement is a direct result of the Group Areas Act whereby black people were not permitted to live in white

69

areas and were forced by the government to move to other areas. However, the original residents refused to be resettled at Vlakfontein township (today's Mamelodi) because they would not have been able to grow crops there or graze cattle. They were eventually resettled on the farm Klipgat, northwest of Pretoria.

This area became part of Bophuthatswana, an 'independent homeland', but, because they were not Tswana speaking, the villagers were marginalised and the settlement slowly disintegrated. Tourists who had been attracted to the village – largely because of its wonderfully colourful architecture – stopped visiting, and the once booming trade in beadwork virtually disappeared, until 1997 when the National Cultural Museum, and the residents of the Ndebele village themselves, decided to revitalise the settlement.

Today, there is much to see, particularly the famous Ndebele murals on the walls of the houses, the extraordinary beadwork and the traditional clothing worn by the women. The houses are built in the traditional manner and, during a tour of the village, traditional skills are explained and demonstrated. Because the homes are privately owned, permission to enter must be obtained from the residents. Their privacy should be respected at all times.

ARTS AND CRAFTS

The Art Factory

Part of Groot Marico's attempts to pull itself into the twentieth and twenty-first centuries has been the development of their home industry and arts and crafts. Some 30 people are involved in the Art Factory, which encourages local artists of all sorts.

Community Conservation

In the past, many black communities were removed from their land, not just because of the Group Areas Act, but also to make way for game reserves. Often, these communities received little or no compensation for their land, with the result that for years, in many areas, black people considered conservation organisations and game reserves to be part of the apartheid system, and therefore did not support them in any way.

However, in recent years, much has been done to try to rectify the situation and to include black communities in conservation and tourism-related activities. Local people have either become directly involved in the management of many of the game reserves, have granted some of their land to tourism or conservation programmes or become partners in various developmental projects. By staying in these establishments or visiting the reserves, tourists make a contribution to the communities who are often living in abject poverty in the areas surrounding the game reserves. The mission of the North West Parks Board is people-centred: 'To conserve wild animals, plants and landscapes for the benefit of the people.'

Together, they organise an annual, local art, music and dance festival where visitors can see communities making wooden furniture and wood carvings from indigenous trees, do needlework, pottery and other crafts.

MADIKWE

Madikwe Game Reserve

Madikwe is managed on the principle that wildlife resources should be used to benefit local communities. The idea is that if local communities can gain real benefits from the reserve by way of jobs, business opportunities and increased economic and social status, then the conservation of wildlife and the environment can be achieved as a secondary spin-off. There are three main stakeholders involved in the running of the reserve: the North West Parks Board, the private sector and the local communities.

The community provides feedback to the other stakeholders regarding their problems and development needs. They also identify community-based projects such as schools, clinics and community centres, which can be funded through dividends generated by the park. They manage these projects through community development associations.

Many communities bordering Madikwe were affected by the establishment of the reserve. In the past, there have been a number of land claims on Madikwe and the support and participation of these communities in the running of Madikwe is thus crucial to the long-term viability of the reserve. The sense of local 'ownership'

created around Madikwe now ensures that wildlife is viewed as a valuable asset.

There are plans for tented camps, campgrounds, a traditional dancing area, a tourist information centre and a heritage trail. In addition, the incorporation of tribal land into the Madikwe Game Reserve on a conservancy basis is currently being negotiated. The game reserve carries the Big Five and a number of other wild animals, and there is accommodation at the Madikwe River Lodge and the Ramorjana community-operated luxury tented camp, both of which supply benefits to the local black communities. There are also excursions to local tourist attractions, such as the black neighbourhoods, to see drama and traditional dancing provided by the community.

THE PILANESBERG

Pilanesberg is one of the largest volcanic complexes of its kind, with rare rock types and structures which make it a unique geological feature. The volcano last erupted about 1 300 million years ago. In 1979, this crater became the Pilanesberg National Park, home to the Big Five, more than 7000 animals, including 24 of the larger game species and more than 350 bird species.

It is believed that, for millions of years, people lived side by side with animals within the protection of the ancient volcano and today the surrounding communities still play a significant role in the national park, benefiting from the thousands of tourists who visit annually.

There is a strong educational ethic within the park, and children from surrounding communities – and further afield – visit the park in order to learn more about nature and conservation. There are many luxury lodges and self-catering tented bush camps and, apart from the abundant wildlife, there are fascinating geological and archaeological sites in the area.

KLERKSDORP

Bosworth Rock Engravings

These spectacular rock engravings, near Klerksdorp, are located on privately owned land, which means that visitors need to book in order to see them. The engravings and paintings consist of both abstract figures and symbols, as well as depictions of the animals that would have been found here by the San inhabitants. One of the most famous of these paintings is of a charging rhinoceros. Also in the area, are more recent engravings carved on 26 April 1884 by General Piet Liebenberg who apparently spent some time with his son nearby, tending their herds of sheep. The site is a national monument.

WOLMARANSSTAD

TOURS AND EXCURSIONS

The Diamond Route

In the old days, diamond and gold prospecting were common pastimes all around the northern and eastern parts of the country. The Diamond Route runs from Wolmaransstad in the North West Province all the way to Kimberley in the Northern

Cape along the N12. A number of private diggers and diamond cutters can be visited in the towns between, so visitors can discover not only the modern diamond diggings, but also get some idea of the life of the old diggers and prospectors.

Mine Tours

Many foreign visitors associate South Africa with the production of gold, so a visit to some of the largest gold mines in South Africa is a must. The tours take visitors deep into the belly of the earth to see the extraction of the precious metal, and it is also possible to attend a gold-pouring session. However, tours are usually run only once a week and must be arranged a week in advance. Contact any of the local tourism offices in the province.

POTCHEFSTROOM

The Pioneer Route

Because many of the towns in the North West Province are steeped in Afrikaner/Voortrekker history, the historic Pioneer Route in Potchefstroom – which was the original capital city of the Zuid-Afrikaansche Republic – is probably a good place to discover a little background of this period of South African history.

There are 14 museums and national monuments in the town and 60 buildings of architectural and other interest. The tour takes you to a variety of these places, and will more than likely include the Andrew Carnegie Library, City Hall, the Göetz Fleishack Museum and the Main Potchefstroom Museum and Totius House.

The Göetz Fleishack Museum is the only remaining example of the early town houses erected in Potchefstroom around the New Market Square between 1850 and 1855. The Main Museum contains changing exhibits with cultural history and art as themes. The Totius House museum was the home of well-known Afrikaans poet and theologian, Totius, and contains many of the poet's personal belongings. The restored homestead of President MW Pretorius is a handsome Cape-style structure that recalls an urban Boer culture that has long since disappeared.

TAUNG

Taung means Place of the Lion, but it is better known as the site where the famous Taung child skull was discovered in 1924.

The Taung Skull Heritage Site and Blue Pools

With the discovery of the Taung skull found in the Buxton quarries in 1924, a controversy began that lasted more than 25 years and put South Africa in the frontline of new discoveries in the study of human origins. Until Professor Raymond Dart stunned the world with the discovery of the skull, most scientists had focused their attention on Asia in their search for the origins of humankind. From a block of rock sent to him from the Buxton lime works near Taung, Professor Dart had chipped a small skull of a six-year-old child – the first early hominid from Africa. The skull displayed both ape-like and human-like anatomical features and

revolutionised the study of human origins. It also added further weight to theories that *homo sapiens* originated in Africa. Dart named this fossil *Australopithecus africanus*. Today, a commemorative plaque notes the precise site of the find in the lime quarry. From the site, there are breathtaking views of the surrounding area.

In contrast to the white dusty powder of the quarry are the nearby Blue Pools surrounded by picturesque caves and azure streams. Visitors can also take a walk through a re-opened mine shaft, but beware the bats. There are also charming picnic sites among the high cliffs, making this a popular spot for day visitors and for hiking and abseiling.

VRYBURG

Vryburg likes to call itself 'The Texas of South Africa', which may give you some idea of the culture of the people living in the area. Today, it is the agricultural heartland of North West Province, but it was originally proclaimed in 1882 as the capital of the ill-fated Republic of Stellaland.

One of the most interesting things that happen in Vryburg is the annual agricultural show – the third biggest in the country – where there is a variety of outdoor sports events, from hang gliding to off-road racing. It is here that you will get a good insight into the lives of local farmers, an opportunity to taste some of the best home-baked goodies and view the pride of the local agricultural produce. For a less contemporary or more historic perspective of farmers and farming practices, the local Arnold Theiller Agricultural Museum will take you back in

7

time to when farmers were still pioneers and used oxen to plough their lands.

RUSTENBURG ARTS AND CRAFTS

Rustenburg Art Ramble

This ramble is close enough to Johannesburg and Pretoria to be a favourite weekend drive for Guateng residents and it is possible to visit many well-known local potters and artists in their own studios. The Art of Africa gallery specialises in indigenous wood carvings and also stocks soapstone carvings, gemstone necklaces, pottery and other items while the Schutze German Crafts gallery has selected antiques, furniture and the best fudge. Craft Planet Creations are made from recycled fabric at Phokeng, in a remote part of the North West Province. The factory specialises in customised dyeing, screen printing, sewing, handweaving and African needlepoint.

Boekenhoutfontein, Paul Kruger House and Museum

This was once the farm of President Paul Kruger and can be visited as part of the Rustenburg Ramble. Four period buildings have painstakingly been restored and are open to the public. A tour through this house will give visitors a historical perspective on this period of Afrikaner history. Bread is baked every Saturday in an old Dutch oven, and a walk in the grounds provides great bird-watching opportunities and the chance to see the exceptional indigenous flora.

TOURS AND EXCURSIONS

The Magalies Meander

Part of the Magalies Meander falls within Gauteng and part within the North West Province but, either way, this area is definitely worth the excursion from Johannesburg. The Magaliesberg range is a range of geological splendour dating back 2 300 million years. Because of its natural beauty and abundant wildlife, the area has been inhabited by humanity for thousands of years. Today, it is quite heavily populated and, as always in areas of wonderful scenic beauty, there are a number of artists and craftsmen in the district, great restaurants, and hideaways to spend the night. There are little shops selling crystals and gemstones, oregon pine furniture, candles and candlesticks made by pensioners, watercolour painters, and potters. Look out for historical gold mines, berry farms and indigenous nurseries.

NORTH WEST
GENERAL

North West Parks and Tourism Board, PO Box 4488, Mmabatho 2735; tel: (018) 384-3040, fax: (018) 384-2524, e-mail: nwptb@iafrica.com

MAFIKENG
GENERAL

Mafikeng Tourism Information and Development Centre, PO Box 4488, Mmbatho 2735; tel: (018) 384-3040, fax: (018) 381-6058

MUSEUMS AND GALLERIES

The Molema House (*see* Mafikeng Tourism Information and Development Centre above)

Sol Plaatjie's House (*see* Mafikeng Tourism Information and Development Centre above)

Sol Plaatjie's Newspaper Office (*see* Mafikeng Tourism Information and Development Centre above)

Mafikeng Museum, PO Box 526, Mafikeng 2745; tel: (018) 381-6102

PLACES OF WORSHIP

St John the Evangelist Anglican Church (*see* Mafikeng Tourism Information and Development Centre above)

HISTORICAL AND ARCHAEOLOGICAL SITES

Kanon Kopjie (*see* Mafikeng Tourism Information and Development Centre above)

Mafikeng Cemetery (*see* Mafikeng Tourism Information and Development Centre above)

Mafikeng Anglo-Boer War Concentration Camp (*see* Mafikeng Tourism Information and Development Centre above)

Concentration Camp Cemeteries (*see* Mafikeng Tourism Information and Development Centre above)

The Ruins of the Old Mfengu Settlement (*see* Mafikeng Tourism Information and Development Centre on this page)

MONUMENTS

The Kgotla of the Barolong Boora Tshidi (*see* Mafikeng Tourism Information and Development Centre on this page)

GROOT MARICO
GENERAL

Groot Marico Information Centre, PO Box 28, Groot Marico 2850; tel: (014252) ask for extension 85

See also Potchefstroom Tourist Information and Development Centre, on page 76

TOURS AND EXCURSIONS

Mampoer Tours (*see* Groot Marico Information Centre above)

Schoemanati, Schoemansdrift (outside Potchefstroom), contact Boet Schoeman, tel: (018) 291-1354, cell: 082 927 0012

Marico Valley Mampoer, Groot Marico, contact Pieter Roets, tel: (014252) ask for extension 2212, cell: 083 7008538

M&M Mampoer Farm, Groot Marico; tel: (014) 503-0365

Tobacco Tours (*see* Groot Marico Information Centre above)

Herman Charles Bosman Literary Society (*see* Groot Marico Information Centre above)

Marico Bosveld Tours, PO Box 28, Groot Marico 2859, tel: (14252) ask for extension 85

HISTORICAL AND ARCHAEOLOGICAL SITES

Gaditshwene Iron Age Ruins (*see* Groot Marico Information Centre above)

7

CULTURAL VILLAGES

Kortkloof Tswana Village (see Groot Marico Information Centre on page 75)
Mapoch Ndebele Village, tel: (012) 341-1320, fax: (012) 341-6146

ARTS AND CRAFTS

The Art Factory (see Groot Marico Information Centre on page 75)

MADIKWE

Madikwe Game Reserve, PO Box 10, Nietverdiend 2874; tel: (01477) 8-0891 or (018) 365-9027

THE PILANESBERG

Pilanesberg National Park, PO Box 1201, Mogwase 0314; tel: (014) 555-5355/6/7/8, fax: (014) 555-5525

KLERKSDORP

Klerksdorp Tourist Information Centre, PO Box 1941, Klerksdorp 2570; tel: (018) 464-3148
Bosworth Rock Engravings, contact Roelf Marx at the Klerksdorp Museum, tel: (018) 462-3546

WOLMARANSSTAD
GENERAL

Wolmaransstad Municipality, PO Box 17, Wolmaransstad 2630; tel: (018) 596-1067

TOURS AND EXCURSIONS

Diamond Route (see Wolmaransstad Municipality above)

Mine Tours, contact Jan Schutte, tel: (018) 632-5051

POTCHEFSTROOM

Potchefstroom Tourist Information and Development Centre, PO Box 912, Potchefstroom 2520; tel: (018) 293-1611, fax: (018) 297-2082
Pioneer Route (see Potchefstroom Tourist Information and Development Centre above)

TAUNG

Taung Skull Heritage Site and Blue Pools, PO Box 743, Delareyville 2720; tel/fax: (01405) 4-1975

VRYBURG

Vryburg Municipality, PO Box 35 Vryburg, 8600; tel: (05391) 78-2200

RUSTENBURG
GENERAL

Rustenburg Tourism Information, PO Box 1993, Rustenburg 0300; tel. (014) 597-0904

ARTS AND CRAFTS

Rustenburg Art Ramble (see Rustenburg Tourism Information above)
Boekenhoutfontein, Paul Kruger House and Museum (see Rustenburg Tourism Information above)

TOURS AND EXCURSIONS

Magalies Meander, PO Box 374, Magaliesberg 1791; tel: (014) 577-1733, fax: (014) 577-1732

About the province

The Northern Cape is the largest province in South Africa, with the smallest population in the whole country; there are only 0.8 million people spread out over a massive 361 800 square kilometres. The province has only one city, Kimberley, and, for the rest, there are wide, open, semi-arid spaces, with a poor transport infrastructure. Despite this, however, the Northern Cape has a stark beauty unlike anywhere else in the country.

The far north of the province borders Namibia and the Kalahari Gemsbok National Park, and it is here that the last surviving groups of San (Bushmen) can still be found living in a natural environment (*see also* box on page 80). It is sometimes possible to meet the descendants of the original San, Khoi and Nama people in these, and other parts of the region.

Much of the present tourism focus is on the incredibly harsh natural environment that once a year, mainly in the Namaqualand region, erupts into a floral wonderland. But there are also a number of exciting projects in the pipeline that will offer tourists an opportunity to meet some of the local inhabitants.

IN THE NORTHERN CAPE

- most of South Africa's diamonds are found;
- you may have an opportunity of meeting some of the few remaining San (Bushmen);
- the mighty Orange River flows;
- every year in spring, Namaqualand's famous wild flowers transform the landscape, drawing thousands of visitors from all over the world.

This chapter

- **Kimberley** The diamond capital.
- **Kuruman and surrounds** The heartland of the province.
- **Namaqualand** Land of the San, Khoi and Nama people.

KIMBERLEY

By the turn of the nineteenth century, Kimberley had become the diamond capital of the world, an event that subsequently had an enormous effect on the entire country: for instance, it was Kimberley's diamond millionaires who were largely responsible for financing the Witwatersrand goldfields – which, in turn, have played a pivotal role in the development of the country. During the early days of the diamond rush in Kimberley, there were up to 30 000 diggers labouring day and night in a frenetic quest for wealth. Today, even though Kimberley is a modern city, there are still some remnants of its rough and tough mining camp days.

MUSEUMS AND GALLERIES

Kimberley Mine Museum and the Big Hole

The discovery of diamonds on Colesberg Kopje started one of the greatest of all diamond rushes, the end result of which was the Big Hole. This hole is among the largest man-made, or rather hand-dug, excavations in the world. The hole may be viewed from an observation platform and is now the focal point of the Kimberley Mine Museum.

The museum includes a fascinating cultural history museum that whisks you back to a time when the town was a bustling, rip-roaring mining camp. This is South Africa's largest, full-scale open-air museum and the complex is dotted with reconstructed buildings of yesteryear. One of the great treasures to be found is Kimberley's first 'house', a prefabricated wooden structure imported from England in 1877 and transported by ox-wagon to Kimberley. Genuine diamonds can be viewed in the Diamond Pavilion.

Sol Plaatjie's House

Renowned author and journalist, Sol Plaatjie, started his writing career by recording the events of the Anglo-Boer War, and he went on to make significant contributions to South African journalism and literature. (See also page 64.)

He was the first black South African to write a novel in English and, as a founder member of the African National Congress, was also the party's general secretary. He once occupied a house in the centre of Kimberley, at 20 Angel Street, which is now a national monument and is being turned into an institute for the study of African languages. Before Kimberley's forced removals, this district was known as the Malay Camp.

The Duggan-Cronin Gallery

Amateur photographer Alfred Duggan-Cronin's interesting collection of photographs was taken between 1919 and 1939 when he worked his way through southern Africa, photographing the indigenous peoples. The more than 8 000 photographs are today a priceless and irreplaceable historical record. There are so few people remaining today who still adhere to their old customs, or who dress in anything other than Western-style clothing except on ceremonial occasions, that it is fascinating to see this magnificent exhibition depicting such a valuable part of the subcontinent's past.

Robert Sobukwe's House

Robert Mangaliso Sobukwe was the founder and first president of the Pan Africanist Congress (PAC), and spent nine years imprisoned on Robben Island (see page 94). In 1958, Sobukwe had broken away from the ANC's stance of passive resistance to the apartheid government, and rallied massive support for the 1960 anti-pass protests. Sobukwe was, however, arrested after police had killed 69 people in what became known internationally as the tragic Sharpeville Massacre. On his release from the prison on Robben Island, he spent his last years practising law in Kimberley under a banning order. He lived under house arrest in Naledi Street in Galeshewe and died in 1978.

McGregor Museum

This museum houses a fantastic geological collection consisting of local rock varieties, fossils and minerals, alongside specimens from the rest of Africa and abroad. The building itself was the original sanatorium, built by arch-colonialist Cecil John Rhodes to serve as a hotel and health resort for the wealthier sectors of Kimberley society. During the four-month siege of Kimberley, Rhodes lived in a comfortable suite on the ground floor and the rooms he used are furnished impeccably in the period style.

The sanatorium was later converted into the Hotel Belgrave and, in 1933, was taken over by a Catholic order to serve as a convent. An increasing number of collections made their way to the building after it became the headquarters of the McGregor Museum in the early 1970s, and the museum now houses an Environment Hall, and the lovely chapel has been converted into the Hall of Religions where visitors can view exhibits pertaining to the five major religions – with themes of ancient beliefs, living religions, biblical biology and the history of religion on the diamond fields.

With the acquisition of the botanical records and the recollections of the Griqua chief, Jan Pienaar, a fully fledged history department was established.

KURUMAN AND SURROUNDS

The name Kuruman apparently comes from the name of a San (Bushman) chief, Khudumane, who once lived in the area. Missionary Robert Moffat arrived there in 1821 and, along with another missionary, acquired land from the chief of the Tlapins and established a mission that subsequently became the best-known mission station in Africa. It was from this humble beginning that much of the area around modern Kuruman developed.

ARCHAEOLOGY

Wonderwerk Cave and Rock Paintings

Wonderwerk Cave is located on the private farm bearing the same name, Wonderwerk, approximately 43 kilometres south of Kuruman. The cave was originally occupied by the San, evidence of whom can be seen in the form of extensive rock paintings which adorn the walls of the cave. These rock paintings were executed with the red and yellow ochres that are found in the area.

Excavations have revealed a history that stretches back over some 800 000 years from the present day. Stone Age handaxes, cleavers, remains of grass bedding, engraved stones and the bones of animals – many of them now extinct – have been found in the cave.

Many of the artefacts recovered from the cave are now housed at Kimberley's McGregor Museum (see this page).

MUSEUMS AND GALLERIES

Moffat's Mission

Many eminent people, such as David Livingstone setting off on his historic journeys of exploration, used Moffat's mission station as a base and there are, in fact, the remains of the famous wild almond tree under which Livingstone supposedly proposed to Mary Moffat. Moffat's house has been carefully restored, as have many of the other buildings. Built in 1831, the original church – with its mud floors, great wooden beams and thatched roof – is still in use. The manual printing press that printed the first Tswana bible is also still clanking away.

Guidelines to meeting the San

Meeting the few remaining San groups can be problematic for a number of reasons. Firstly, many groups live in inaccessible and isolated parts of the country. Secondly, and perhaps more importantly, visitors need to understand that, for many years, these people have been either ignored or harassed, chased from their land, abused and generally treated very badly. In the past, some 'tour operators' who had access to the San, also treated them rather poorly, and today even governments continue to disregard these indigenous people of southern Africa and their plight. They are generally poverty-stricken, dispossessed of their land, and in a constant state of insecurity.

There are a few organisations, however, that have been attempting to assist the San in reclaiming their land and helping them regain some sort of livelihood and dignity. If you would like to meet the San, be aware of and sensitive to the many problems they have had to – and continue to – contend with.

There are initiatives under way to help the San: development projects and programmes will allow tourists to meet these fascinating people and it is possible that these projects, if well managed, could go a long way to helping them. Because of the past treatment of the San, it needs repeating that they are human beings, not merely unusual attractions trotted out for the benefit of tourists. When choosing a tour operator, try to find out whether the San will benefit from your visit and how significant an interaction you will be able to have with them. Find out how long your tour operator has been working with the particular group you are planning to visit and ask the operator or guide about the issues surrounding land tenureship. However, at this time, some of the better projects involving the San are in a state of flux, mainly because there are major complications around land tenureship – particularly in the Kalahari Gemsbok National Park. While these issues are still being debated, it has been quite problematic for meaningful tourism projects to be firmly established. It could probably take some time for these issues to be resolved.

For more information and advice regarding the San and tours, contact the San Institute in Cape Town (see page 83).

NAMAQUALAND

A good way to visit and experience the wonders of Namaqualand is to go on a 4x4 trail. Although you do not necessarily need a four-wheel-drive vehicle to get around, it could be more comfortable, and you will be able to see places you would probably not otherwise reach. A new 4x4 trail is in the process of being set up, which will take visitors to some of the remote Nama villages where you are able to meet local people and experience something of their culture. Ask at the Springbok Tourism Information Office for tours that are community based (see page 83).

MEETING THE PEOPLE

The Kalahari Adventure Centre

For a number of years, this organisation has been working at putting together a 'cultural experience' where visitors can spend two nights with three San families. During the day, visitors walk a little way into the desert with the San trackers and learn about their hunting and gathering lifestyle and, at night, there is a chance to sit around the campfire with them and talk about their culture and life experiences.

The people of Springbok

A number of community tourism projects have recently been initiated in the Namaqualand district that involve people of Nama and Khoi descent. At the time of going to print, most of the projects – designed to bring smaller, less advantaged communities into the tourism fold – are

still in the initial planning and pilot project phases. There are, however, some exciting and interesting developments, which will, in time, offer tourists access to communities who have descended from some of the oldest indigenous populations in southern Africa. Already in operation are a number of guesthouses or other accommodation options with communities or families. Ask about Pella, Eksteenfontein, Paulshoek Tourist Camp in the Leliefontein Reserve – where there is also a Methodist church and parsonage, both of which are national monuments – and Riemvasmaak in the Richtersveld National Park. Contact the Springbok Tourism Information Office for further details (see page 83).

Nama Cultural Heritage Programme

Assisted by non-government organisations, local communities are in the process of recording sites of cultural, historical and archaeological importance in the Richtersveld region. At Eksteenfontein and Khubus, there are small community cultural museums that document local history and culture.

The people of the Richtersveld

The Richtersveld, in the semi-arid northwest corner of the Northern Cape Province, lies in the bend of the Orange River on the border of Namibia. Four communities living here offer the opportunity to experience Nama culture. 'Kom Rus 'n Bietjie' ('Come Rest a While'), a community guesthouse at Eksteenfontein, is managed by the local Women's Forum, and serves traditional meals. At Sandrift, another community project on the banks of the Orange River offers great angling opportunities and, on the border of the Richtersveld, is the settlement of Khubus, with its quaint community museum. Lekkersing also has a community guest-house where visitors can experience true Nama hospitality. Because many of the projects are still in their start-up phase, it may be a good idea first to contact the Springbok Tourism Information Office for details of the cultural experiences and background information on the Nama people (see page 83).

The People of Pella

Pella was founded by the London Missionary Society in 1814 as a sanctuary for the KhoiSan people who had been driven out of Namibia. During 1872, the mission was abandoned because of terrible drought and was only re-opened six years later. Today, Pella is still a small settlement whose people live much the same way as they have for hundreds of years. Stop at

the Pella Kultuur-en-Koffiekroeg, run by Elizabeth and her family, where you can drink the old traditional *moerkoffie* (hand-ground coffee) and stay over in old *matjies-hutte*, Khoisan shelters – traditionally made from skins, but today generally made from hessian wrapped around a wooden frame that is easily moved from place to place. Lunch and supper are cooked by the old matriarch and consist of traditional local fare – but you will need to let them know a little in advance if you want full meals.

There is also a wonderful old Roman Catholic Cathedral that took two missionaries seven years to complete – not surprising considering that they built it from pictures in a German encyclopedia. Some of the first date palms in the country were planted in the walled garden, and they produce a uniquely flavoured date, which is sold in wooden boxes by mail order throughout the country. This small oasis is set in the middle of a sun-baked desert. The soil is vividly coloured by minerals, and a spring has brought life – figs, grapes and pomegranates – to this stark and amazing landscape.

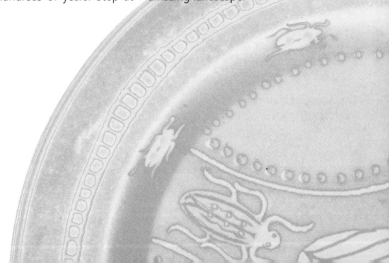

NORTHERN CAPE
GENERAL

The Northern Cape Tourism Authority, Private Bag X5107, Kimberley 8300; tel: (0531) 82-2657/2643, fax: (0531) 81-2937

KIMBERLEY
GENERAL

Diamantveld (Diamond Fields) Regional Tourist Information Centre, PO Box 1976, Kimberley 8300; tel: (0531) 82-7298, fax: (0531) 82-7211

Kimberley Tourism Information, Private Bag X5017, Kimberley 8300; tel: (0531) 3-1434 or 2-2657

The Regional Tourism Information Centre, Private Bag X6088, Kimberley 8300; tel: (0531) 82-7298; fax: (0531) 82-7211

Kimberley Mine Museum, Tucker Street, Kimberley; tel: (0531) 3-1557/8

McGregor Museum, 12 Atlas Street, Kimberley; tel: (0598) 3-0680

Sol Plaatjie's House, 20 Angel Street, Kimberley; (see Diamantveld Regional Tourist Information Centre above)

The Duggan-Cronin Collection, PO Box 316, Kimberley 8300; tel: (0531) 3-2645

Robert Sobukwe's House, Naledi Street, Galeshewe, Kimberley; (see Diamantveld Regional Tourist Information Centre above)

KURUMAN
GENERAL

Kuruman Information Office, Main Street, Kuruman; tel: (05373) 2-1095/6/7, fax: (05373) 2-3581

ARCHAEOLOGY

Wonderwerk Cave (see McGregor Museum on this page)

MUSEUMS AND GALLERIES

Moffat's Mission, The Moffat Mission Trust, PO Box 34, Kuruman 8460; tel: (0537) 12-1352

NAMAQUALAND
GENERAL

Springbok Tourism Information Office, PO Box 5, Springbok 8240), tel: (0251) 2-2011, fax: (0251) 2-1421, e-mail namakwaland@intekom.co.za

MEETING THE PEOPLE

The Kalahari Adventure Centre, PO Box 20, Augrabies 8874; tel: (054) 451-0177, e-mail: info@augrabies.co.za

The San Institute (Cape Town), PO Box 12995, Mowbray 7700; tel: (021) 686-0795

Nama Cultural Heritage Programme, contact the South African Cultural History Museum, 25 Queen Victoria Street, PO Box 61, Cape Town 8000 ; tel: (021) 424-3330

Transform (a non-government organisation working with local communities), contact Mr Floors Strauss, cell: 083 457 1976

Pella, contact Springbok Tourism Information Office (see above) or Robford Tourism, PO Box 44454, Claremont 7800, Cape Town, Tel/fax: (021) 683-6761, email: robford@mweb.co.za

8

WESTERN CAPE

About the province

The Western Cape is an area of great beauty and enormous cultural diversity. The province's 3.9 million people have the highest literacy and lowest unemployment rate in the country – yet there are still massive discrepancies between rich and poor.

Because this is where the European colonists first established a permanent settlement on the southern tip of Africa, this is where you will find some of the oldest established towns, mission stations and small communities. Here, too, generations of farmers and fishermen, working in often harsh and hostile conditions, have carved a life for themselves in some of the most dramatic landscapes. Generally speaking, the result has been the development of hard-working, tough, sometimes rather eccentric – but always friendly and hospitable – communities with a deep commitment to the land.

Many people make the trip all the way down to the tip of Africa simply in order to see Cape Town and its fabled beauty but,

if you are interested in getting to know and understand South Africa and her people, the province has much to offer and you should expand your horizons by travelling further out into the Klein Karoo and up the Garden Route.

IN THE WESTERN CAPE

- you are most likely to meet people from the so-called coloured community;
- you are most likely to meet the Cape fisherfolk;
- most of the slaves were brought ashore here before they were sold;
- you could see the Karoo mermaid;
- the top attractions include Table Mountain, fynbos, whales, and vineyards;
- the Afrikaans language developed.

This chapter

- **Cape Town:** The Mother City and surrounds.
- **The Garden Route:** The southern coast.
- **The Klein Karoo:** Ostriches and caves.

CAPE TOWN

The most obvious of the Mother City's landmarks is Table Mountain, around which life in the city seems to revolve. It was the sight of Table Mountain that the old seafarers most looked forward to during the early voyages of discovery that rounded the Cape of Good Hope.

Known at that time as the 'Tavern of the Seas', the city is today still regarded as a place that people are drawn to in order to refresh, repair and revictual – in much the same way as it was for the old sailors. It is a truly beautiful city, filled with excellent restaurants, theatres, art galleries, museums and, of course, a fascinating diversity of people. As a result, Cape Town is widely considered to be one of the top travel destinations in the world.

The original inhabitants of this region, the San (Bushmen) and the pastoral Khoi (Hottentot), have long since been integrated, one way or another, into other cultures, including that of the Europeans who arrived to settle in the Cape around 1652, and into the slave communities who came from as far afield as Indonesia, Malaysia and India. They also integrated into the black communities who were moving southwards down the coast of South Africa. It seems as if Cape Town has always been a place where people from all walks of life, from many countries around the world, of different race, culture and language have come together.

In the early days, it was this integration of humanity which led to the development of the language that is now known as Afrikaans. Slaves, farmers and labourers – all of them from different backgrounds and cultures – needed to be able to communicate with one another, and so a version of the official Dutch began to develop, until, finally, the clergy, officials, traders and aristocrats all adopted Afrikaans. It has since become one of the country's eleven official languages.

Cape Town is probably one of the most cosmopolitan of all South African cities, the tranquil environment drawing people from all over the world. Be that as it may, many visitors find that, in its sophistication, the city does not offer many opportunities to meet black people or learn about its indigenous cultures.

TOWNSHIP TOURS

One sure-fire way to meet the local people is to take a tour into one of the massive sprawling townships that surround Cape Town. It is, however, not advisable to go into these townships unless you are accompanied by someone who knows their way around. While most of the areas are entirely safe, it is easy to get lost and end up on the wrong side of town.

Unlike Johannesburg and Durban, Cape Town's townships do not have many established 'sites' or 'venues' of historical interest to visit. Most of the tours that are on offer focus more on community projects, visiting people, shebeens and taverns with which tour guides have established an association.

Most people also visit only the townships of Langa and Khayelitsha, although some do venture into other areas too. Bordered by three massive motorways and a railway track, all running into and out of the city, Langa is Cape Town's oldest formal black township – but all these routes bypass Langa itself, which has only one entrance and one exit to service the thousands of people who live there. During apartheid, this arrangement made it easier for the government to control the people living there. It is also possible to visit some of the hostels in the area and see how they have developed over time.

Bo-Kaap

Cape Town has an active Muslim community who can boast a fascinating history and who have contributed much to the development of the city. The first Muslims who were brought to the Cape were slaves, prisoners and political exiles captured in places such as Indonesia, India, Malaysia, Sri Lanka, Madagascar and elsewhere in Africa.

The origins of the Bo-Kaap date to the mid-1700s, but it was only after the emancipation of the slaves in 1834 that many freed slaves started settling in the 'upper city' that is now commonly known as the Bo-Kaap. In 1952, the area was declared a 'coloured area' in terms of the Group Areas Act, and reserved as a residential 'suburb' for the Muslim community. Today, parts of the area have been declared a national monument and it is possible to wander the streets and soak in something of what life was like for this community throughout the last century.

Although it is generally quite safe, it is always better to go with a guide, preferably someone who knows the community or who was raised there, and who can provide you with an insight into everyday life. Most of the tours will take you to the local mosque, which offers visitors a glimpse of what a pivotal role religion plays in this small community.

Do remember that followers of Islam follow strict codes of dress and behaviour, and visitors are advised to respect these age-old customs (see also page 157).

Make a point of visiting the Bo-Kaap Museum, which – built in 1760 – is the oldest house in the area, still retaining its original form. The museum gives some background to both the origins of the Bo-Kaap community and the contemporary coloured community of Cape Town.

District Six Museum

District Six was once a vibrant and cosmopolitan community of mainly working-class people from different cultural, religious and racial backgrounds, all living together. The population of District Six grew, but the municipal authorities at the time failed to provide adequate services or facilities, and much of the area began to deteriorate. In 1950, the apartheid government passed a law that forced people into racial groups and District Six, convenient as it was to the city, harbours and factories, was declared a 'whites only' area. Approximately 60 000 residents were consequently relocated and their homes were razed to the ground.

Today, the area is largely an empty and desolate expanse of land that stretches across the hillside at the foot of Devil's Peak. Apart from the odd church or religious building, little remains of the original District Six except memories – memories kept alive by what has to be one of the most vibrant museums in the country. The museum is presently housed in the old Methodist Mission on Buitenkant Street. The church is often called the 'freedom church' because of the stand it took against the apartheid government, and is a real 'people's museum', put together by ex-residents of District Six to commemorate the area and honour those who fought against the forced removals of the Group Areas Act. The museum also provides a space for the community to come together and share their experiences.

The District Six Museum – so popular that it is looking at upgrading and expanding – is very much a 'living museum': not only are there new exhibits added which rotate as new information and technology becomes available, but the community is also currently engaged in land restitution issues resulting from the loss of their land during the apartheid days.

Abalimi Bezekhaya Project

One of the main aims of the Abalimi Bezekhaya Project is the greening of the Cape Flats area. Following the forced removals of the Group Areas Act at the height of the apartheid years, people were dumped on the vast, flat wasteland of the Cape Flats and, very soon, what little vegetation there was had been used for firewood or destroyed to make way for housing – leaving the area sandy, dusty and largely denuded of any real greenery.

Abalimi has been running a training course in vegetable growing and assisting people to establish vegetable gardens – both communal and private – thereby making an enormous contribution not just towards creating jobs in areas where unemployment is rife, but also towards putting food on people's tables.

Other greening programmes initiated by the project are the Indigenous School Gardens Project, and the School's Environmental Education and Development (SEED) Programme whereby school children are encouraged to grow indigenous trees in the grounds of their schools. Abalimi has also been working with the committee of the Victoria Mxenge Self-help Housing Development Scheme, assisting them to establish gardens and greenery around the new housing programme. Most township tours cover the social and/or historic perspectives, but the difference with Abalimi is that they also provide an environmental perspective.

Khayelitsha Craft Centre

On a weekly basis, women from the Khayelitsha community and surrounding areas bring their art and crafts to this bustling centre to sell. Everything, from handmade leather shoes, printed T-shirts, beadwork, basketry and traditional items of clothing, are sold directly to the public from this vibrant self-help centre – and prices are usually much lower than you could find elsewhere in the city. Thursday is the day when the crafters arrive with their new stocks, but the shop is open throughout the week, and there are usually music or dance performances to entertain shoppers.

Philani Women's Project

It is a South African social phenomenon that women, often single, are most often the sole bread-winners in a family. Without skills, and often without much formal education, there are few opportunities to find employment; the women of the Philani empowerment project are taught skills that help them to provide for themselves and their families.

The women at the centre are taught to use waste material, such as fabric off-cuts, to weave mats and other soft furnishings depicting scenes from life in the township.

Nyanga Open-air Meat Market

The meat market is a real eye-opener for people not used to African township lifestyles. Experience the daily bustle, the way of life, the lively banter, the exuberance of the market. In contrast to the immaculate meat counters found in most supermarkets, the open-air meat market has carcasses slapped out on make-shift tables – and just about any type and part of an animal may be found on sale here. It may sound rather disgusting to Western sensibilities but, as a cultural experience, it is hard to beat, and shows a facet of urban Africa that few people know exists.

Food Kitchens

The township food kitchens provide an invaluable service to people who are otherwise unable to provide a daily meal for their families. Many of the kitchens' organisers are determined not to accept 'handouts' because these tend to keep the beneficiaries dependent on charity rather than empower them. So, where possible, people are required to perform a token service, such as peeling potatoes, in return for their meals. This discourages a culture of non-payment, which became a means of protest during the apartheid years, but which is today causing financial problems for local governments throughout the country.

Spaza shops

The small spazas are a phenomenon in townships and rural areas, which were entirely unserviced by the apartheid government. In order to assist township residents, small-time entrepreneurs started bringing basic items of daily necessity into the townships and selling them from either their own homes, or from temporary shacks, so that residents no longer needed to travel into the main centres to buy their everyday consumables. The spazas are good places to buy cooldrinks and sweets while travelling around the townships on a hot day, and it is a good way to make a small contribution to the development of the area and its people.

Shebeens and Taverns

Most of the organised tours operating in the city take visitors to Cape Town's shebeens and taverns. Even if it is hardly the 'real thing', there is a restaurant-cum-club in the CBD, Shebeen on Bree, where visitors drink from tin cups and eat 'authentic' fare from tin plates, which gives at least some idea of the township shebeen experience, if you are too nervous to venture into a township.

Golden's flowers

'Golden', as he is known, arrived in the townships after he had left his rural home to find work in the city. The only work he could find was as a gardener, but one day Golden had a dream in which he was told by his ancestors to go to the rubbish dump to collect flowers. Predictably, there were no flowers growing on the rubbish dump, but there were thousands of scraps of plastic bags and cooldrink cans. And so Golden began creating 'flowers' from these. He has become so successful that he now sells his pieces all over Cape Town, and can be visited at his township home and workshop.

Imiziamo Yethu

Mandela Park, an informal settlement right in the middle of the somewhat upper middle-class, predominantly white, seaside village of Hout Bay, is the home of a unique community tourism project.

The Imiziamo Yethu tour – the name means 'Our Collective Effort' – is a walking trail that starts with an explanation of the issues around the formation of this informal settlement, and of the problems experienced by both sectors of the communities, both black and white, living in the Hout Bay area. This tour is exceptional in that it focuses on a small area and a small community, and is run by two men, one a black ex-political activist (Kenny Tokwe) who spent some time in detention, and the other a white ex-soldier (Craig Hepburn), who are now working together to help this disadvantaged community of about 6 000 people by introducing tourism into their area. It is a pleasant change to be able to walk – rather than drive – through an informal settlement and be able to speak to the residents. The tour organisers may be reached through Green Turtle Safaris (see page 113).

Urban Safaris

This novel way to experience Cape Town starts when you are fetched from wherever you are staying, and ends when you decide you have had enough – usually in the early hours of the morning.

This 'safari' adventure takes away all the stress of trying to find a party in town. Guests are ferried by minibus to many of Cape Town's popular nightspots, and there is a ready-made party on the bus as you travel from place to place. It is especially pleasant not having to queue or pay cover charges and there are drinks aplenty on board. At an hourly rate, with people who really know the city, an urban safari gives you a comprehensive idea of Cape Town by night (and by day, on request).

The night-time venues in Cape Town are endless, and the trips may be tailored to your tastes: there is a mainstream tour to the more popular spots, and an alternative tour to the less visited night-time venues – some of which are quite exhilarating, others rather seedy.

MUSIC AND DANCE

Contemporary Cape Town is largely about entertainment and enjoyment, and the city is crammed with good venues and restaurants that host music and cabaret shows where you can hear just about any type of music and enjoy any type of dance or theatre.

The Coffee Lounge

The Coffee Lounge, situated in the centre of Cape Town, is the place to visit for some sense of Cape Town's laid-back, kinda-cool, a-little-trendy atmosphere. This eccentric venue is three storeys high: the first floor is an excellent coffee bar furnished with the '50s furniture that was once popular in many a suburban home; the second is a crazy gallery, and the third a theatre that staunchly supports South African artists and performers – where you can listen to vibey music and watch late-night movies.

8

The theme here is undoubtedly local is lekker (local is cool). Since the many budget cuts to the performing and visual arts made by the government, South African artists are finding it difficult to make a living, and many have left the country to work overseas. With this drain on local talent, places such as The Coffee Lounge have become invaluable as venues for new, up-and-coming, as well as established artists. Tuesday night is comedy night, and every other night of the week (except Sundays and Mondays when it is closed) you have a chance to see South African artists perform, or watch one of the movie classics – many of which have a South African theme.

Nico Theatre Complex

'The Nico', as it is fondly known by Capetonians, is the focus of Cape Town's mainstream entertainment and also the country's first large, multi-purpose centre for the presentation of the performing arts. An impressive 1 200-capacity opera house is used for ballet, symphony and musicals – and, occasionally, opera – and there are two other smaller theatre venues. On average, there are about 600 performances a year, and a full calendar of children's shows performed in the grand foyer.

The Rainbow Puppet Theatre

This 110-seater theatre at the Waldorff School in Constantia sees a variety of performances by professional puppeteers using assorted puppets, including glove, shadow and rod puppets. Performances are sure to enthral the entire family.

Cape Magic Entertainment and Theatre for Africa

Cape Magic Entertainment is a new theatre company that specialises in promoting entertainment with a South African flavour using wildlife and cultural themes, and performing at specially selected historic venues, such as Cape Town's Castle. Two of their most popular productions are *KwaManzi* (Place of Water), a powerful play filled with animal imagery and storytelling that evokes the soul of Africa, and *Ghosts of the Castle* that tells the story of the ghosts that haunt Cape Town's Castle of Good Hope. Be sure to keep an eye out for where they will next be performing.

Kirstenbosch Summer Concerts

The National Botanic Gardens at Kirstenbosch, with their magnificent displays of fynbos, are not only famous as one of the top botanic gardens in the world, but have also become well known for the sunset concerts held on the lawns in summer. These are a hot favourite with locals who pack picnic baskets – and the kids – into the car and head off for a late afternoon and evening of live music that may include jazz, big bands, blues, a little light classical, and occasionally traditional Cape Malay music.

Maynardville Open-air Theatre

The romantic garden theatre of Maynardville is only open during the Summer Shakespeare Season when Shakespearean performances are performed on a charming little stage set under a starry Cape sky.

The Wine Estate Theatres

A few of the bigger wine estates have their own amphitheatres that stage a range of popular entertainment such as plays and live music. Spend the afternoon wandering around the Spier estate or the Oude Libertas – both are located in the Stellenbosch area – and enjoy the concerts out under the stars.

The Green Dolphin

This excellent venue situated in the popular Victoria & Alfred (V&A) Waterfront well deserves its undoubted reputation as one of the prime jazz spots in the whole of Cape Town. Here, you can hear live jazz played by some of South Africa's top jazz musicians almost every night of the week. The food is outstanding too, so booking is essential.

South Africa's Darling

The small town of Darling, some 80 kilometres up the west coast from Cape Town, has become a hive of cultural activity and a satirical experience of South Africa. The focus of attention is 'Evita se Peron', an old railway station converted into a theatre, restaurant, pub and place of general entertainment (perron is the Afrikaans word for 'platform').

Evita Bezuidenhout is a fictional character, dubbed 'the most famous white woman in South Africa', who was created by internationally renowned South African satirist, Pieter-Dirk Uys, in the days of apartheid. Uys used her 'as a means to cheat the censor system of apartheid and confuse the establishment'.

From having been an ambassador to the fictional homeland of Bapetikosweti, Evita, an Afrikaans matron, now owns her own theatres: Peron No. 1, a small intimate theatre that seats 80 and is famous for its collection of 'boere-kitsch' (farmers' kitsch) on the walls that reflects some of the most extraordinary (and often politically incorrect) historical milestones in South African history.

Peron No. 2 is a restaurant-cum-bar used for cabaret, and its round tables can seat about 105 people for lunch and dinner. Extra venue space is provided outside in the sheltered courtyard or on the station veranda alongside the railway line.

Evita se Kombuis (Evita's kitchen) serves egte boerekos (real Afrikaans farm food), as well as traditional Cape dishes such as bobotie, waterblommetjiebredie, curry, roast lamb, chicken, quiche and pudding. Nearby is the 'Bapetikosweti Duty Free Shop'.

Evita's garden is a sight. Boerassic Park, as it is known, is a work in progress that also provides an open-air venue for shows. This satirical garden has huge trees, pretty local blooms – and exquisite plastic flowers from Taiwan – and is dotted with figures of past Afrikaner leaders in the guise of garden gnomes.

Darling, however, is also a focus during the September wild flower season, when visitors to the area can experience the magnificent showing of the 1 500 species of wild flower that grow here.

89

The Drum Café

Be cool, eat food, listen to poetry, jive to marimbas and try your hand at *djembe* (African) drumming. Jam sessions are held every Wednesday and drumming lessons every Monday, Wednesday and Friday at 6pm. The Drum Café also sells drums and undertakes repairs.

Eziko

Eziko is a cooking and catering training centre which trains unemployed men and women in basic cooking and catering skills. It is situated in one of Cape Town's oldest townships, Langa.

Its 60-seat restaurant is open from 12h00–17h00 but it will also open later and over weekends if there are bookings for more than 15 people.

There is a basic 'winter' menu of what could be termed 'township food' which offers dishes such as lamb stew, dumplings and vegetables, samp and beans, and fried chicken with vegetables – a truly African feast which consists of *Ijinja* (traditional ginger beer) that is served on arrival, *Imbanjana zegusha* (Langa's lamb riblets), *Amaphiko enkukhu aqhol-weya asezik* (special fried chicken wings), spinach and maize balls topped with spicy tomato, pumpkin fritters and many other dishes.

There are also tempting side dishes on offer, which incorporate such exotic fare as *biltong* and dried mango salad. The range of desserts on the menu includes warm *vetkoek* topped with honey and roasted nuts, and icecream served with creamy Amarula sauce.

Mama Africa

A menu of traditional 'African' fare, such as *sadsa* (a stiff maize porridge eaten by hand) and relish, and live music (including jazz) every night except Sundays. The beat starts at 10.30pm and stops late – very late...

Africa Café

They do the whole 'Africa thing' at the Africa Café: drums, staff in traditional clothes, and a communal feast. The theme is more African than South African, but it's fun and good value for money.

MUSEUMS AND GALLERIES

There are a seemingly endless number of museums and galleries in Cape Town and in the suburbs, ranging from those dedicated to the military, the police, education, wine and culture, to the medical profession. There are also smaller community museums that focus on the history and people of a particular location.

South African Museum

The controversial and lifelike exhibits of South Africa's early inhabitants, the San – cast from living subjects in the early 1900s – are some of the displays for which this museum is best known. There are also dioramas of reptiles and the fossil-rich Karoo, offering some insight into humankind's evolutionary history. With whale watching becoming a popular pastime along the South African coast, the extraordinary Whale Well – echoing to the sounds of whale song – is of particular interest.

Mayibuye Centre

The collection of material relating to the anti-apartheid struggle may be viewed at the Mayibuye Centre by appointment only but, to make sense of South Africa's past (and its present), it is well worth the effort to view the photographic archives, films, tapes, videos, posters, banners, art and historical papers housed in this centre at the University of the Western Cape.

South African Cultural History Museum

The building that today houses the South African Cultural History Museum was once the Slave Lodge that housed the majority of the colony's slaves throughout the 176 years of slavery at the Cape. Over the years, it also served, less formally, as the local brothel, and it was only after 1818 that it became the premises for the Supreme court and was later used for various other government purposes.

Many of the exhibits reflect the many influences of a variety of cultures on South Africa's cultural heritage, but there are also displays that shed some light on the early Egyptian, Greek and Roman civilisations. In the courtyard of the museum are the tombstones of Dutch governor Jan van Riebeeck and his wife, Maria, who are best remembered for the part they played in bringing the first white settlers to South Africa.

Hout Bay Museum

This is a real community museum that has an active education function. Set as it is in a valley once entirely forested (the Dutch word *hout* means wood) on the side of a mountain covered in fynbos, with a river nearby and the seashore down the road, the village and its small museum is bound to have a strong environmental focus. But there is much more to it than that. The museum also makes use of all the historic and cultural resources in the area, and trails and courses run from the museum take in the ancient Khoi middens in nearby Llandudno, discussing the Khoi's close relationship with the environment, their use of tools and so on, up to the abandoned manganese mine, and round and about Hout Bay.

There is an outstanding audiovisual show, as well as an exhibit about the building of Chapman's Peak Drive, an engineering masterpiece running around the sheer cliffs from Hout Bay to Noordhoek.

Simon's Town Museum

Simon's Town has generally been known as a naval port since 1814, and the museum covers the history of this seaside town, including the story of the 7 000 locals who were removed from the area under the Group Areas Act.

A special display and audiovisual show are dedicated to the Able Seaman 'Just Nuisance', a famous great dane dog that was officially commandeered into the Royal Navy here, and a number of educational talks on subjects such as penguins and whales, and evidence of Simon's Town's long and historic connections with the sea.

There are also guided walks through the cobbled streets of the town and an interesting tour of the Old Burying Ground, possibly one of the oldest extant cemeteries in the country.

South African National Gallery

The permanent collection on exhibit at the South African National Gallery focuses on South African art. It includes beadwork and an indigenous sculpture collection. There are also works of European artists on display.

The Castle of Good Hope

The present Castle (the original was a fort of earth and timber) was built to hold and safeguard the farmers and other settlers within its walls in times of trouble in the early days of the colony's existence. Its pentagonal structure is typical of the Dutch military fortifications of the day, and today the Castle is one of Cape Town's most famous landmarks.

Mondays to Fridays see the Changing of the Guard and Ceremony of the Keys – with guards often in full regalia and accompanied by a military band – and guided tours take visitors down into the dungeons where criminals of one sort or another were held in the old days.

Many of the period rooms house collections of paintings and furniture dating from the 17th century to the mid-19th century. The most famous of these is the William Fehr Collection – part of which may also be viewed at Rust-en-Vreugd manor house in Buitenkant Street – that depicts the Cape of Good Hope as the crossroad between East and West, and includes furniture, porcelain and silver. Also housed here is the international study centre and a changing programme of contemporary art, multimedia installations and photographic exhibitions.

Houses of Parliament

Tours around the Houses of Parliament take visitors to see the stately offices of South Africa's law-makers. The original building was established in 1885, but was enlarged in 1910 and has been extended several times since then, the last time being during the 1980s to accommodate State President PW Botha's controversial three-chamber parliament. The galleries, parliamentary museum and Africana library are open to the public while parliament is in session during the first six months of the year. One-hour tours are conducted during the recess between July and December. Visitors are requested to dress appropriately.

WORLD HERITAGE SITE

Robben Island

Although the most popular attraction on the famous penal settlement where South Africa's first black president, Nelson Mandela, was incarcerated is the cell in which he lived for 13 years of his 27-year imprisonment, there are many other fascinating features on the Island.

Visitors can only see the island as part of an official tour group, but the tour itself covers the entire history of the island, including its days as a leper colony (there are 1 500 leper graves), a military base during World War II, through to the present. A ferry carries visitors to the island and the tour, by bus, takes you past the 'house' of Robert Sobukwe, founder of the Pan African Congress, who lived in enforced isolation on the island for years, to the limestone quarry in which political prisoners were forced to work, and finally to the notorious B-section in which Mandela's cell is situated.

Guides, once themselves political prisoners on this very island, offer a fascinating insight into the lives of prisoners on the island. Overnight visitors can now be accommodated in the old wardens' quarters on Robben Island.

MARKEtS

Camphill Village Market

Farm produce, organic and biodynamic products, and anything vaguely healthy may be purchased at the market held on

The Cape Winelands

Ever since the early Dutch colonists first planted vines at the Cape, Cape Town seems to have become immersed in the production (and consumption) of wine. There are a few wine estates in the Constantia Valley of the Peninsula, but the Cape's most famous winelands lie beyond the city limits in the valleys of the hinterland.

Many of these well-established estates offer not only wine tasting, but also guided tours during which visitors observe the wine-making process (bottling, labelling and cellar storage), and may even talk to some of the winemakers – or at least people who are involved with the craft – before finishing with a taste of the wine.

Each estate has something to offer: a restaurant, museum, gallery, theatre or farm stall, or all of the above. Although most of the more popular wine estates and farms fall within the parameters of the three established routes around Franschhoek (16 venues), Stellenbosch (21 cellars) and Paarl (20 members), some of the smaller, lesser-known farms are also worth visiting – even if it is simply to avoid the summer crowds and experience a more intimate look at one of the Cape's most famed industries.

In previous years, many of the wine estates were involved in rather controversial labour practices, but some now participate in the new South Africa in a more meaningful way by enabling permanent workers to acquire title to their own homes – a situation denied them in the past. In this way, the more progressive estates are not only trying to break the traditional tie between the insecurity of farm housing and employment, but also to shift at least some wealth to previously disadvantaged communities. As part of the project, one or two estates are assisting their labourers in producing wines – bottled under their own label – from their own land.

It is possible to tour some of these farms, meet the 'new owners', and talk to them about their past and how they feel about the changes taking place. Of course, you are able to purchase the home label when it is available. This is really a wine route with a difference and is far more down to earth than many of the bigger, more commercial establisments found here. These alternative tours can be arranged through Grassroots Tours (see page 113).

the first Sunday of every month at Camphill Village near Atlantis. This is the place to buy wholesome foods such as home-made bread, yoghurt and icecream, cosmetics and a range of hand-crafted knick-knacks.

Greenmarket Square

Greenmarket Square is almost as famous in Cape Town as Table Mountain. Originally established as the farmers' market in the early 1700s, the old cobbled square in the heart of the city accommodates one of the country's oldest flea markets, and is well known for its arts, crafts, curios and hand-made clothing and jewellery.

The Pan African Market

This market in Long Street in the City Bowl is said to be one of the largest of its kind in South Africa, exhibiting a range of African curios, art and craftwork. Approximately 54 traders are housed in the market precinct and many of the artisans work in their on-site studio shops. A café, Amuka ('wake up'), on the first floor serves traditional African food.

Association for Visual Arts

The Association offers workshops, concerts and lectures, and runs a large and vibrant exhibition space for both experienced and emerging artists.

Holistic Lifestyle Fair

A place to 'get the hang' of laid-back Cape culture is the holistic Lifestyle Fair that takes place at the Observatory Community Hall on the first Sunday of every month.

On sale are a number of esoteric products, aromatherapy treatments, other alternative health treatments and crafts. Fair organisers also hold workshops and show movies.

MEETING THE PEOPLE

The Kalk Bay Fishermen

As with many of the world's small fishing communities, the fishing communities along the coast of False Bay lead rather difficult lives, reliant as they are on weather and sea conditions and the availability of fish stocks. On a usual tourist route, visitors would not normally find it easy to meet or spend time with these communities.

However, a project – run by Grassroute Tours (see page 113) – introduces the fishermen of Kalk Bay to visitors, who can spend part of a day with them out on a working fishing boat. Generally, you are not treated like a tourist, but are expected to pull your weight and fish with the rest of the crew. On stepping ashore, the fishermen teach you how to gut your fish – if you really want to – and then cook it over an open fire and eat with the fishermen's families. It is a unique way to integrate with the local community, and the meal-time stories are worth every discomfort you may have experienced on the sometimes rather choppy seas. Be sure to wear old clothes and remember that there are no special privileges. If you want to know even a little about the life of a fisherman, you need to live it for a day. Bait up your hand line.

THE 5LAVE ROUTE

The first slaves were imported to the Cape from the West African countries in 1658, hailing the start of a sad period of South African history that only ended with the emancipation of slaves around 1834, by which time there were about 38 000 slaves in the country. Despite its historical significance and the important role played by slaves in the development of the country, the slave past has all but been ignored in South Africa – until recently.

In the remote areas surrounding Cape Town are some of the most beautiful, quaint and underrated little hamlets that began as mission stations and to which many slaves fled once they were freed. Many of these villages, for years ignored by the apartheid government, have remained much the same for centuries. Some of them still have the central village square, the church, the occasional watermill (some have now been restored) and rows of exquisite cottages that were once homes to freed slaves or members of the indigenous population who converted to Christianity. The villages are indeed beautiful. Cows graze in the pastures, the thatch-roofed cottages are white-washed, and many of the people living here are direct descendants of the original inhabitants.

Elim

Elim is a little Moravian mission settlement some 200 kilometres from Cape Town in the heart of the Agulhas Plain. The church, with its simple Moravian architectural style, stands amid 12 fountains and 70 palm trees and is the centre of this coloured community. The village has the only monument in South Africa that commemorates the freeing of the slaves in 1834. Elim's tiny community of 416 in 1847 grew to a population of about 700 by 1840, and it continued to grow as more freed slaves arrived to settle here.

Today, Elim's small band of residents are restoring their village, offering visitors a peep into their unique history. The village will also become part of a more extensive Slave Route currently being formalised to assist these long disadvantaged communities and bring them into the tourism fold.

Each year, just before Easter, all of the cottages that line the road are white-washed. Some are original two-roomed, thatched, mission-style Elim *huisies* (Elim thatchers are sought-after craftsmen), such as those once occupied by the freed slaves. The original slave cemetery was recently rediscovered, and many of the gravestones still bear the impersonal names – such as January or September – given to slaves by their masters according to the month in which they arrived or were sold. Men and women are buried on separate sides of the graveyard. The stone grinders of the restored watermill are still used today to grind wheat, and the flour from the mill is used to bake traditional Elim *mosbolletjies* (small, spicy bread-like balls) as well as the most delicious biscuits.

Some of the rarest wild flower species are picked and sold from Elim, and the community has put aside a plot of land as a nature reserve, through which a small hiking trail runs. Accommodation in the village is with families in cottages or in more 'formal' accommodation in nearby towns, which needs to be arranged in advance.

Suurbraak

The small hamlet of Suurbraak (meaning 'sour marsh') is set in a well-watered little valley at the foot of the Langeberg. After a rather mundane drive, you turn a corner – and there stands the little village, with village square and a cluster of cottages that extends for no more than a kilometre. Cattle graze in the nearby fields and chickens run around in the main road, and modernisation seems to have passed this village by. Although there is electricity, many residents still use their old wood stoves for heating and cooking.

The original settlement of indigenous Attaquas (one of the Khoi groups) was discovered early in the 1600s when the Dutch first arrived in the Cape. The Attaquas were pastoralists and traders, who had named their settlement 'Xairu', which means 'beautiful'. The Dutch called the area 'paradise'. The London Missionary Society finally established a mission here in 1809, and the cottages were built and inhabited by those who accepted 'the new order' and converted to Christianity. Many of the current residents are direct descendants of the original inhabitants. Until 1960, both white and coloured families lived in what had by then become known as Suurbraak (named for the surrounding sourveld and the brack water in the area), but, once it was declared a coloured area by the apartheid government, the white population was forced to leave. Some have since returned to the area.

The quiet and rather lovely village, with its giant oak trees, fruit trees, small plots of vegetables and squawking chickens, has taken on an air of excitement. People are renovating their homes and other buildings in the village, many of which have been declared national monuments. A small coffee shop sells local specialities as well as local handicrafts such as fine embroidery and other artworks and crafts. The children in the district are being trained as tour guides and can take visitors on walks through the hamlet and its surroundings. Although there is no formal accommodation here, it is possible to stay with one of the local families if you arrange it beforehand.

Genadendal

Genadendal is the oldest Moravian mission station in the whole of Africa and was established to try to convert the Khoi clans to Christianity. It is situated in an area known as Baviaanskloof (Ravine of the Baboons), and, isolated as it is in a pristine scenic environment, it is almost as if time has passed the inhabitants of Genadendal by. Life in this beautiful village is still much the same as it was when the Dutch first landed at the Cape. Although this was not a slave community, the mission did provide a haven for freed slaves.

One of the first teacher training colleges for coloured people was established in Genadendal, but it was forced to close its doors during the apartheid years. People in the area worked on the nearby farms and, as with many of the hamlets in the Western Cape that began as mission stations, the present population consists largely of village elders. There is little employment in the area and the farm work is seasonal, so the young people inevitably leave for better opportunities in the bigger centres.

Genadendal's church square is still intact, as is the more than 100-year-old church. Services are held here every Sunday and the community plays German brass musical instruments. The local museum tells the fascinating story of the village, the old watermill has been restored to perfect working condition, and a magnificent grove of ancient oak trees planted by the original inhabitants of the mission still stretch their arms heavenwards. The quaint little coffee shop and restaurant serve local dishes, bobotie, roast mutton or beef with beans and other home-grown vegetables, and also braais (barbecues).

Melkhoudtsfontein and Stilbaai

The original inhabitants of the Melkhoudtsfontein and Stilbaai area were Strandlopers ('beach walkers'), part of the broader group of Khoi. These hunter-gatherers lived in the area, harvesting marine and other natural resources found along this stunning stretch of coast that lines the Agulhas Plain, and there is still much evidence of their existence here. Still in use are the *vywers*, or ancient fish traps: dams made from boulders built to form a barricade between the high- and low-water marks. The traps are maintained in their former condition and, according to fishermen's lore, only the person who maintains the trap may take the fish caught in it.

For many years, the inhabitants of Melkhoudtsfontein, descended largely from the original residents, seemed to belong nowhere. Their village was not part of the local authority, and the result was that the community was entirely marginalised: they had no facilities, no electricity, they received no assistance whatsoever, and they became some of the most destitute of the region's fisherfolk.

In recent years however, the people of Melkhoudtsfontein have put themselves on the map with some innovative tourism projects. They have established their own botanic garden – one of the first ever in a township – called the Soete Inval Botanical Gardens (it is fitting that their Khoi ancestors were traditionally known as outstanding gardeners). The garden contains many plants of traditional medicinal and culinary use, and boasts most of the fynbos species found in the province. Viewing is particularly good from July through to October. The little churchyard is dotted with the graves – many decorated with sea shells – of fishermen who drowned. The community has also upgraded the fishermen's houses and developed not only a community centre, but also the 'Soete Arbeid Craft Shop' where one can sit and chat to the locals. Many handmade local crafts are on sale at the shop, which also stocks hand-ground coffee and other local dishes such as *vetkoek* (a bread-like bun deep-fried in oil).

These enterprises and other tourism-related projects have received much national and international acclaim as successful social development projects.

99

Stilbaai is one of the most ideal places for spotting whales along this coast and, between July and October, boasts the highest gathering of whales in the world.

An extraordinary number of eels also populate the many streams in the area, and many have become incredibly tame. It is possible to hand-feed them, and this is usually done at the historical Palinggat Residence, one of two national monuments in the town that serve as outstanding examples of Strandveld architecture.

Amalienstein

This little village, with its landmark church, is a focal point in the Ladismith district. It began its history around 1838 when the South African Missionary Society bought land for the establishment of a missionary station at Zoar. Zoar became quite famous overseas from about 1842, which was during the period that Rev Radloff was in charge of the mission, and many people from the coloured community came to settle there. But the little farm of Zoar could not support the more than 1 000 residents and further land – farm called Elandfontein – was bought by the Berlin Missionary Society with money left to them by Frans Stein (hence the origination of the name Amalienstein).

Over the years, the little village has been dogged by controversy due to a rift that may have had its roots in problems between the South African Missionary Society, who undertook to maintain the buildings and the land, and the Berlin Missionary Society, who took responsibility for the religious well-being of the people

of Zoar. The rift in the district caused such disruption it resulted in families splitting. Over the years, this small but pretty village became poor and people living there had little hope of employment.

In 1992, a non-government organisation, known as LANOK, was approached to manage and develop the farm, which had fallen into a state of disrepair, for the people of Zoar. Today, the Amalienstein farming activities include vineyards, plums, soft citrus, nectarines, peaches, and a dairy section.

There are a number of wonderful attractions around Amalienstein, which have been developed for tourism and to encourage people to visit the area with a view to assisting the local community with employment opportunities. The Evangelic Lutheran Church is a beautiful landmark in the nearby Seweweekspoort ('seven weeks pass') valley, dating back to the eighteenth century. A visit to the church and graveyard is really worthwhile.

Another place to visit is the birthplace of the famous South African poet and writer, CJ Langenhoven. His home was in the Hoeke valley, a mere seven kilometres from Amalienstein. There are also numerous hiking and mountain bike trails in this picturesque, if sometimes arid, countryside.

Waenhuiskrans (Arniston)

Today Arniston is a trendy little seaside village where many Capetonians have their smart beach homes. But originally this fast-growing little village was known as the fishing village of Waenhuiskrans, which took its name from the nearby, massive seaside caves people said were large enough to house a wagon. *Waen, huis* and *krans* are the Dutch/Afrikaans words for 'wagon', 'house' and 'cliff' respectively.

The more interesting and beautiful part of the village is still the Waenhuiskrans section of the town which, perched overlooking a wide blue bay, with its original little thatch and whitewashed fishing cottages, has been declared a national monument. But, as with most of the original fishing villages, the communities are poor and hardy. In order to help put the village on the map, provide an education service and uplift the local community, locals from the coloured community formed a fishers' union, which takes visitors on a 'cultural tour' through their village. Visitors are met at the nearby Arniston Hotel and their first stop is the monument to those who died during the wreckage of the Arniston, a ship which sank offshore and from which the other part of the village takes its name. Visitors are given the history of the Arniston before going down to the little harbour. Here, more is explained about the lives and history of the little fishing community, the importance of fish and the dependence of the community on fishing.

The next stop is the actual fishermen's village known locally as Kassiesbaai, where the local tour guide will tell visitors all about the origins of the village, the people, the structure of their homes and the involvement of the National Monuments Council in trying to preserve the village. An interesting part of the tour is visiting a local family at home, where you learn about

how these communities live and feel about their circumstances, politics past and present, sport or just about anything else. There is also a visit to the church, which is built in the same way as the fishing cottages, the local shop run by a retired old fisherman and, finally, the Kassiesbaai Craft Centre where visitors can enjoy a cup of tea. This area is most famous for its whale-watching opportunities, and where better than from a spot chosen by fishermen years ago as a place with a perfect view of the sea.

THE GARDEN ROUTE

The earliest known inhabitants of the coast that stretches along what is now known as the Garden Route were the 'Strandlopers' ('beach-walkers'), hunter-gatherers who lived mainly along the beaches; the Khoikhoi, who lived largely on the plateaus; and the San who occupied many of the caves along the mountainsides. Obviously there were crossovers between the groups, and today there is still evidence of these early, but now long gone, inhabitants. The name 'Outeniqua', for example, is derived from a Khoi word meaning 'man with honey', and middens up and down the coast give some idea of what their lives were like.

The arrival of Europeans and black groups also had a distinct influence and added to the diversity of cultures to be experienced in these areas.

Many of the towns and villages dotted along the Garden Route are quiet, sleepy little settlements that, in season, attract holidaymakers intent on escaping life in the big city. Knysna, for example, is most famous for its lagoon, resident artists and its magnificent forests. Although the area was once thick with indigenous yellow-wood and stinkwood, in recent years, much has been replaced by exotic commercial plantations.

For all its beauty, Knysna and its surroundings is perhaps fast becoming a prime example of South Africans at their most insensitive in their frenzy to establish a 'place in the sun'. The authorities have, for generations acceded to overdevelopment in the name of 'improvement' and profit-making at the expense of the natural environment. But this 'development' has also spawned groups of environmentalists and social activists who are working hard to improve the conditions along the Garden Route.

MOSSEL BAY

Tarka Township

The houses in Tarka Township just outside Mossel Bay, for many years a coloured township, are some of the oldest in Mossel Bay, dating back to 1898. The houses were built with locally excavated stones, and held together with clay and sand instead of cement. The history of Tarka and its people, and the role they have played in the development of Mossel Bay, are related in the old photographs in the Culture Museum in the Bartolomeu Dias Museum Complex (see page 103). First see the photographs, and then see the real thing.

Cape St Blaize Cave and the Khoi Village

The pastoral Attaquas were a group of Khoi who were living in the area around Cape St Blaize when the Portuguese explorer Bartolomeu Dias landed here in 1488 while on his voyages of discovery around the African coast. These early inhabitants were the reason he gave Mossel Bay its original name of 'Bay of the Herders' or 'Bay of the Cowherds'.

The Khoi village being established at the foot of the caves is still very much in its developmental stages and is a small private initiative. Obviously, there are no longer any genuine Khoi people in the district – most were integrated into other groups many years ago – but the 'village' of reconstructed Khoi homes does give some background and insight into Khoi life in the past. On occasion, the village owners organise a concert or re-enactment of scenes from the lives of the early Attaquas, and of particular interest is the explanations of the wedding celebrations and the death and burial ceremonies. There is also a small, outdoor restaurant.

Even though boardwalks have been constructed to protect the nearby Cape St Blaize cave, a national monument in its own right, the cave certainly has a more authentic feel to it than the village. Situated on a superb lookout point, it is thought that it was originally used between 100 000 and 70 000 years ago as a shelter for people who hunted and collected shellfish, bulbs and honey.

The most likely occupants of this cave and, quite probably, many other shelters along the coast, were groups of about 15 San – or, perhaps, Attaquas.

Muller's Farm

This farm, not far from Mossel Bay, provides a rather unusual opportunity actually to see a working farm typical of so many in the southern Cape. Visitors can spend a day on the farm, take an ostrich tour, or ride a tractor, and experience at least some of what it means to be a farmer here. Fresh farm produce is on sale, and the gallery at the homestead shows work by local artists.

Bartolomeu Dias Museum Complex

Four museums make up the Bartolomeu Dias Museum Complex: the Maritime Museum – its marine history played a significant role in the development of this community – the Shell Museum and Aquarium, the Culture Museum and the Granary.

The Granary, which is a reconstruction of the original built in 1786, contains exhibits of old wagon trails, mountain passes and fynbos, while the Shell Museum and the Aquarium were erected beside the Post Office Tree in 1902; a fascinating exhibit explains how man uses shells.

The Culture Museum depicts the heritage of the people of Mossel Bay and includes exhibits of its earliest inhabitants, the Khoi and the San. The Maritime Museum houses a beautiful replica of the caravel used by Portuguese explorer Bartolomeu Dias to cross the Atlantic more than five centuries ago. There are also displays of early maps, shipwreck salvage, coins and gemstones.

Post Office Tree

A large milkwood tree on the hillside in Mossel Bay became an important landmark for sailors passing the Cape in the early days of the settlement. In 1500, a certain Pedro de Ataide left an important letter in a shoe, or an iron-pot (no one has decided quite which), at the foot of the large tree. The letter was found in 1501 by João da Nova, a commander of an East India fleet en route to India, and he took it with him. This started the tradition of 'post office trees' in South Africa, where sailors could place their letters for calling ships to collect and deliver.

Today it is still possible to post a letter in a shoe (albeit a copy made out of stone) under the tree and it is specially franked in commemoration. The original old milkwood tree has now been declared a national monument.

Hartenbos Museum

The Hartenbos Museum is in the village of the same name, on the outskirts of Mossel Bay. Walking from room to room in this amazing little museum, you almost feel as if you are a Voortrekker. Life-like dioramas recall the way of life during the Great Trek, showing a family loading their wagon for the long journey ahead, unpacking each night and getting ready to sleep, as well as various daily functions such as repairing the wagon, fighting off hostile people, playing, singing and dancing. One of the last scenes depicts a fairly stereotypical, but dignified President Kruger, who is a central figure in the display. There is also a traditional shop circa 1930.

Lazaretto Cemetery

The Lazaretto Cemetery, which is situated close to the sea, is the final resting place of residents who played a significant role in the development of Mossel Bay. Most of the graves are worn and eroded by the ravages of time and the sea, and the oldest decipherable grave headstone dates back to 1809.

Malay Graves

Another interesting site is the old Malay graves not far from the Old Post Office Tree. This piece of land was granted to the mostly slave Muslim community well over 100 years ago, for a graveyard. The graves were rediscovered in 1968.

Crime and Disaster Tour

Unsurpassed in originality, the Crime and Disaster Tour is a delight. It would spoil the show to reveal too much about this tour, but it takes visitors through the dark side of Mossel Bay's history: a brutal murder, the ghost lady of the harbour, shipwrecks, and an unexplained disappearance in the course of justice.

Mossel Bay Tourism will put you on the right trail (see page 114).

Cultural Dance Groups

Three 'dance troupes' operate in Mossel Bay, each from a different cultural sector of Mossel Bay's community. The Mossel Bay Coons is a group of coloured folk who, in the true Coon festival tradition, don their colourful outfits to sing, dance and play banjo, drums and guitars. Another is the Pafani maAfrica group who perform all the traditional Xhosa dances, while the third is the Hartenbos Voortrekker Dance Group who dance in the manner of the old Boer tradition. The three groups represent the three main cultural groups who converged on the area in the past, and contributed to its development.

The groups – who can be hired out for tour groups – usually perform on specified occasions, but they are often asked to perform at venues around the city or at festivals. Information may be obtained through the Mossel Bay Tourism (see page 114).

The Garden Route is renowned not only for the warm hospitality of its people, but also the exceptional seafood and other culinary delights, so to get to know the locals, pop into one of the delightful little eateries and strike up a conversation with the regulars.

Jazzbury's

This restaurant prides itself on providing 'modern, cross-cultural South African fare' and is the place to go if you would like to try fine southern Cape wines and local fare such as mopane worms, curries, prawns, oysters and ostrich.

GEORGE

The George Museum

Although you don't usually expect to find fairies in a museum, one of the most enchanting exhibits of the George Museum is the fairy exhibition – a series of exquisite paintings by local artist Ruby Reeves. Considering the amazing floral diversity and innumerable plant species found covering the mountains, hilltops and valleys in the area, it is not difficult to see where she got her inspiration. Another interesting diversion is the story of the region's early timber enterprises, which have played such a prominent part in George's history. It is rather fun to see what towns looked like 'in the old days', and George Museum also has a gallery of photographs of the town's past.

The Southern Cape Herbarium

Housed in the same building as the George Museum is the Southern Cape Herbarium, best described as a library of pressed flowers that have been collected from all over the southern Cape. The herbarium has a strong educational basis and there is an on-going programme of courses for the public. Staff are actively working to preserve the valuable areas of fynbos from the bulldozers introduced by developers up and down the Garden Route.

A small display depicts how the early botanists – the indigenous Kwena and San people – used plants, and in the museum grounds is a charming ethno-botanical garden where the plants used by the early people for medicinal and culinary purposes are cultivated.

The Herbarium staff will show you around and explain which plants the Voortrekkers used for coffee or for sweetener, and which plants the San or Kwena used to 'clear the blood' and so on. It may, however, be a good idea to telephone beforehand because staff are often away on field trips.

KNYSNA
TOWNSHIP TOURS

Knysna Township Trail

The Township Trail is a four-hour off-road walk that takes you into the heart of the old, established townships of Knysna. There are numerous opportunities to meet members of the community and learn about their lives. There is also a stop-off with Mary, a storyteller, who explains many of the interesting Xhosa customs, such as the circumcision ceremonies, and the reasons why three-month-old children have a little piece of their finger chopped off. She explains the significance of traditional beer and, if there is any brewing while you are there, you have the opportunity to taste some.

Apart from the visit to Mary, there is no set route or any other facilities laid on for the visitor. If, for example, you are interested in seeing a pre-school, they will take you to one; if you would like to see dancing, the students practise every afternoon and you can go along and watch; if you want to visit a *sangoma*, there are many in the township. As a result, the trail is probably one of the more authentic and informative.

This trail is part of a community development project in Knysna's townships. The income goes directly back into the project to finance a number of social programmes, such as an education centre in a Rastafarian community (one of the stop-offs during the trail), a pre-school, a *sangoma* school, a small dance

10

troupe called Our Future, and a tour-guide training programme for teenage students from underprivileged communities. There is also a bursary fund to cover the costs of the students' final tour-guide exams.

Hornlee Nature Reserve

The small coloured community of Hornlee outside Knysna has won numerous awards for the little botanic garden and nature reserve that were established by a group of students from the nearby school. The children, assisted by their teachers, worked closely with their community to establish this little garden in a small valley that was once an eye-sore of a garbage dump. As the garden grew, so the surrounding community began to take increasing pride in its surroundings. Visit the garden, the school and the surrounding community and discover how the garden has changed people's perceptions of their environment.

ARTS AND CRAFTS

Knysna Painting Holidays

As you walk through Knysna, it seems as if every second shop is selling arts or crafts of some sort. Many of the objects on sale are handmade, and the area seems to attract artists, weavers, potters, cabinet-makers, woodcarvers and any other crafters. It is even possible to go on a 'painting holiday' with well-known artists Dale and Jenny Elliott, who offer basic and advanced painting courses, Corporate Therapy art courses, Right-Brain Art Weeks, Outdoor Painting Weeks and much more.

The Old Gaol Complex

The Old Gaol was the first government building in Knysna and originally housed convicts employed to work on the road from Knysna to Prince Alfred's Pass. During the Anglo-Boer War, the gaol was picketed and sandbagged to provide a shelter for people from the outskirts of Knysna who were fleeing from the Boers. The premises was declared a national monument in 1991, and today it is a hive of activity and an important meeting place for the Knysna community. Locals gather at the wonderful café called The Old Gaol, but there is also the Angling Museum (people in this area are avid fishermen), the Knysna Art Gallery and a gift shop to visit. Occasionally, there may be buskers' evenings at The Old Gaol, where you can sit back and enjoy the compositions of the street musicians.

The Old Nick

This old shop is situated in the old trading store that was once the only store between Knysna and Humansdorp. The pottery available here is hand-thrown, decorated and fired on the premises, and there is a working weaving museum where old power looms from the last century are still used to produce beautiful woven items, such as rugs and cloths.

The Timber Route

Much of Knysna's early life evolved around forestry – and, to a large extent, it still does. The interesting Timber Route takes you to the studios, galleries, workshops and factories of woodworkers, carvers, wood merchants and the Reenendal Community

Entrepreneurs, a group of underprivileged people who produce handmade wooden products and crafts of all sorts. Information and bookings can be made through the Knysna Tourism Bureau (see page 115).

THE KLEIN KAROO

The Klein Karoo may be semi-arid, but it is a very productive farming district. Apart from the ostriches for which it is most famous, the alcohol industry here produces all sorts of beverages, from wine and port, to the more 'traditional' tipples such as witblitz (white lightning) and buchu brandy (made from the leaves of the buchu bush).

OUDTSHOORN

TOWNSHIP TOURS

Matjoks

Townships in the Oudtshoorn district are known as the Matjoks, and tours tell the 'untold stories' of the area. Visitors are taken to Bridgton and Bongolethu – meaning 'My Pride' – where they may meet the people and see for themselves how one of the most prosperous communities of the Garden Route and Klein Karoo has developed from the remnants of apartheid.

CULTURAL VILLAGES

Gamkaskloof

Although not a cultural village in the strictest sense, Gamkaskloof is certainly one in the broader context. It seems almost unreal that, in modern times, people lived in the Gamkaskloof Valley, almost completely isolated for more than 100 years. The earliest inhabitants were Stone Age people, but the first white farmer to settle in the valley was Petrus Swanepoel who set up farm there in 1830.

Eventually, a small pioneer settlement of 16 farms was established. There was no road into the valley, and the only access or exit was on foot or by donkey. All goods were carried in and out through the Gamka River gorge. As a result, the community became rather insular and increasingly uninterested in the outside world. The valley was given the Afrikaans name,

Ostriches

There are three main ways to see ostriches: simply drive past in a car (the birds seem to line the road), visit an ostrich show farm, or go on an ostrich safari. A fourth option, however, is to visit one of the working ostrich farms (some now take visitors), but be warned: many people may consider some of the practices rather brutal.

Unlike the past, when the main marketable feature of the ostrich was its feathers, every part of a bird is now used: feathers are still used by the fashion industry; meat is sold as a tasty, low-fat protein food; ostrich biltong (dried meat) is a popular delicacy; the hides are used for a variety of fashion and curio goods; bone meal is an extremely valuable fertiliser; and, of course, the live birds are a major tourist attraction.

Wine, Port and Witblits

A wine route runs through the Klein Karoo from De Rust (east of Oudtshoorn) to Montagu in the west. The area is one of eight wine regions in the country; although the production is fairly small, the wine and port are classed along with the best in the country. *Witblits*, a highly alcoholic drink made at some of the farms, features prominently in the folklore of the Voortrekkers, with many hilarious accounts relating to bouts of drinking. Brandy generally has a 43% alcohol content, but *witblits* has 50%. So, if you are planning a tasting trip, beware the kick. And plan to stay somewhere close by overnight.

Although some farms produce *witblits* commercially, it is still distilled in the traditional way in many places, by boiling the grapes over a coal fire in copper pots. If left to distill for about three years, *witblits* can be made into brandy. In the Calitzdorp area, a port festival is held every year – and there are many farms where you can taste port throughout the year.

Die Hel (The Hell), by a stock inspector in about 1940, when he would make his two-monthly rounds to inspect livestock and had to climb down 'the ladder' to get into the valley, and complain bitterly that this was indeed 'Hell'.

A road was finally constructed in 1962, and the people of Gamkaskloof began to leave. As the valley emptied and its citizens ventured into the outside world, many sensational, and sometimes unfounded stories appeared in newspapers and magazines about this community that time seemed to have forgotten. The last active farmer finally left Gamkaskloof in 1991. Most of the land in the Gamkaskloof is now under the protection of Cape Nature Conservation, which realised that the wealth of cultural history left behind by this small community – living here in isolation as if it was still the 1800s – should not be lost. Today, visitors may still see the abandoned homes and farms, but the town has not really been developed as a tourist destination, and, even though there is now a road into the valley, the trip is arduous and you will probably need a sturdy car.

Contact the Cape Nature Conservation officer based at the historic farm, Ouplaas, for more details (*see* page 116).

ARTS AND CRAFTS

The Klein Karoo National Arts Festival

This annual festival for the visual and performing arts is fast becoming a contender as one of the most outstanding festivals in the country. Although it has a strong Afrikaans component, this is where you will see some of the most exciting 'stars' of contemporary arts in South Africa. People converge from all over the country for a few days of dance, drama, music, crafts, art – and just to meet the friendly, and often eccentric, folk of the Klein Karoo.

Oudtshoorn's Mermaids

If anything really captures the essence of the people of Oudtshoorn, it has to be the mermaid in the bell tower of the CP Nel Museum. Although the town is inland – in a semi-desert – there have always been legends of *watermeidjies* (water maids or mermaids), and the older coloured folk of the district have, for decades it seems, frightened children into obedience with threats that the *watermeidjie* would carry them off – much like the bogeyman.

The Klein Karoo experienced terrible floods in 1996 and, shortly thereafter, a wag on the local radio station reported that a mermaid had washed out at the bottom of one of the small waterfalls in the district. Within days, hundreds of people from all over the country – and, so the story goes, media representatives from as far afield as Zimbabwe and Namibia – flocked to see the mermaid. Some visitors claimed that they had not heard the news, but had been told about the mermaid by their ancestors in dreams. On finding no mermaid, many people felt duped but, with the sense of humour that seems to characterise the people of the area, the CP Nel Museum obliged. An old window display mannequin was dressed like a mermaid and propped up in the museum – to more-or-less everyone's delight. Later, when the fuss had died down, the townsfolk decided to haul the mermaid up into the bell tower above the CP Nel Museum where, lit up at night, she still resides today.

But the strange mermaid story does not end there. On researching the phenomenon of the 'mermaid rush', a local anthropologist discovered that there are four known sets of San rock art in the area that unmistakably depict mermaids – and these date back thousands of years. Mermaids have obviously been in the district for a long, long time.

CP Nel Museum

Named after a local businessman who amassed a fascinating array of weaponry, early motor cars, war medals, and a private shell collection, these exhibits are all housed in the building once occupied by a boys' high school. Also on display is an intriguing collection of fashion items from the opulent era of Oudtshoorn's feather boom. Being in the centre of what was once the heart of a thriving ostrich feather industry, some displays tell the story of ostrich farming, but there is also one of the world's finest collections of old bottles on show.

The ghosts of feather palaces

It seems that Oudtshoorn has always been a place of rather eccentric people. At the turn of the century, during the boom in the feather industry, people made enormous amounts of money. Many spent their money on opulent homes – each more extravagant than the last. The result was what are known today as the 'Feather Palaces', with their sandstone turrets and towers, wrought-iron railings, fretwork and lacework, papier mâché pressed ceilings, fireplaces and elaborate stained-glass windows. Many of these, such as Mimosa Lodge, Pinehurst and Rus en Urbe – or Foster's Folly, as it is known – still stand today.

Foster's Folly

Foster's Folly was built by Mr J Foster, a local attorney, member of the Cape Legislature, rumoured playboy and general high-roller. He is rumoured to have kept both a wife and mistress, in separate parts of this large mansion. When the feather boom crashed, so did many businessmen and farmers, and Foster apparently committed suicide in the cellar of his home.

But that version of the story is not interesting enough for the inhabitants of Oudtshoorn, and another version has it that he didn't really commit suicide; he only pretended to – and later attended his own funeral in disguise. He was, however, never seen again, and his grand home became a girls' boarding school, then a guesthouse, and is presently being converted into a hotel school.

In a bizarre twist to Foster's tale, a local photographer was taking pictures in one of the rooms of Foster's Folly in 1997 when he heard footsteps down the passage. A woman – wearing the inevitable long white dress – appeared, carrying what he thought may have been a small baby or a doll. She greeted him as she passed into the next room. Once his assignment was over, he went to say goodbye – but the room was empty. As can only happen in a place like Oudtshoorn, research is now afoot to discover who the ghost could be. Early speculation was that it should have been a male ghost, since Foster supposedly committed suicide there, but people say that it may be his wife or his mistress – or even one of the wayward schoolgirls.

Arbeidsgenot

Arbeidsgenot in Oudtshoorn was the home of CJ Langenhoven, one of several accomplished people who made the town their home. Langenhoven, an attorney, prolific writer and champion of the Afrikaans language, wrote the old South African national anthem, *Die Stem van Suid-Afrika*, in 1918.

On his death, his wife presented Arbeidsgenot to the South African nation, and it is now open to the public. The house is filled with Langenhoven's personal belongings, including many gifts given him by readers, such as the little carving of Herrie, an elephant that features in one of his books.

The Cango Caves

The Cango Caves are among the most commercially developed in the country but, be that as it may, they are internationally renowned as one of the world's great natural wonders and few visitors to this subterranean wonderland ever leave disappointed. The story goes that the entrance to the caves was discovered in 1780 by a herdsman who told his master, Barend Oppel, about them.

Together with a local road builder and farmer named Jacobus van Zyl, they explored the caves. Van Zyl was lowered into the cave with a flickering flame torch, and discovered a massive chamber, 98 metres long, 49 metres wide and 15 metres high, and tall formations such as what is now known as Cleopatra's needle, a 9-metre-high stalagmite that is 150 000 years old.

Matjiesfontein

Matjiesfontein began its life as an insignificant little wayside rail station in the wilds of the Karoo over a century ago, but it grew to attain fame throughout the country. This delightful village was developed by Jimmy Logan, the son of a Scottish railway official who, in the late eighteenth century, gained the refreshment room concession at the Matjiesfontein siding. Between 1884 and the outbreak of the Anglo-Boer War, he built the village of Matijiesfontein into a celebrated Victorian health and holiday resort frequented by the rich and famous.

Cecil John Rhodes, the infamous colonist, was a frequent visitor, as was the well-known South African author Olive Schreiner, who visited and stayed so often that today the cottage she stayed in is named the Olive Schreiner Cottage. Presidents and aristocrats from the Cape Colony all visited and stayed at Logan's fine home, Tweedside Lodge. By 1920, when James Logan died, the small village was no longer fashionable (it had been by-passed by the National Road at the end of World War II) and finally sank into obscurity – until 1968, when it was bought by a well-known hotelier who saw the potential in the graceful Victorian buildings.

Today, the Lord Milner hotel has been restored to its former elegance and there are 14 beautifully restored bedrooms, antique-filled public lounges and a library that opens onto spacious courtyards and verandas. There is also a lovely old Victorian country pub, a post office, and at the train siding across the dusty little street is a museum stuffed with Victorian memorabilia. Logan's General Store is now a coffee house, behind which is the original Logan's Masonic Lodge – probably the oldest building in Matjiesfontein.

There are few other places that are worth visiting for a glimpse into South Africa's Victorian colonial past.

11·

More than 30 caves have been found since those early days, and they contain amazing limestone dripstone formations. The Grand Hall, a later discovery, stretches 107 metres across and the highest dripstone formation is a column of 12.6 metres. It is unlikely that the early inhabitants of the cave ever ventured very far into the caves, but at the entrance to the caves is a small section of original San paintings, testimony to the fact that the caves were once inhabited by South Africa's earliest residents.

MONUMEN⊤5

Statue of the Boer

As you drive towards Vlakteplaas outside Oudtshoorn, you may wonder what is looming on the hillside. As you draw closer, you will see a massive, elaborately carved statue of a Boer standing on a grave site. He is wearing a hat and is carrying a carefully sculpted pocket watch – but over time he has lost the hand that once held a pipe. Although there certainly is a story to be told here, no one is saying what it is.

In small, conservative communities such as this one, it may be considered blasphemous to have an image of yourself erected on your grave, particularly such an enormous one. Perhaps this is why no one wants to be associated with the statue.

Slave Dam

At the top of the Kammanassi mountains stands a large dam hand-built by slaves who completed it in 1834. This is a very pretty spot, much favoured by picknickers and the setting for many tales and legends of yesteryear told by the locals.

MEETING THE PEOPLE

Bernhard's Taphuis

The Taphuis is one of Oudtshoorn's many good restaurants – but there's a difference. It not only serves food, but also has a cigar menu. The cigars come from such exotic destinations as Cuba, Switzerland, the Philippines, Dominican Republic and other enthralling places. The menu also includes The Serengeti, which is described as South Africa's top cigar brand and ideal for beginners – and a great memento of a visit to South Africa.

CAPE TOWN
GENERAL

Cape Town Tourism, PO Box 1403, Cape Town 8000; tel: (021) 426-4260/7/8, fax: (021) 426-4266

TOWNSHIP TOURS

Bo-Kaap Community Guided Tours, contact Shireen Narkedien, tel: (021) 422-1554

Bo-Kaap Museum, 71 Wale St, Cape Town; tel: (021) 424-3846

District Six Museum, tel. (021) 461-8745

Grassroute Tours, PO Box 51701, Waterfront 8002; tel: (021) 424-8480, fax: (021) 424-8481, e-mail: grasrout@iafrica.com

Green Turtle Tours and Safaris, 15 Victoria Avenue, Hout Bay; tel: (021) 790-7671, cell: 082 882 7884

One City Tours (Mandalay), contact Paula Gumede, tel: (021) 387-5351

Siyaya Group Tours (Gugulethu), contact Xolile Somdaka, tel: (021) 637-9625

Eziko Cooking & Restaurant, P O Box 38, Langa, 7455; tel: (021) 694-0434; fax: (021) 694-6711

Abalimi Bezekhaya Project, Private Bag X12, Observatory, 7935

Khayelitsha Craft Centre, PO Box 135, Thornton 7485; tel. (021) 361-5246

Philani Women's Empowerment Project (see Cape Town Tourism above)

The Nyanga Open-air Meat Market (see Cape Town Tourism above)

Imiziamo Yethu (see Green Turtle Tours above)

Urban Safaris, contact Jochen, cell: 082 930 5747, 082 757 9145

MUSIC AND DANCE

The Coffee Lounge, 76 Church Street, Cape Town; tel: (021) 424-46784

Nico Theatre Complex, DF Malan Street, Foreshore, Cape Town; tel: (021) 421-7695, fax: (021) 421-5448

The Rainbow Puppet Theatre, Waldorff School, River Road, Constantia; tel: (021) 783-2063, 706-2738

Cape Magic Entertainment, PO Box 6939, Roggebaai 8012; tel: (021) 421-1878, fax: (021) 419-7790 (dinner and show on request for groups only)

Kirstenbosch National Botanic Gardens, Rhodes Drive, Newlands; tel: (021) 761-4916

Maynardville Open-air Theatre, cnr Church/Wolfe streets, Wynberg; contact Jenny at the Nico Theatre Complex, tel: (021) 421-5470; for bookings, contact Computicket, tel: (021) 430-8010

Oude Libertas Amphitheatre, Adam Tas Road, Stellenbosch; tel: (021) 808-7473

Spier Theatre, tel: (021) 809-1165, e-mail: spier@iafrica.com

The Green Dolphin, Victoria & Alfred Waterfront; tel: (021) 421-7471

Drum Café, Caledon Studios, 84 Harrington Street, Cape Town; tel: (021) 461-1305

Mama Africa, 178 Long Street, Cape Town; tel: (021) 424-8634

Africa Café, 213 Lower Main Road, Observatory, tel: (021) 447-9553

Evita se Peron, tel: (02241) 3145, e-mail: evita@iafrica.com

MUSEUMS AND GALLERIES

South African Museum, Queen Victoria Street, Cape Town; tel: (021) 424-3330

Mayibuye Centre (by appointment only), University of the Western Cape, Modderdam Road, Bellville; tel: (021) 959-2954, fax: (021) 959-3411

South African Cultural History Museum, 49 Adderley Street, Cape Town; tel: (021) 461-8280, fax: (021) 461-9592

Hout Bay Museum, 4 St Andrews Road, Hout Bay; tel: (021) 790-3270

Simon's Town Museum, The Residency, Court Road, Simon's Town; tel: (021) 786-3046

South African National Gallery, Government Avenue, Cape Town; tel: (021) 465-1628, fax: (021) 461-0045

The Castle of Good Hope, Castle Street, Cape Town; tel: (021) 469-1249/50

Rust-en-Vreugd, 78 Buitenkant Street, Cape Town; tel: (021) 469-1160, fax: (021) 462-3750

Houses of Parliament, Government Avenue, Cape Town; tel: (021) 403-2911

Robben Island Tours, tel: (021) 419-1300

MARKETS

Camphill Village Monthly Market, Camphill Village (near Atlantis) off the N7; tel: (021) 572-2345, fax: (021) 572-2238

Pan African Market, 76 Long Street, Cape Town; tel: (021) 424-2957

African Craft Market (Khayelitsha), tel: (021) 54-2693, 361-5246

Association for Visual Arts, 35 Church St, Cape Town; tel: (021) 424-7436, fax: (021) 22-1477

Holistic Lifestyle Fair, Observatory Community Hall, Station Road, Observatory; tel: (021) 448-7166

Zenele Enterprises (Khayelitsha), tel: (021) 361-1840

Kuyasa Bufazi Women's Project, tel: (021) 694-2006, 556-1511

THE CAPE WINELANDS

Winelands Information, tel: (021) 876-0686

Franschhoek Wine Route, tel: (021) 876-3062

Paarl Wine Route, tel: (021) 872-3605

Stellenbosch Wine Route, tel: (021) 886-4310

See also Grassroute Tours on page 113.

MEETING THE PEOPLE

Kalk Bay Fishermen (*see* Grassroute Tours on page 113)

THE SLAVE ROUTE

Elim Tourism Bureau, PO Box 33, Elim 7284; tel: (02848) 806, fax: (02848) 750

Amalienstein Tourism Information, PO Box 36, Ladismith 6655; tel: (028) 561-1000, fax (028) 561-1419

Suurbraak Tourism Information, PO Box 132, Suurbraak 6743; contact Gerhard Voges, tel: (0285221) 806/611

Genadendal Tourism Information, PO Box 137, Genadendal 7234; tel/fax: (028) 251-8582

Melkhoudtsfontein Tourism Information, PO Stilbaai 6674; tel: (02934) 42602, fax: (02934) 42549

Waenhuiskrans Tourism Information, Waenhuiskrans Fishers' Union, PO Box 351, Bredasdorp 7280; tel. (02847) 5-9156/9737; or contact Tony Murtz, tel. (02847) 5-9300

THE GARDEN ROUTE
GENERAL

Garden Route Tourism, PO Box 1514, George 6530; tel/fax: (044) 382-7078, cell: 083 743 9290

Wilderness National Park, PO Box 35, Wilderness 6560; tel: (044) 877-1197, fax: (044) 877-0111

Meiringspoort Adventures, tel/fax (044) 241-2087

Die Gat Safaris, PO Box 72, De Rust, 6650; tel/fax: (044) 241-2406

MOSSEL BAY

Mossel Bay Tourism, PO Box 1556, Mossel Bay 6500; tel: (0444) 91-2202, fax: (0444) 91-1912, e-mail: Info@mb.lia.net

Tarka Township (*see* Bartolomeu Dias Museum Complex on page 115)

Cape St Blaize Cave and the Khoi Village, 3 16th Avenue, Mossel Bay 6500; tel: (044) 691-1648, cell: 082 572 9161
Muller's Farm, tel: (0444) 98-1022, cell: 082 494 6403
Bartolomeu Dias Museum Complex, Private Bag X1, Mossel Bay 6500; tel: (0444) 91-1067, fax: (0444) 91-1915
Post Office Tree (see Mossel Bay Tourism on page 114)
Hartenbos Museum, PO Box 3, Hartenbos 6520; tel: (044) 601-7200
Lazaretto Cemetery (see Mossel Bay Tourism on page 114)
Malay Graves (see Mossel Bay Tourism on page 114)
Crime and Disaster Tour (see Mossel Bay Tourism on page 114)
Cultural Dance Groups (see Mossel Bay Tourism on page 114)
Jazzbury's Restaurant, 11 Marsh St, Mossel Bay; tel: (0444) 91-1923, fax: (0444) 91-2268

GEORGE

George Tourism Bureau, PO Box 6530, George 1109; tel: (044) 801-9295, fax: (044) 873-5228
George Museum, Private Bag X6585, George 1109; tel: (044) 873-5343, fax: (044) 874-0354
Southern Cape Herbarium, tel: (044) 874-1558 (see also George Museum above)

KNYSNA
GENERAL

Knysna Tourism Bureau, 40 Main Street, Knysna; PO Box 87, Knysna 6570; tel: (044) 382-5510, fax: (044) 382-1646, e-mail: knysna.tourism@pixie.co.za

TOWNSHIP TOURS

Knysna Township Trail, PO Box 897, Knysna 6570; cell: 083 269 8501, fax: (0445) 2-2609
Hornlee Nature Reserve, contact Bronwyn Maree, tel: (0445) 82-6107

ARTS AND CRAFTS

Knysna Painting Holidays, contact Dale and Jenny Elliot; 105 Bayswater Drive, Leisure Isle, Knysna 6570; tel: (044) 382-5646, fax: (044) 384-0006
The Old Gaol Complex, cnr Main and Queen streets, Knysna; tel: (044) 392-6138
The Old Nick, PO Box 437, Plettenberg Bay 6600; tel: (044) 31395, fax: (044) 30521
The Timber Route (See Knysna Tourism Bureau on this page)
Reenendal Community Entrepreneurs (See Knysna Tourism Bureau on this page)

THE KLEIN KAROO

Greylands Ostrich Farm, PO Box 744, Oudtshoorn 6620; tel/fax: (044) 272-6428
Klein Karoo Wine Route, contact Calitzdorp Co-op Winery, tel: (044) 213-3301, fax: (044) 213-3328
Die Poort Winery, tel: (02934) 5-2406, fax: (02934) 5-2347

OUDTSHOORN
GENERAL

Oudtshoorn Information, Queens Hotel Building, Baron Van Reede Street; PO Box 255, Oudtshoorn 6620; tel: (044) 272-2221, 279-2532/3, fax: (044) 272-8226
Cape Nature Conservation, PO Box X658, Oudtshoorn; tel: (044) 279-1739
Buchu Tours, 113 Victoria St, Oudtshoorn; tel/fax: (044) 272-0076

11

TOWNSHIP TOURS

Matjoks (see Oudtshoorn Information on page 115)

CULTURAL VILLAGES

Gamkaskloof, contact Cape Nature Conservation, tel: (04436) 736

ARTS AND CRAFTS

Klein Karoo National Arts Festival, tel: (044) 272-7771, fax: (044) 272-7773, e-mail: karoofees@pixie.co.za

CP Nel Museum, 3 Baron van Reede St, Oudtshoorn; tel/fax: (044) 272-7306

Oudtshoorn's Feather Palaces (see Oudtshoorn Information on page 115)

Foster's Folly (see Oudtshoorn Information on page 115)

Arbeidsgenot (see Oudtshoorn Information on page 115)

Cango Caves, tel: (044) 272-7410, fax: (044) 272-8001

MONUMENTS

Statue of the Boer (see Oudtshoorn Information on page 115 or the CP Nel Museum on this page)

Slave Dam (see Meiringspoort Adventures on page 114)

MEETING THE PEOPLE

Bernhard's Taphuis, 10 Baron Van Reede Street, Oudtshoorn; tel: (044) 272-3208

FREE STATE

About the province

The Free State is possibly one of the most underrated areas in South Africa. Surrounded by six provinces and the independent mountain kingdom of Lesotho, the Free State lies at the very heart of the country. While some areas of the province are fairly flat and somewhat mundane, the southeastern region is set against the majestic and towering Maluti mountain range of Lesotho, and has much to offer a traveller with an interest in the people of South Africa. The approximately 3.1 million Free Staters are renowned for their friendliness and hospitality, and the area remains entirely untouched by commercial tourism.

IN THE FREE STATE

- everything is made of sandstone;
- you are most likely to meet people of Sotho and Tswana origin;
- every cave has a story to tell;
- you will meet good, solid, salt-of-the earth Afrikaans farmers;
- you will see large open spaces, rocky koppies so characteristic of the area, and fields of maize, pumpkins and sunflowers.

THIS CHAPTER

- **Bloemfontein:** The capital.
- **The Southeastern Free State:** The region to the southeast of the capital bordering Lesotho.

BLOEMFONTEIN OR 'MANGUANG'

'Manguang', the Tswana name for Bloemfontein, means 'Place of the Cheetahs', which says something about the surrounding countryside in the days before settlers, farmers and hunters tamed the inland plains of the country. The literal translation of the Afrikaans word 'Bloemfontein' is 'flower fountain' perhaps referring to the fact that where the city now stands there was once a spring that, at various times throughout history, provided a source of water for the San (Bushmen) and the teeming herds of game they hunt-ed, for the Sotho farmers and, later, the Voortrekkers and settlers.

Most tourists with an interest in the Anglo-Boer War head for the battlefields of neighbouring KwaZulu-Natal (see page 171) without realising just how important and central to the war the Free State was. During the Anglo-Boer War, the British in fact occupied Bloemfontein, leaving a legacy of British features in what had formerly been the capital of a Boer republic. There are numerous monuments and museums in the capital that testify to the province's pioneering past, but which also honour the opposing armies and innocent victims of the Anglo-Boer War.

MUSEUMS AND GALLERIES

Bloemfontein Tourism Information (see page 129) can help you plan the five-kilometre walking tour that takes in 25 places of historical interest, including the First Raadsaal, the National Women's Memorial and War Museum, and the National Museum.

The First Raadsaal

This is Bloemfontein's oldest building which still survives in its original state. Built in 1849 and constructed as a school, the humble one-roomed building was home to the last three presidents of the former Orange Free State.

National Women's Memorial and War Museum of the Boer Republics

Approximately 26 000 Boer women and children died in British concentration camps during the Anglo-Boer War, and they are commemorated here in a striking 36.5-metre sandstone obelisk. The War Museum is dedicated to the Boer soldiers who took part in the war between Boer and Brit, and exhibits include items and weapons made by Boer prisoners during their incarceration.

National Museum

While one of the delights of the National Museum is the beautifully reconstructed turn-of-the-century Bloemfontein street scene, by far the most interesting exhibits are the archaeological displays that include the Florisbad skull discovered at Florisbad

Spring approximately 50 kilometres from Bloemfontein in the 1930s. Florisbad Man is believed to have been an ancestor of the San people who lived here between 50 000 and 35 000 years ago. The cultural displays in this museum include a unique collection of costumes, beadwork, traditional utensils, artefacts and instruments used by the Sotho people.

The House of Bram Fischer

Bram Fischer was a son of Bloemfontein, born in the Free State in 1908. In 1965, he was arrested and sentenced to life imprisonment under the Sabotage Act. He was detained by the apartheid government on Robben Island, and finally transferred to a hospital in 1975 after being diagnosed with cancer. He died exactly a year later. He was a member of the South African Communist Party and a lawyer in both the Treason Trial and the Rivonia Trial, which saw Nelson Mandela and his ANC colleagues served with life sentences. It is possible to visit the house at 72 Reitz Street which, between 1910 and 1946, was owned by the Fischer family.

MUSIC AND DANCE

The Sand du Plessis Theatre

The Sand du Plessis Theatre is home to opera, ballet, drama and musical performances in Bloemfontein. It is worth attending a performance just to see what is considered by many as one of the most modern theatres in the world. This

R60-million complex, with its façade of massive glass panels, features works of art as part of the decor.

Heidram Drama Group

Look out for any performances by this community group of young actors, most of whom come from disadvantaged backgrounds. Members of the company range in age from 14 to 40 and, as well as acting, the group takes care of all the technical elements of their productions, providing the lighting, props, sets and production designs – largely because there is seldom enough money to call in the experts.

But this does not mean that the group is second-rate. Quite the contrary. The Heidram Drama Group has performed in many competitions and festivals where, through the years, they have won several awards. Most of the money they make is ploughed back into new productions. Some of the country's top actors started their careers with Heidram.

SOUTHEASTERN FREE STATE

In this area, sandstone is a part of the people's lives. It always has been. From ancient times, people inhabited many of the sandstone caves that characterise the area. Painted records of antelope and lion, little bands of hunters, comets and trance dancers weave across the cave walls, evidence of Africa's earliest ancestors, the San. The caves were also used by later inhabitants hiding from marauding warriors, by Boer and British soldiers, and, for centuries, as shelters for people and their livestock during bad weather. There is sandstone everywhere, and not just in its natural state. Across the veld, enormous, beautifully hewn sandstone posts are used for fencing. Buildings, from lowly cattle sheds to gracious homes with wide verandas, have been built from the local stone, and each cave, farmhouse and outbuilding tells a story – as do the locals.

Free State farmers are great storytellers, known for their hospitality and, sometimes – although all too often as a result of broad generalisation – their rigid political views and Calvinist religious beliefs.

THE LANDSCAPE

The Caves

There are caves of every shape and size across virtually the entire southeastern Free State. Many are on private land and few are used on a permanent basis. The caves that are indeed used are generally occupied by traditional healers who, at the calling of their ancestors, go to the caves to learn their craft before being sent back to help their people. It is not necessary to take a guide with you when you visit these caves, but it is always more interesting if you have someone who can either translate for you, or at least give some explanation of the proceedings.

Many of the caves in the area are used by traditional African healers, but many more are not inhabited today although they once were. It is a unique sensation to stand in these massive, and often eerie,

11

overhangs in the hills, imagining the lives of past inhabitants: the Boer women secretly cooking and caring for their children, hiding for months at a time in caves while their men were out fighting the British in the surrounding hillsides; and perhaps the very first inhabitants, the San, or Bushmen, who left endless records of their passing on the cave walls and overhangs throughout the region.

The healers using the caves are often dressed in traditional costume, which can seem quite outlandish to outsiders. But this is Africa at its most authentic. Still, visitors are always welcome as long as they are sensitive and respectful of the customs.

Locals may need to observe some rituals on entering the caves, but as outsiders, and particularly white outsiders, nobody expects you to know any better. It is usually quite acceptable to wander around the caves, but be sensitive and do not talk loudly or go peering into areas that are clearly being used as private living areas. If there is a ritual or ceremony taking place, ask if you can attend – it is seldom that you will be turned away – and take your place quietly at the back. The general rules are to be polite, use your common sense, and be sensitive to the situation. Always ask before you take photographs.

Although it may seem a little incongruous, a local white person sometimes organises parties or performances by well-known South African bands in some of these 'healers' caves', and it is quite something to experience the crossover of cultures. These performances happen entirely on an ad-hoc basis. If you would like to attend, ask people in the nearest town. As in most small towns, someone usually knows someone who knows someone who knows what's going on.

Rose Cottage Cave

Rose Cottage Cave, near Ladybrand in the west of the region, is a sandstone cave with a story that is still being unlocked. The site is in the process of being excavated and researched by the University of the Witwatersrand Department of Archaeology and, layer by layer, researchers are slowly exposing its secrets. The first people to inhabit the cave were thought to do so almost 100 000 years ago. So far, archaeologists have found that more recent inhabitants – people who inhabited the cave more than 10 000 years ago – hunted not just zebra, black wildebeest and eland but also animals that are now extinct, such as the blue buck, Cape horse and quagga, which once roamed these hills.

Through sophisticated dating procedures executed on the cave's old hearths, researchers have found that the wood burnt by the early inhabitants included alpine plants and proteas. It seems, though, that less than 10 000 years ago, this vegetation was replaced with woodland of the type now common in the area. The rock art found in the cave, although not the best in the region, is quite fascinating because some paintings are of freshwater fish that have never occurred in the Ladybrand area. An ancient cowry shell from the east coast has also been excavated – suggesting that our Stone-Age ancestors either travelled far or had really remarkable trade networks.

Modderpoort Priory

In 1869, before the establishment of the beautiful Modderpoort Priory near Ladybrand, the Anglican missionaries who founded the mission station, set up home in a small cave. The tiny cave was formed by a fall of enormous sandstone rocks from the mountains above. Apparently, the priests went to an excessive amount of trouble and expense to make the cave habitable, but never quite got it right, and the cave remained cold and damp – a fact which, no doubt, prompted them to construct the lovely sandstone buildings of St Augustine that grace the mission estate today. Even today the cave is rather miserable, but is still occasionally used as a chapel. There are rumours that, during the years of apartheid, this cave was used to hide members of the ANC before they were smuggled out of the country via nearby Lesotho.

In the Priory graveyard, close to the graves of the early Anglican priests, is the grave of the famous Basotho prophetess, Anna Mantshupa Makheta, who died in 1904. The grave is usually easy to find – it is the only grave with a Victorian Gothic tombstone covered in small clay bowls, little piles of maize, flowers, coins and strings of beads, placed there by the thousands of pilgrims who come from all over southern Africa to pay her homage. A diviner and seer and a contemporary and relative of the great Basotho leader Moshoeshoe I, Makheta is famous for having predicted

that the Basotho would win a major battle against the British and that, following a disastrous drought, a rich harvest would ensue. This came true. The Sotho won the battle and, dramatically, the next day, the heavens opened and welcome rains ended the drought – securing Makheta's reputation as a prophetess. Despite many rumours and misinformation about her, there is no evidence that she ever lived or worshipped in the historic little Modderpoort cave-cum-chapel.

However, to this day, black people in their thousands make the pilgrimage to Modderpoort to pay their respects and ask Makheta's blessings. They stop at the cave, at her grave, and at a water well she is said to have loved and where she dreamed many of her famous dreams. It does seem likely that she converted to Christianity, considering she has been buried in the Anglican mission graveyard. While Mantshupa Makheta is not well known among South Africa's white population, to many blacks Modderpoort is South Africa's answer to Lourdes.

Magul se Gat

High in the Korannaberg is Magul se Gat, a cave that is part of the Korannaberg hiking trail near Marquard. Magul, a local Basotho bandit, and his band of renegade thieves – also rumoured to be cannibals – terrorised the early farmers and settlers in the flatland before retreating back to his hideout in the mountains. Unable to capture him, the farmers finally drilled holes into the top of the cave to blast him out with dynamite. When the smoke settled, they stormed the tiny entrance to the cave – but it was empty. Magul and his band had escaped through a secret entrance at the other end of this tunnel cave. The hiking trail passes right through the cave, although there is a separate path for those who suffer from claustrophobia and don't want to walk through the long, dark passage.

The Salpeterkrans

Tucked away in a steep valley outside Clarens is the Salpeterkrans – also known, among many other names, as the Fertility Cave – which is reputed to be the largest overhang in southern Africa. The cave has been used since ancient times, first by the San, and later by the local Sotho and other African people, particularly traditional healers who go there to study, perform their ancient spiritual rites and worship. Many of the local black women say that, if a woman is finding it difficult to conceive, she should visit the cave and, after 'speaking with the ancestors' – usually through the mediation of a traditional healer – she will fall pregnant.

The mouth of the massive overhang is protected by an enormous pile of fallen rock and could easily be missed, except for the thin trails of smoke from small cooking fires winding out into the sunlight. On entering the cave, it is customary to place a candle on a rocky outcrop and light it in honour of the ancestors. Next, you walk in a clockwise direction around the outcrop. During the walk you are supposed to leave all bad thoughts behind before proceeding.

The cave itself is enormous and, over the years, healers, initiates and other inhabitants have built low stone walls demarcating temporary living areas. Some of these areas are thought to have been built by earlier herdboys to protect the livestock. In some places, the floor of the cave has been excavated by healers to obtain the precious white clay they use for a variety of purposes.

'Called' by their ancestors, many healers come from all over the country to undergo their tuition in the cave. They wear traditional attire of brightly coloured cloths, beads and dried bones, and the inflated bladders of various animals are tied around their limbs. Visitors are most welcome, and little notice will be taken of you. You may ask to consult with one of the healers and have the bones thrown (a small donation is always appreciated). Try to catch somebody's eye – often a smile is all that is needed – and approach only when someone indicates that you should.

Mount Mautse

Since the early 1970s, hundreds of black people have been going to pray to God and their ancestors at these caves situated near Ficksburg. This apparent crossover between Christianity and the older spiritual practices is a common feature of African religions and, in the eyes of the people, is apparently without contradiction. Many Sotho people follow the ancient belief that the spirits of the ancestors finally come to rest in the mountains, and Mount Mautse is particularly important. It is believed that the spirit of the great Sotho king Moshoeshoe resides here, at the site of some of his victorious battles against the Boer settlers.

In some of the caves, there are small statues of Mary and Jesus, while other caves are used for learning the traditions and rituals of a healer or fortune-teller. The healers say that people from all denominations are welcome to create their holy places in the caves. It is indeed a spiritual experience to watch devoted worshippers praying and lighting candles, and songs echo softly through the caves. There are usually local folk cooking their food over small smoky fires and you will see them washing their clothes and going about their daily business – all while the worshippers pray. If you want to learn more, approach someone and ask. It is fascinating to hear the stories of their lives.

Holkrans and Christmaskrans

Holkrans is an uninhabited cave situated in the Meiringspoort Nature Reserve at Meiringspoort, close to Fouriesburg. The entire population of women and children of Fouriesburg hid from British soldiers during the Anglo-Boer War in this cave, and only returned to the town after the war had ended. The cave is an enormous overhang in the wall of a large and strange 'tunnel' formed by thousands of years of water erosion, and cannot easily be detected. Apparently, during the War, the British troops often heard what they thought were people whispering in the hills around the deserted town of Fouriesburg, but could never locate them. The Boer women and children who hid in Christmaskrans, a

cave in the Senekal district, were not as lucky. On one Christmas Day during the War, after weeks of deprivation, the women apparently decided to brew coffee as a treat for themselves and their children. Unfortunately, the British soldiers smelt the coffee, and tracked down the women and children, many of whom were sent to prisoner-of-war camps.

Rock Art

There is plenty of evidence in the southeastern Free State of the San (Bushmen), the indigenous people who once wandered freely and hunted widely throughout the country.

The San began to withdraw from the area – and finally disappeared – as groups of Bantu and settlers moved in. But they left a vast legacy of paintings on the walls of caves and overhangs throughout the region. Studies have revealed that some San were still in the area at least until the early to mid-nineteenth century, and it was recorded in the 1860s that a San painter, still carrying his painting materials, was among those killed by a Boer commando in the Witteberg reserve. With this evidence, it is clear that the San were in contact with the Boers, but it seems they also saw the arrival of the British because there are a number of paintings depicting soldiers in red-and-blue tunics and horses to be found in the area.

In the Fouriesburg district alone, there are no less than 22 farms where rock art can be found. (In many areas there are also dinosaur fossils.) In Koerland in the Fouriesburg area, there are interesting paintings of a lion hunt and, at Wynford, there are paintings of dolphin. Other paintings can be found at Reineveld and Avondzon. There are also paintings at Holkrans (*see* page 123), as well as in the Golden Gate Highlands National Park, and a famous painting of the White Lady can be seen in a cave near Ladybrand.

To see other examples of indigenous rock art, ask at any of the local information or publicity offices, or at your hotel or guesthouse. Most locals know where some examples of rock art can be found, and unless you know your way around, or know what you are looking for, it is always better to go with a guide.

Few of these sites are officially protected and there has been much vandalism to these priceless works of art – so please be especially careful not to damage them in any way.

CLARENS AND FOURIESBURG

Apart from the numerous sites of San rock art dating back thousands of years, there are literally hundreds of modern artists and crafters, shops, galleries, and weaving, pottery and painting studios throughout the region, so keep your eyes open for them. One of the better-known areas for art and crafts is Clarens. The little town is renowned not only for the quality of its craft shops, but also for its annual art festival.

The Qwa-Hands Centre in QwaQwa, a little further east – near Clarens and the Golden Gate Highlands Reserve, serves as a retail outlet for many rural crafts

people and you can pick up some local and traditional work at reasonable prices.

The Castle

The Free State is full of what you may call 'characters' who reflect, in one way or another, the diversity of its people and their culture. One such character took it upon himself to build a Scottish Castle in the early 1980s, complete with turrets, in the middle of the Free State. He was unable to complete the task and, about 18 years later, the castle stands abandoned and at the mercy of the elements. It is possible to visit the ruins and, while the walk can be rather strenuous for the unfit, it only takes about two hours. Take it slowly as the breathtaking views of the Maluti mountains are well worth the effort.

Cinderella's Castle

Another 'character' took it upon himself to build a small castle using 55 000 beer bottles. This castle, which is still standing, can be seen in Naupoort Street in Clarens at the Maluti Lodge Hotel. There is also a curio shop.

Basotho Cultural Village

This village is set in spectacular surroundings and it is 'commercial' – in the sense that many of the traditions are enacted for visitors and people do not live there permanently. The South Sotho and Zulu cultures are quite different in many ways, and the Basotho village is perhaps not as busy as the cultural villages in KwaZulu-Natal. Rather, it has a quiet charm that reflects the easy-going nature of the Sotho people.

The authentic village depicts not only the culture and historical background of the Sotho nation from its inception, but also offers some insight into the contemporary lifestyles of modern Sotho people. Some of the homesteads encountered on a walk through the village have been built in Western style, there is invariably a radio blaring from inside, and the modern furniture is used in a colourful manner that is uniquely African. There are demonstrations on how huts are decorated, the making of clay pots, basketware, the crushing of maize, food preparation and a taste of home-brewed beer. Traditional games are played and visitors can take a two-hour hike with an *ngaka* (traditional doctor) who will explain where the medicinal plants are found and their customary uses. The hike also takes visitors past original San rock paintings. Also on the site of the homestead is a museum, curio shop and tea garden – and don't miss the fascinating audiovisual show screened on arrival.

Overnight accommodation is available and you can either cater for yourself, or order a special 'Sotho Experience' – with food and drink prepared and served in the ways of the forefathers.

Carolina Lodge

As with other rural areas, if you want to learn something about the people and culture of an area, try to stay in a small bed-and-breakfast establishment or with a family who will offer you first-hand opportunities to interact with the locals. There are literally hundreds of good B&Bs and guesthouses on the farms in the region.

Carolina Lodge is a real family affair – and Free State hospitality at its best. Owned by Rose and John Bailey, it is a great place to stay if you have children. Farm animals abound: there are dogs and cats and birds and rabbits and guinea-pigs and cows and horses all over the place. Rose is a registered tour guide, who knows everyone in the district, can take you anywhere you want to go, and introduce you to anyone you want to meet. A ritual in the Bailey household is tea and fruitcake on the lawn in the late summer afternoons in true farm style. Winter can be very cold and even snowy in these areas, and on cold winter's evenings the fire is lit and everyone gathers round with mugs of coffee or glasses of sherry. These occasions are uncontrived and very conducive to getting to know the Free Staters. The food is old-style family fare and the accommodation is either in rondavels or in the beautiful, old, stone stables that have been converted into cosy bedrooms.

Bokpoort

Bokpoort farm has been in the Roos family for four generations, and Chris and Sunette are determined to hang onto their heritage here. Because of Bokpoort's proximity to Lesotho and its resident cattle rustlers, Chris has, in recent years, suffered enormous stock losses, making cattle farming an increasingly unviable proposition. In the manner so characteristic of Free State farmers, Chris, loath to sell or leave his family farm, opened a guesthouse and started Snowy River Horse Trails, now extremely popular. Guests can ride out into the wilderness and surrounding farmlands in much the same way the early trekkers did, or Chris could escort you on horseback to the nearby village of Clarens to meet the resident artists and visit the local 'watering holes'. There are also special trails for students and backpackers.

Chris and Sunette breed mustangs (which are called Basotho ponies here), tough and solid horses used by the Basotho for getting around the rough mountain terrain of nearby Lesotho. These ponies are ideal mounts for inexperienced riders and know every nook and

Basotho Blankets

The Basotho Blanket is a modern extension of the time when the Basotho wore traditional coverings of animal skin. Today, the blanket is everyday wear for the Basotho people, and is commonly seen in the Free State.

The use of the blanket can be traced back to the 1800s when the Basotho first came into contact with Europeans. These early blankets were white and smeared with red ochre, and were followed in time by small 'five-and-a-half-feet square' blankets of shoddy reused yarn from old woollen coats and clothing and, finally, the patterned blankets. Most of the designs of the modern 'traditional' blankets have remained unchanged for 50 to 80 years or even longer, but although they have no stigma today – virtually everyone wears them – these blankets once indicated a lowly status,

For instance, in 1925, when the Prince of Wales visited Lesotho, people wearing blankets were assigned to the back of the crowd and were not allowed near the prince: *Kobo morao!* – Blankets at the back! It was at about this time, too, that missionaries, evermindful of the heathen connotations of the skin kaross, began to discourage wearing blankets. With the growth of urbanisation, blankets came to

be associated with rural people, but in the 1980s the blanket took an upward swing, especially among Basotho migrant labourers who would not easily part with them as they not only signified identification with their community, but revealed their class, standing in the community, marital status, and geographical origins.

Blankets are used for a number of ritual purposes. A young bride, for instance, must wear one wrapped about her hips until her first child is conceived. A newborn baby is wrapped in a special blanket, and this blanket is then often used to carry the baby on the mother's back. A woman should always cover her shoulders at funerals and church gatherings, especially in the presence of her male in-laws. A husband gives his bride a wedding blanket, and another on the birth of the first child, and so it goes on.

The design and colour of the blankets also carry significance: the *Poone*, or maize, design implies fertility for both men and women, and the cabbage leaf is a sign of prosperity. The way a blanket is worn is important too, and it is believed that, if stripes are worn horizontally instead of vertically, this can stunt the growth, development and wealth of the wearer.

cranny of the surrounding valleys. Because Chris is an instructor, the trails are easily accessible for even the most nervous of novices. The food provided on the trail is prepared in true pioneer fashion – cooked outdoors over an open fire.

The accommodation is rustic but comfortable and there are self-catering cottages as well as The Stable restaurant, and – for the more adventurous – mountain bikes for hire.

Rustler's Valley Music Festivals

When the annual Rustler's Valley Music Festival first started, it was considered by many local Free Staters a very 'odd place to visit'. This was because it drew hundreds of people (read 'hippies') who wore different clothes, drove different cars (if they drove at all) and generally behaved in a 'different' manner. But the locals seem to have grown accustomed to this odd lot, and the festival has grown from strength to strength. They now hold two festivals, one in Easter and one, with an African Jazz theme, over Christmas and New Year.

Rustler's is, in many ways, similar to the Splashy Fen (see page 166) festival that is held in KwaZulu-Natal. Like its Drakensberg counterpart, it consists of four days of camping out, listening to music and hanging out in nature. While the focus of the festival is music, in addition to the live bands, it includes markets, activities – for instance aromatherapy and reflexology – and entertainment such as drumming, juggling, and making musical instruments such as marimbas.

CLOCOLAN

Ben Nevis

This small B&B near Clocolan is one of the many places in the region where a visitor can experience authentic farm life on a farm growing asparagus, cherries, plums, peaches, vegetables, olives and pumpkins. The farm produces its own cherry wine (the first cherry trees were planted here in 1927), cherry and peach liqueurs, preserved and bottled products, as well as dried and fresh fruit. The hospitality on the farm is quite overwhelming and visitors may choose either the B&B option (supper may be provided on request), or experience farm life by staying in a large farmhouse at a cheaper rate. There are walking trails, many indigenous trees and birds, and San paintings.

Evening Star

Originally bought in 1870 when white farmers moved into the so-called 'conquered territory', the farm was purchased in 1889 by the Catholic Order of Mary and a monastery was erected. Some 200 metres to the east, St Leo's College was established. St Leo's was the first school to offer secondary education in the Free State. One of the early missionaries among the Basotho was a Father Gerard, who was beatified by Pope John Paul II during his visit to the nearby state of Lesotho in 1988. Church authorities have restored the chapel of Father Gerard, which is now used by locals for regular services and weddings.

Although Evening Star is not a homestay in the traditional sense of the word, it does provide accommodation in the form of one small, private cottage of the sort enjoyed by honeymooners. The cottage is perched up behind the monastery overlooking the slopes of this wild and romantic mountain and the rolling farmlands and koppies beyond. The farm, in the Cloete family since 1921, is currently owned by Johan and Lizette Cloete, who have taken a keen interest in restoring the old monastery. Many of the floors in the buildings are still made of cattle dung, and the farm – which is part of the Metsiawang Conservancy near Clocolan – has been declared a National Heritage Site.

Lizette, who is a keen potter, has turned part of the monastery into a gallery. She also runs a tea garden where she serves the most refreshing home-made lemonade.

FICKSBURG

More than anything else, the Free State is about farming. The people often live fair distances from each other, or in the small towns scattered throughout the region. Much like small-town communities throughout the world, the local folk are often conservative, hard-working and somewhat suspicious of strangers.

In the Free State, however, this doesn't stop them from being friendly and helpful. Look out for the many home industries and farm stalls dotted along the roadside.

The Cherry Festival

The southeastern Free State is famous for the cherries that grow well in the cool and mild winter temperatures. Cherry season runs from about 20 October to 30 November but, because most of the cherry orchards are tucked away on the deep, well-drained soils of the mountain slopes, travellers on the lookout for the profusion of cherry blossoms in September, will seldom see them. A number of farms make their own cherry wine, liqueurs and other products.

The annual cherry festival is held in Ficksburg and has been running for approximately 60 years, making it the oldest produce festival in the country. If you want a real sense of this farming community, the Cherry Festival, usually held in the third week of November, should be on your agenda.

There are also annual agricultural shows, an asparagus festival and a number of harvest-related festivals that take place in this part of the Free State.

FREE STATE
GENERAL

Free State Department of Arts, Culture, Science and Technology, Private Bag X20506, Bloemfontein 9300; tel: (051) 405-4680, fax: (051) 405-4873

Bloemfontein Tourism Information, PO Box 639, Bloemfontein 9300; tel: (051) 405-8490

BLOEMFONTEIN
MUSEUMS AND GALLERIES

The First Raadsaal, St George's Street, Bloemfontein; tel: (051) 447-9610

War Museum of the Boer Republics, Monument Road, Bloemfontein; PO Box 704, Bloemfontein 9300; tel: (051) 47-3447

National Museum, 36 Aliwal St, Dan Pienaar, Bloemfontein 9301; tel: (051) 447-9609, fax: (051) 447-9283

The House of Bram Fischer, 72 Reitz Avenue, Westdene, Bloemfontein 9301; contact Bloemfontein Tourism Information above

MUSIC AND DANCE

Sand du Plessis Theatre, corner Markgraaff and St Andrews streets; tel: (051) 447-7771

SOUTHEASTERN FREE STATE
GENERAL

See Free State Department of Arts, Culture, Science and Technology above

THE LANDSCAPE

To view the Rose Cottage Cave, Modderpoort Priory, Magul se Gat, Salpeterkrans, Mount Mautse, Holkrans and Christmaskrans, contact Rose Bailey (see Carolina Lodge below)

CLARENS & FOURIESBURG

The Castle, contact Rose Bailey (see Carolina Lodge below)

Cinderella's Castle, contact Rose Bailey (see Carolina Lodge below)

Basotho Cultural Village, Private Bag X826, Witsieshoek 9870; tel/fax: (058) 721-0300

Carolina Lodge, contact Rose and John Bailey, PO Box 143, Fouriesburg 9725; tel: (058) 223-0552/1066

Bokpoort, contact Chris and Sunette Roos, PO Box 25, Clarens 9707; tel: (058) 256-1181, cell: 083 628 5055

Rustler's Valley Music Festivals, contact the Festival Convenor, tel/fax: (051) 933-3939

CLOCOLAN

Ben Nevis, PO Box 141, Clocolan 9735; tel: (051) 943-0031

Evening Star, contact Johan and Lizette Cloete, PO Box 155, Clocolan 9735; tel: (051932) 3240

FICKSBURG

Cherry Festival, contact Ficksburg Tourism Information, tel: (051) 933-2322

EASTERN CAPE

About the province

Since the 1994 elections, the former homelands of Transkei and Ciskei have been re-incorporated into South Africa, becoming part of the Eastern Cape. Parts of the province suffered tremendously during the apartheid years and are still struggling to find their feet. The area, however, has a fascinating history, a magnificent natural environment and an interesting mix of people. Of the 7.3 million people living there, the large majority is Xhosa-peaking. Many Xhosa – especially rural communities – still live according to tradition. Although this 'Cinderella province' is the second poorest in the country, it is one of the most beautiful places to visit.

THE EASTERN CAPE

- is the birthplace of Nelson Mandela;
- is the ideal place to meet Xhosa in their traditional rural environment;
- offers the most unspoilt, wild and dramatic coastline in the country;
- is where the 1820 British Settlers came ashore at Algoa Bay (Port Elizabeth);
- is within touching distance of the hot arid plains of the Great Karoo;
- is where a coelacanth, a fish thought to be extinct for 70 million years, was netted in 1938.

This chapter

- **Port Elizabeth and surrounds:** The Friendly City and its surrounding farmlands.
- **Graaff-Reinet and Nieu-Bethesda** The oldest town in the province and the Owl House.
- **Grahamstown:** City of Angels and its historic past.
- **East London and surrounds:** The harbour city and its environs.
- **The Wild Coast** of the former Transkei.

PORT ELIZABETH & SURROUNDS

The sea port city of Port Elizabeth was founded as a staging post for the British immigrants of 1820, and named in memory of the young wife of acting British governor Sir Rufane Shawe Donkin. Sir Rufane built a stone pyramid to his wife, who died in India at the age of 28, on the hill overlooking Algoa Bay, and the monument, with its touching inscription, still stands there today. But Port Elizabeth is not merely a city of tragic romance; nor is it simply a harbour city founded by settler communities. The city was a hot-bed of political and social resistance during the years of apartheid and was the first city in the country to elect a non-racial city council. In terms of populations, it is the fifth largest city in the country with about 1.1 million citizens.

MUSEUMS AND GALLERIES

Port Elizabeth Museum

Many people visit this museum because of the aquarium housed in the same complex, but it also has a tropical house and a snake park and covers the natural history of Algoa Bay, plus the maritime history and cultures of the area. One of the interesting features is Amaskiko, an exhibition of traditional storytelling and local culture.

The Donkin Heritage Trail

The Donkin Heritage Trail is a good way to experience the feel of the city, both old and new. There are innumerable historic buildings, monuments, fine architecture, homes, statues, gardens and churches, many with links to the 1820 Settlers, which give visitors an insight into the colonial history of the city. The Campanile at the entrance to the harbour is a monument to the 1820 Settlers and houses a carillon of 23 bells that ring the changes every day at 08h32 and 18h02 (evidently, the bells are a little out). (See Tourism Port Elizabeth on page 145).

Castle Hill Museum

Castle Hill Museum, perched on the side of the steep hill, is the oldest house in Port Elizabeth. Built in 1827, it contains period furniture and a wonderful collection of dolls. The long row of terraced Victorian settler cottages facing Donkin Street have been restored, but are now mainly used as business premises.

King George VI Art Gallery

This gallery has extensive permanent collections of British, Oriental, and South African art. Much of this last originates from the Eastern Cape region. There is also an international printmaking collection.

ARTS AND CRAFTS

Wezandla Gallery and Craft Centre

This is a good place to pick up crafts made by mainly rural crafters, both local and from other African countries. There is a large craft area with many interesting items on sale, and there is an art gallery exhibiting the work of locals. This is a good place to buy traditional South African ingredients for the pot.

GRAAFF-REINET & NIEU-BETHESDA

Graaff-Reinet is the oldest town in the Eastern Cape. The small town, with its buildings of white-washed walls and green shutters, boasts 200 national monuments – more than any other town in South Africa. Today Graaff-Reinet, which is set in the middle of a nature reserve, is committed to the conservation of its buildings and of the surrounding environment. There are numerous museums, art galleries, churches, old shops and stately homes – from Cape Dutch to Victorian houses and quaint Karoo cottages. Some of the more prominent landmarks include:
• The beautiful Drostdy, once home of the landdrost and now an award-winning

hotel. It includes Stretch's Court, a row of cottages dating from 1855;
- Reinet House, a cultural history museum built in the Cape Dutch style. In the yard is a huge grapevine planted in 1870;
- The Dutch Reformed Church, built in 1886, and thought by many to be one of the most imposing and beautiful churches in South Africa;
- The Old Library with its art and pioneer photographic collection, rock-art reproductions and fossilised remains of Karoo reptiles that inhabited the area 200 million years ago;
- The Hester Rupert Art Museum, which started out as a church and today houses the work of 106 South African artists;
- The Jan Rupert Centre, a Neo-Gothic building that is now home to a cottage industry which concentrates on the spinning, knitting and weaving of locally produced wool.

In order to appreciate the very essence of the town of Graaff-Reinet, ask at the Publicity Association (see page 145) for copies of the charming Stoep Stories, one-page leaflets that include stories about Graaff-Reinet as told by many of the old-timers. One delightful such story relates how a house in Bourke Street was rented by a farmer who went off to fight for the British in the Anglo-Boer war, leaving behind his pregnant wife and small daughter. The new baby began to arrive during a night in 1901 and, because a curfew had been imposed, two lantern-bearing soldiers were sent to the black township to collect the midwife. 'To her dying day,' goes the story, 'Old Spaas, the midwife,

spoke with pride of the time she marched between two soldiers all the way from her home in the black township through the streets of the town to deliver the baby girl in Bourke Street. Today that baby is a grandmother and great-grandmother well over ninety years old'.

After driving through the hot Karoo and along the seemingly endless road to Graaff-Reinet, it may be tempting to head for the nearest hotel, but a good alternative is to stay with a family providing a bed-and-breakfast alternative. There are a number of old landmark houses that date back to the early 1700s and many of the district's families have lived on their farms for generations. Many of the farms have old family and farming records dating back to the 18th century, and can give you unique and personal insights into the lives of South Africans living in this harsh, but beautiful environment.

Clifton Country House
One of the oldest houses in the district is situated in Pretorius Kloof on the Sunday's River. Originally known as De Klipfontein, it was bought by Willem Sterrenberg Pretorius in 1819. The house has since changed hands a number of times and was renovated following a fire in about 1933. This pioneering house and farmland boast wonderful vineyards and fruit trees dating back to the 19th century.

Bloemhof Guest Farm
Bloemhof farm was bought by ancestors of the Murray family from Voortrekkers who left the area at the start of the Great Trek

in 1838. Evenings on the farm are filled with stories and myths about the farm, the area, and the six generations of Murrays who have lived here.

Doornberg Guest Farm

A grove of 200-year-old oak trees surround the homestead of this well-known farm set deep in the heart of the Sneeuberg mountains. Gravestones belonging to the family date back to the 1780s and the farm has now been owned by five generations of the Van Heerden family.

One of the fun activities on the farm is a trip with Peet van Heerden in a cart drawn by an obstinate cart-horse called Jasper.

Karoo Fossils

Along the slopes of the koppies to the west of Graaff-Reinet, lie ancient river channels and, as elsewhere in the Karoo, the fossilised bones of mammal-like reptiles. These reptiles lived in what was once, millions of years ago, the prehistoric Karoo marshlands. As the animals died, their bones and skeletons were washed into lakes and pools and rapidly covered in mud. Today, the Karoo shale is composed of this hardened mud and, having been buried for over 200 million years, these fossil bones have become exposed. They provide a unique insight into life in a world before birds and mammals – and long, long before people walked the earth.

The Owl House

Nieu-Bethesda lies in the foothills of the Sneeuberge in an isolated, magnificent part of the Great Karoo. This strange village is famous because of an extraordinary woman, Helen Martin, who was born here in 1898. 'Miss Helen', as she was called, lived a reclusive life, and over the years transformed her cottage, now known as The Owl House, into a wonderland of ground glass, light and colour. In her yard is a collection of hundreds of strange and mythical cement-and-glass figures, which she sculpted with the help of two local workmen.

It was Helen Martin's wish that her work be preserved as a museum. The Owl House, once an object of derision and embarrassment in this small, conservative

The Life of Helen Martin

At one stage in her early life, Helen lived in Graaff-Reinet but returned to the village to nurse her ailing parents. After their death, Miss Helen became increasingly reclusive and, an avid reader of Omar Khayam and William Blake, she turned her attention to Oriental mysticism. She developed a fascination with light and colour and, it was at this point in her life that she began to grind up glass and cover the walls of her house. Once that was done, she moved her work out into what has become known as The Camel Yard where she built her hundreds of mythical figures. As she grew older, her sight started to fail and finally, on a cold winter's morning in 1976, at the age of 78, Miss Helen took her own life by swallowing caustic soda.

little Karoo town, has become the single most important asset of the village of Nieu-Bethesda.

GRAHAMSTOWN OR 'ERHINI'

There are several versions as to the origin of the Xhosa name for Grahamstown – 'eRhini'. Some people say it is the name of a reed that once grew in the area, while others say it was the name of an old Xhosa man who lived in the Stone's Hill area of what is now Grahamstown.

The Untold Story

Graham's Town: The Untold Story – A social history and self-guided tour is a small booklet about Grahamstown produced by a group of women from the Black Sash organisation. It is well worth laying your hands on a copy if you are passing through the Eastern Cape – and particularly if you are spending any time in Grahamstown – as it provides the 'alternative' history of the area and also a number of tours visitors may undertake on their own.

At the height of the turmoil of the 1980s, when Grahamstown – like the rest of South Africa – was reacting to the states of emergency that had been imposed on it by an increasingly oppressive government, the women of the Black Sash decided that, while there was enough information on the white settlers of Grahamstown, there were a number of untold stories about the other people who had played such an important part in building the Grahamstown of today. The book walks visitors

through various landmarks and offers a new perspective on old and familiar landmarks. It also gives an insight into the lives of people, other than settlers, who experienced hardships trying to make a life in this part of the Eastern Cape.

PLACES OF WORSHIP

The Cathedral of St George and St Michael

The stately and imposing structure of the Anglican Cathedral, with its spire and 45-metre bell tower, took 128 years to complete. The original belfry contained three bells, the metal from which was used for the set of eight that now hang in the cathedral. This was the first full complement, and the heaviest, set of bells on the African continent. During the frontier wars, the cathedral was used as a depot for the distribution of arms and ammunition, as well as a refuge and officers' headquarters.

MUSEUMS AND 9ALLERIES

The Albany Museum Complex

The Albany Museum complex consists of five fascinating museums: the Provost Prison, Fort Selwyn, the Observatory, the History Museum and the Albany (or the Natural Sciences) Museum, which is the second oldest museum in the country. On display are traditional Xhosa dress and beadwork, depictions of early man, an Egyptian mummy, artefacts, and exhibits of animals and birds.

The museum specialises in the study of freshwater fish, insects and geology, as well as archaeology.

The History Museum records the family trees of the 1820 Settlers, and also offers a genealogical service to the public. Jewellery, clothing, toys, furniture, porcelain cooking utensils and military memorabilia from the settlers are also on display.

The Observatory was originally a 19th-century home and shop, in which the first diamond found in South Africa was identified by Dr WG Atherstone. The Observatory houses the only camera obscura (still in perfect working order) in the southern hemisphere, and from which visitors can observe the city below,

a Meridian room where Grahamstown time was first set, and rooms containing an array of Victorian furniture.

ARTS AND CRAFTS

The 1820 Settlers' Monument

The hub of the arts festival is the 1820 Settlers' Monument, which was built to commemorate the contribution made by English-speaking South Africans in the development of the country. The Monument is used on a day-to-day basis as an educational, cultural and conference centre. A soaring yellowwood sculpture by South African artist Cecil Skotnes, is the focal point in the Fountain Foyer. The main

The Standard Bank National Arts Festival

From small beginnings, the 'Grahamstown Festival' has grown into what is purported to be the biggest on the African continent and one of the largest events of its kind in the world. Generally regarded as the premier cultural event in Southern Africa, this annual event runs for about 10 days, usually during early July. The plethora of shows and bustle of the festival entirely transforms this usually rather sleepy little university town. The main programme features a selection of disciplines including drama, many forms of dance, music, the visual arts, a book fair, a film festival, open-air craft markets, cabaret, student drama and winter school lectures.

In contrast to the main festival events, there is also the Fringe Festival, which has no selection criteria and often reflects what is happening in grass-root art circles. Every possible venue is used for productions, performances and exhibits, ranging from Gothic chapels, old gaols, fully-equipped theatres and even a converted locomotive shed. The streets are alive with impromptu entertainment of every sort. Accommodation – usually extremely difficult to come by if you haven't booked well in advance – is in hotels, caravans, tents, private homes, boarding school dormitories, university residences, in the townships and on nearby farms.

theatre seats 900 people and there are many conference halls, lounges and open areas equipped for a variety of functions. Also housed here is an art gallery with temporary exhibits and a restaurant.

The Masithandane Association

Grahamstown is an extremely impoverished community with a high level of unemployment. The Masithandane project – meaning 'Let us love one another' – was started in order to help women generate their own income. By teaching the women skills, it has been possible to empower them to take control of their own lives.

Tours organised by Masithandane include an in-depth tour of Grahamstown East, a visit to the gardens, the soup kitchen and a traditional 'Xhosa picnic'. Visitors are also taken to the International Library for African Music where famous ethnomusicologist, Andrew Tracey, introduces them to the vibrant world of African music and musical instruments. The project won the Women in Tourism Award in the Eastern Cape in 1997, and has rekindled and encouraged an interest and pride in indigenous Xhosa culture.

The Masithandane Project

Originally, the Masithandane Association had been administering community soup kitchens in the township areas, and it wasn't hard to notice that – as in many impoverished communities – litter, particularly plastic bags, was an enormous problem. Women were encouraged to collect as many of the offending plastic bags as

they could, and turn them into hats, bags and mats. In order to get the project going, people visiting the soup kitchens were also encouraged to 'pay' for their meals by handing in plastic bags.

With more than enough raw material to work with, the women set to work with a will to master a new skill. More women joined the group and they began experimenting with traditional beadwork. With great imagination and ingenuity, they were soon creating a variety of headgear and other products, which found a ready market, not only in the community, but also both locally and internationally. The project became so popular that visitors buying Masithandane products wanted to meet the women, and so the endeavour expanded to a tentative involvement in tourism. Today, encouraged by their success, Masithandane provides many tourists with their first taste of 'real' South Africa.

EAST LONDON & SURROUNDS

East London is one of the five large harbour cities along South Africa's coastline and much of the city has developed around the port and its activities. During the apartheid era, East London was set right between the 'independent' homelands of Ciskei and Transkei. Like other cities throughout the country, East London is surrounded by townships and informal settlements that continue to grow as rural people leave their homes and move to the urban centres looking for work. Against this African backdrop, there are still many reminders of the city's links to the white settlers, particularly the English and Germans.

TOWNSHIP TOURS

Unlike some other South African cities, East London has no 'sites' in the township that you can visit on your own. Most of the places of interest that relate to the apartheid struggle are outside the city. But that does not mean it is not interesting to visit East London's townships. Each township has its own particular atmosphere and history, so it is useful to go with a guide who can take you to the two major townships of Duncan Village – or Gompo Town, as it is known – and Mdatsane, which, after Soweto in Gauteng (see page 15), is the second largest black township in South Africa. If possible, go with someone who knows the culture well and who can give you a first-hand background on local traditions and customs and point out the transitions taking place in the culture as people move from the rural backgrounds into urban township life. A good guide will be able to fill you in on things such as dress, face-painting, customs such as *lobola* – or bride wealth, which is still a very important feature of modern life – and who can perhaps explain the *abakweta* and circumcision ceremonies. There are some good community projects to be visited, and most guides have a favourite that they will support. A stop-off at a community project also gives visitors some idea of the difficulties faced by township dwellers and the ways in which, through the projects, people are attempting to deal with their circumstances.

Steve Biko's House, Grave and the graves of the Bisho Massacre

Steve Biko, born in Ginsberg on the outskirts of King William's Town, was a vocal advocate of black consciousness who believed that blacks had to liberate their minds from apartheid and the effects of institutionalised racism and white liberalism. Many people believe that the brutal murder of Steve Biko while in police custody in Port Elizabeth was the catalyst that sparked the death knell of apartheid.

It is possible to visit both Biko's small matchbox home – complete with asbestos roof – and his grave on your own, but the experience will be much more rewarding if you go with a good guide who can relate the story of Biko's struggle for black freedom. Some of the tours visit the clinic started by Biko in King William's Town, before moving to Port Elizabeth to the cell in which he was interrogated, his grave site and to the Steve Biko statue recently erected in East London to commemorate his death. Within 24 hours of the unveiling of the sculpture, right-wing activists had defaced it – generating the kind of debate that characterises South Africa's heritage. Other related sites are the graves – in the same graveyard in which Biko rests – of many of those who were massacred in Bisho in one of the most tragic debacles of the apartheid years. It is also possible to visit the offices of the *Daily Dispatch*, where editor Donald Woods, Biko's great supporter, was based before leaving the country, and even meet members of the Biko family and some of his acquaintances.

Fort Hare University

Fort Hare University also needs a guide – mainly because it can be frustrating to find your way around. The university has seen many of South Africa's leaders and Nobel Peace Prize Laureates pass through its doors. Mandela received the prize in 1992, Archbishop Desmond Tutu in 1984 and Albert John Luthuli in 1961; all attended Fort Hare. Other eminent people associated with the university include presidents Robert Mugabe (Zimbabwe), Sir Seretse Khama (Botswana) and Ntsu Mokhetle (Lesotho). Originally built as a fort in 1847, the university opened its doors in 1916 with just 20 students, and today there are nearly 6 000. It also houses the ANC archives and a magnificent library, and the De Beers Art Gallery boasts a remarkable collection of African Art.

Qunu

Qunu is the village where Nelson Mandela, South Africa's first black president, was born. The house in which he lived no longer exists, but visitors are shown the plot where it once stood and the nearby graves of his parents. There are plans to build a museum in or near the village but, in the meanwhile, it is still possible to visit the school he attended. Mandela has built a holiday home in the village.

CULTURAL VILLAGES

There are few cultural villages in the Eastern Cape, possibly because so much of its population still live the way they have for hundreds of years – and there has been no need to develop special 'cultural' or 'historical' villages for tourists. However, people living traditional lives are often

40

The prophetess Nongqawuse

Amid the turmoil of the Frontier wars, a young Xhosa girl claimed she had had visions of 'New People' who told her that the dead were preparing to rise again. They would bring with them amazing new cattle – but only if the people first killed all their cattle and destroyed their 'impure' crops. Hailed as a prophetess, Nongqawuse set in motion what became known as the great Xhosa cattle-killing and crop burning that resulted not only in mass starvation within a period of 15 months, but also in the tragic downfall of the Xhosa nation as an independent entity. She had claimed that

on a certain day, the sun would rise blood red and, at midday, it would turn back, leaving the earth pitch black. Following a terrible storm, the unbelievers (including the Europeans) would be destroyed, at which time the dead would rise up and there would be peace and plenty in the land. Many Xhosa even tried to persuade the whites to kill their cattle.

It has been proposed that the site where Nongqawuse is believed to have lived and where she made her prophesies be set aside in remembrance of this traumatic and terrible event that changed the course of history.

notoriously difficult to access, so the few 'cultural villages' in the province are indeed quite useful.

Khaya la Bantu

This Canadian-financed project is still rather small, but quite authentic. The village, which is open to visitors, is in fact the homestead of a family who has been living on this working farm for generations. It has thus not been 'created' for the tourist market, but developed through negotiations with the families who have agreed to allow tourists to visit them in their small rural, thatch-roofed homes to learn more about the Xhosa culture. Visitors are accompanied by interpreters – mainly teachers or nurses – who can help with the language and explain the construction of the small mud homesteads, the process of thatching, slaughtering animals for the ancestors and other culturally important ceremonies. There is usually traditional singing and dancing and, during the sheep shearing season, the owners of Khaya la Bantu will organise a demonstration. Because the village is small (it consists of only two families), it is possible to have a far more intimate cultural experience than one would normally encounter in the Eastern Cape.

MUSEUMS AND GALLERIES

Anne Bryant Gallery

The Gables, a lovely old Edwardian home, was bequeathed to East London by Mr Edward Bryant on the death of his beloved wife on condition it be turned into an art gallery. Apart from the magnificent art collection that is widely representative of South African art from 1880 to the present, the building itself is also worth visiting. The wooden floors, spacious rooms with pressed-steel ceilings and stained-glass windows are wonderful examples of post-Victorian architecture.

East London Museum

This museum, ranked among the best of its kind in Africa, has much to intrigue visitors, but is best known as the home of the coelacanth, thought to have been extinct for 70 million years. The first coelacanth netted off Chalumna Mouth in 1938 is now on display here, but the museum is also home to the world's only remaining dodo egg. The flightless dodos, once common on the Indian Ocean island of Mauritius, became extinct when they were slaughtered in their thousands by early settlers and the crews of passing ships. The last of these all too tame birds were seen in the 1680s, although a related species survived on various other islands for about another century.

Other interesting displays in the museum include an exhibit on humankind through the ages, a beautiful marine shell collection, a display on the Xhosa, Mfengu and other traditional cultures, a maritime exhibit that includes the lifeboat and other relics off the *Oceanos*, a modern ship that was wrecked off the coastline in 1991, as well as pieces off other wrecks. There is also the story of the colonial settlers, including the German immigrants.

42

The Amathole Museum

One of the many things people will remember about the outstanding Amathole Museum (formerly the Kaffrarian Museum) in King William's Town is Huberta, a hippo that captured the hearts of South Africans when she trekked some 700 kilometres down the coast of South Africa between 1928 and 1930. This famous hippo started her travels somewhere in the Richard's Bay area of KwaZulu-Natal and, at some stage in 1930, took up residence for six months in a river near the village of Port St Johns on the Wild Coast. The river – ironically named Mzimvubu, meaning 'Place of the Hippo' – had not seen a hippopotamus for many years. After upsetting a great many people by overturning their boats, grazing in their gardens and providing endless amusement, Huberta wandered southwards – to her death. She was shot by hunters on the banks of the Keiskamma River. Her days of wandering over, Huberta now rests on permanent display in the museum.

Huberta, however, is not the only thing to see in the museum. There are a staggering 40 000 mammal species, including a rare black lechwe from Zimbabwe (only one other is known in the world), a webfoot hare from Calvinia and a record 5.5-metre giraffe.

The Xhosa gallery has beautifully crafted examples of traditional beadwork and interesting displays of Xhosa and Khoisan culture.

Lock Street Gaol

This gaol, now a quaint shopping complex selling crafts and curios, was the first women's gaol in South Africa. Built in 1880, it was in this gaol that Winnie Madikizela-Mandela (former wife of Nelson Mandela) was incarcerated during the apartheid years. It also housed one of South Africa's most notorious women criminals, Daisy de Melker, who was hanged for poisoning three of her husbands with arsenic.

Latimer's Landing

In the early 1900s, Latimer's was a wooden wharf situated just upstream of East London's First Creek. Latimer's was known as the Fishing Quay, and what was then known as First Creek is now the Dry Dock. Latimer's Landing is named after Marjorie Latimer, a former curator of the East London Museum who helped identify the coelacanth. Today, Latimer's Landing is East London's waterfront development on the banks of the Buffalo River. Every Saturday and Sunday there is a flea and craft market at the Landing.

MONUMENTS

You could see a lot of forts, blockhouses and monuments, ruins and lonely graveyards when travelling through the Eastern Cape, especially if you're somewhat off the beaten track, as there are more than 200 in the region. Even though many of the forts were temporary affairs and the sites since lost, there are still a number of important and fascinating forts to be seen. By following the forts, you can follow the progress of a decisive period in South African history when the Xhosa fought bitterly against the settlers. The eastern frontier of the Cape Colony was marked by continuous unrest from 1779 until 1879.

The Kei River was the scene of intense conflict during the period 1877 to 79, and a number of forts were built as garrisons. These included Kei Mouth, Fort Buffalo in the Tyityaba Valley, Fort Warwick at Mpetu, Fort Union and Fort Linsingen at Ebb-and-Flow. And this was just one small area. There are numerous other forts up and down the province. At the old garrison town of Fort Beaufort is the famous Martello Tower built during the Frontier wars. It is built inland and away from the coast and appears to be the only one of its kind in the world. The officers' mess at the fort is now a military museum.

THE WILD COAST

The Wild Coast stretches about 280 kilometres along a magnificent stretch of coastline lined with thick indigenous forests, grassy hills rolling down towards the beaches, sweeping estuaries teeming with fish, long white beaches, and majestic waterfalls that crash over jagged rocky ledges into the rivers and sea. The Wild Coast is home to many Xhosa communities whose lifestyle has changed little in centuries. They are also some of the most impoverished people in the country, many of them relying on the natural environment to sustain them, and there are real concerns that, in the long term, this could have disastrous environmental and social consequences. Few employment opportunities exist in these areas, which places increasing pressure on the natural heritage of the province.

CULTURAL VILLAGES

Isinamva Cultural Village

Near to Mount Frere in the heart of the rural landscape is a 'cultural village' with a difference. This is a real village – not one set up for tourists, but one where tourists can experience the authentic day-to-day lives of Xhosa people.

On arrival, guests are greeted with the typical, rural Xhosa hospitality. Early in the visit there is usually 'story time', the traditional means of educating young people (and now visitors too). The people share their history – their origins, the forced removals from their original homes, and the events that shaped their lives, both negatively and positively. If you are really lucky, you may be entertained with fairy tales, the stories, which have educational and cultural meaning, that were traditionally told by grandparents to children in the old days.

Guests take part in all the day-to-day running of the homestead: they are invited to cook with the women and to participate in the household chores. They milk cows, herd goats and, during the planting season, help in the fields. Women and children fetch water from the springs.

There is also the opportunity to meet the tribal authorities, as well as visit schools, day-care centres, traditional healers and other development projects in the area.

As is the case when visiting any other rural community, go prepared to respect the code of conduct and traditions of the people, and you will walk away with an inspiring cultural experience.

MEETING THE PEOPLE

Amadiba Adventures

Amadiba Adventures is based in one of the most beautiful, unspoiled coastal areas in southern Africa, among some of the most traditional communities in the country. 'Amadiba', as the project is commonly known, is a community-based tourism initiative that was set up to bring the benefits of tourism to communities who have long been excluded from these activities.

Their first project is a horse trail. Riding horses has a low impact on the environment and one of the aims of the project is to assist local people to earn a living, while at the same time protect the priceless heritage on which they live. By using horses owned by the locals, there has been no need for the enormous capital outlay often required to get projects of this nature off the ground.

The trail leaves from the Wild Coast Casino Hotel on the border of the Eastern Cape and KwaZulu-Natal, and winds south along the magnificent and unspoilt beaches, through small villages, past shipwrecks and on to the Mtentu River on the northern border of the splendid Mkambati Game Reserve, and then back again.

The trail takes six days during which time you will not only see some of the most stunning views in the country, but also have the chance to sit around the fire and chat to locals about their lives and traditions. The Amadiba Horse Trail provides visitors with an opportunity to interact with rural Xhosa people in a meaningful way. All the facilities and services are provided and owned by self-employed individuals in the form of small 'businesses', which are the basis of the trail. The project is structured in such a way as to spread the benefits of tourism among as many people as possible, each of whom is trained for his or her particular job. About 60 people along this stretch of coast participate in the project. They hire out their horses, ferry people across rivers in canoes, provide accommodation, a laundry service and catering, guide fishing, canoeing and cultural tours, grow food and build overnight and hiking huts and other facilities. If you are not mad about horse riding, there is also a wonderful hike along much the same route.

Your experience will assist in developing sustainable and responsible eco-tourism focused on real community ownership and participation.

EASTERN CAPE
GENERAL

Eastern Cape Tourism Board, PO Box 186, Bisho 5605; tel: (040) 635-2115 or 636-4055, fax: (040) 639-2756 or 636-4019, e-mail: ectb@gateway.nis.za

Tourism Port Elizabeth, Lighthouse Building, Donkin Reserve (opposite The Edward Hotel in Belmont Terrace, Central); tel: (041) 52-1315, fax: (041) 55-2564

PORT ELIZABETH & SURROUNDS
TOWNSHIP TOURS

Calabash Tours, 8 Dollery Street, Central; tel/fax: (041) 585-6162, e-mail: calabash@iafrica.com

Fundani Township Tours, PO Box 21715, Port Elizabeth; tel/fax: (041) 63-1471/1922, cell: 082 964 663, e-mail cultours@iafrica.com

Kaya Lami Tours, contact Sizwe Johnson, cell: 082 424 0581

Walmer Township Tours, contact Mzolisi, tel: (041) 51-2572, cell: 082 970 4037

CULTURAL VILLAGES

Kaya Lendaba (Shamwari Game Reserve), PO Box 91, Paterson, 6130; tel: (042) 203-1111, fax: (042) 235 1224

MUSEUMS AND GALLERIES

Port Elizabeth Museum, Beach Road, Humewood, Port Elizabeth; tel: (041) 56-1051, fax (041) 56-4962

Donkin Heritage Trail, see Tourism Port Elizabeth above.

Castle Hill Museum, 7 Castle Hill, Port Elizabeth; tel: (041) 52-2515, fax: (041) 56-4962

King George VI Art Gallery, 1 Park Drive, Port Elizabeth; tel: (041) 56-1030, fax: (041) 56-3234

Wezandla Gallery and Craft, 27 Baaken Street, Port Elizabeth; tel: (041) 55-1185

GRAAFF-REINET & NIEU-BETHESDA

Graaff-Reinet Publicity Association, PO Box 153, Graaff-Reinet 6280; tel/fax: (0491) 2-4248, e-mail: graaff-reinet@elink.co.za

The Owl House, The Owl House Foundation, Poste Restante, Nieu-Bethesda 6286; tel/fax: (04923) 605

HOME-STAYS

Clifton Country House, contact Gappie and Elsona de Klerk, tel: (0491) 91-0566, fax: (0491) 3-5614, e-mail: clifton@elink.co.za

Bloemhof Guest Farm, contact Walter and Anne Murray, tel/fax: (0491) 91- 959, e-mail: graaff-reinet.blo@elink.co.za

Doornberg Guest Farm, contact Peet and Hanna van Heerden, tel/fax: (04923) 749

GRAHAMSTOWN
GENERAL

Tourism Grahamstown, 63 High Street, Grahamstown 6139; tel: (046) 622-3241, fax: (046) 622-3266 See also Eastern Cape Tourism Board on this page.

PLACES OF WORSHIP

Cathedral of St George and St Michael, Church Square, Grahamstown; contact the parish office, tel: (046) 622 2445.

MUSEUMS AND GALLERIES

Albany Museum Complex, Somerset Street, Grahamstown 6140; tel: (046) 622-2312, fax: (046) 622-2398

ARTS AND CRAFTS

The Standard Bank National Arts Festival, PO Box 304, Grahamstown; tel: (046) 622-4341, fax: (046) 622-3082, e-mail: sbnaf@foundation.intekom.com

The 1820 Settlers' Monument, contact Sharon McGillewie at The 1820 Settlers' Foundation; PO Box 304, Grahamstown, 6140; tel: (046) 622-7115, fax: (046) 622 4457

The Masithandane Association, contact Erica McNulty, PO Box 2240, Grahamstown; tel: (046) 622-8735, tel/fax: (046) 622-5944

EAST LONDON
GENERAL

Eastern Cape Helpline, tel: (047) 532-5691
See Eastern Cape Tourism Board on page 145

TOWNSHIP TOURS

Amatola Tours, 20 Currie Street, Quigney, East London; tel: (0431) 43-0472, fax: (0431) 2-6914

Daily Dispatch Tours, 31-35 Caxton Sreet, East London, 5201; PO Box 131, East London 5200, tel: (043) 702-2000

Fort Hare University, Private Bag 1314, Alice 5700; tel: (040) 602-2247

CULTURAL VILLAGES

Khaya la Bantu, PO Box 6, Mooiplaas 5288; tel/fax: (0431) 851-1011

MUSEUMS AND GALLERIES

Anne Bryant Gallery, 9 St Marks Road, Southernwood, East London; tel: (0431) 2-4044

East London Museum, 319 Oxford Street, Southernwood, East London; tel: (0431) 43-0686, fax: (0431) 43-3127

Amathole Museum, cnr Alexander and Albert Road, King William's Town; tel: (043) 6424506, fax: (043) 642-1569

Lock Street Gaol, Lock Street, city centre

Latimer's Landing, Pontoon Road, East London Harbour, contact Eastern Cape Helpline, tel: (047) 532-5691

Martello Tower, contact Fort Beaufort Information, tel: (046) 645-1555

WILD COAST
GENERAL

See Eastern Cape Tourism Board on page 145.

CULTURAL VILLAGES

Isinamva Cultural Village, PO Box 72, Mount Frere 5090; cell: 083 659 8491

MEETING THE PEOPLE

Amadiba Adventures, contact Travis, cell: 082 657 2524, or Simon, cell: 082 932 1442; tel: (031) 791-0178, fax: (031) 791 0055, e-mail: cropeddy@iafrica.com

KWAZULU-NATAL

About the province

The name 'KwaZulu' means 'Place of the Zulu', while 'Natal' was the name given to the area by Portuguese explorer Vasco da Gama who sighted the coast on Christmas day in 1497.

KwaZulu-Natal, on the eastern seaboard of South Africa, is home to 8.7 million people. The province is perhaps one of the most diverse – both physically and culturally – and something of a melting pot of cultures with influences from not only Africa but also from both the East and West. Even though it is one of the most densely populated provinces, there are still vast areas of magnificent wilderness, small rural villages and pretty country towns with many unique cultural attractions.

IN KWAZULU-NATAL

- meet traditional Zulu people in a rural environment;
- tramp around the Anglo-Zulu and Anglo-Boer battlefields;
- experience the culture – and the sub-tropical heat – of the coastal regions;
- you are most likely to come into contact with Eastern culture.

This chapter

- **Durban and surrounding areas:** Urban black and white culture.
- **Pietermaritzburg and the Midlands:** For years, the province now called KwaZulu-Natal was known as the 'last outpost', and Pietermaritzburg and its surrounds to this day retain strong associations with the colonial past.
- **The Drakensberg:** Rural farming communities and mountain vistas.
- **Zululand:** Home of traditional Zulu and historic battlefields.
- **Maputaland:** Tonga, Zulu and other traditional groups.

DURBAN OR 'ETHEKWENI'

There is some difference of opinion over the meaning of 'eThekweni', the name by which Zulu-speakers know Durban. A few of the rather quaint – and more polite – translations in tourist brochures claim that the name means 'the place where the earth and the ocean meet' and 'the place of the bay'. However, Zulu names are often derived not only from association with the natural environment, but more importantly from their strong identification with their prized Nguni cattle. It is more likely that the name is taken from the shape of Durban Bay which, according to Zulu people, resembles the shape of the hanging testicles of a bull.

Durban, as it is a city, may not seem to be the ideal place to spend a cultural vacation, but it is in the cities – simply by the sheer volume of people who live there – that you will inevitably experience the greatest diversity of cultures. As the largest and busiest city in KwaZulu-Natal, Durban – hot, sweaty, and vibrant – is extraordinarily rich in African urban culture and, perhaps more than any other city in the country, has the feel and pulse of Africa.

Home to the country's largest Indian population, Durban is also where you are most likely to come into contact with South Africa's Indian residents. Indians first arrived in South Africa as indentured labourers to work on sugar-cane plantations in 1860. They have retained much of their rich cultural heritage, which includes beautiful mosques, colourful temples, vibrant festivals, exciting food and dance.

TOWNSHIP TOURS

Many of the great leaders of the apartheid struggle were born, worked or died in and around Durban, and Durban's townships were hotbeds of political dissension and conflict. Nowadays, many of the townships are relatively peaceful, and a visit to some of these areas will offer an interesting background and perspective on township life.

Some 2.5 million people live in Durban's dormitory suburbs, or townships, and each township has its own story to tell in terms of the influence which apartheid had on its formation. Few townships have a decent infrastructure or reliable essential services. Clermont and Lamontville, into which tours are now often taken, were at the forefront of the anti-apartheid struggle during the 1980s and, as a result, these areas were by-passed for development projects

and suffered massive state repression. KwaMashu, to the north of Durban, was established in the 1950s when people were forcibly removed from Cato Manor, today an informal settlement. Umlazi, to the south of the city, is the largest township, with some 1.7 million people. Most township residents commute to the city daily by train, bus or mini-bus taxi. Look out for the wonderful murals on the walls of many of the recently upgraded railway stations.

KwaMuhle Museum

Before setting off on a tour into any of Durban's townships, be sure to visit the KwaMuhle Museum – in the building that once housed the notorious Department of Native Affairs – close to the city centre. The powerful displays provide a fascinating and often heart-breaking link to the city's apartheid past and the misery caused by the absurd laws which rendered the majority of the population second-class citizens in the country of their birth. The exhibits offer some background to the pass laws, influx control and beerhall systems, and there are also displays of Zulu artefacts that have survived the turbulent past.

A particularly interesting permanent exhibit depicts the history of Cato Manor, now a sprawling informal settlement behind Berea, which once saw barbaric forced removals.

Cato Manor

Cato Manor lies about 12 kilometres east of central Durban and was once a bustling settlement of Indians and Africans who co-existed peacefully until the infamous

Group Areas Act expropriated their land for white settlement and forcibly removed people and resettled them in KwaMashu much further away from the city. The controversial Cato Manor area was also the scene of notorious riots of 1949 and 1959, and these are depicted at the KwaMuhle Museum.

Most of the township tours pass through or stop at Cato Manor, but many white Durbanites will probably warn you to stay away from the area. A good, although rather narrow, tarred road winds through it and, compared to many other informal settlements, it is easy to drive through if you want to see how the people of Cato Manor live. If you keep to the main road, you cannot possibly get lost. However, although the road is used by city commuters throughout the day and night, it is probably not a good idea to stop just anywhere if you are on your own. It is much more rewarding to go with a guide – preferably a black guide who knows people in the area and who can take you to meet some of the residents.

Cato Manor is now the site of one of the country's most ambitious urban renewal programmes, but look out for the small, brightly painted Hindu temples which have endured in the lush overgrown vegetation throughout the area's troubled past.

The Gandhi Settlement

Many foreign visitors do not know that the Mahatma Gandhi lived in South Africa, let alone that he was a resident for 21 years, arriving in the country in 1893. In 1903 he established a settlement in Phoenix, about 25 kilometres from central Durban on the northwestern edge of Inanda. This area is now an informal settlement known as Bhambayi (apparently a Zulu version of the word 'Bombay'). On this 100-acre farm – the area was rural in character at the time – Gandhi formulated his political ideas and established his newspaper, the *Indian Opinion*. From here he also organised his struggle against the racist laws of the apartheid government. The inhabitants of Gandhi's *ashram* farmed and led a life of self-subsistence in accordance with his philosophy of *sarvodaya*, or 'the ideal life'.

Sadly, not much remains of the Mahatma's settlement, which was violently destroyed by squatters from the surrounding Inanda township in 1985, when the Indians were forced to flee for their lives. Many of the remaining ruins are now inhabited by squatters but, if all goes according to an ambitious and costly plan, the settlement will be restored and a museum of sorts established. Negotiations are currently underway to resettle the squatters elsewhere. In the meanwhile, even though there is not much to see, it is quite an experience to stand in a room on the floor of which the great leader once slept.

The Gandhi settlement is quite safe to visit with a guide, but it can prove difficult to locate among the rambling shackland if you are on your own.

The Ohlanga Institute and Rev John Dube's Grave

Reverend John Langalibalele Dube was the first president of the African National Congress (ANC). Born in 1871, he was a

14

writer, clergyman, teacher, humanitarian and political leader. He was buried here in 1946, having donated his land to the education trust which he had founded. Originally called the Zulu Christian Industrial School, it is now known as the Ohlanga Institute, a focal point for the education of young black people. The institute, based on Gandhi's settlement, which is only a kilometre away, teaches children to become self-sufficient.

The graves of Rev Dube and his wife are situated on a shady hill overlooking the sprawling townships, Durban city centre and the sea. Again, you will need a guide in order to visit this site because it is rather difficult to find, and it is also necessary to observe the custom of first stopping at the Dube family home to ask permission to visit the graves.

KwaDabeka Hostel

If you are planning to visit the province's rural areas, or have already done so, it would be worthwhile also to visit a township hostel to observe the transitions of a culture. After leaving their rural homes to seek work in the cities, many people found – and continue to find – accommodation in these once notorious hostels. In the past, most of the hostels provided only single-sex accommodation, which in many ways contributed to the demise of the stable family unit among rural populations. These days, many of the hostels are being upgraded and refurbished, and can accommodate couples, as well as families.

KwaDabeka Hostel in Clermont is said to be the largest in the southern hemisphere, housing more than 15 000 people. The conditions under which people lived in this hostel in the past were appalling; even though life is still difficult for many residents, the situation has improved somewhat in recent times. Residents have set up herbalist shops, barber shops, shebeens, dry cleaners and cobbler shops in the central area known, with true Zulu humour, as the 'CBD' (Central Business District). Other traders sell peanuts and various odds and ends from makeshift stalls in the hostel passages. There is always a friendly atmosphere, with music blaring, laundry hanging from the windows and neighbours and friends sitting around chatting.

Merewent and Wentworth

Durban does not have as large a population of so-called coloured residents as Cape Town. A tour through the areas which accommodated the coloured people – displaced after the Group Areas Act was passed by the Nationalist government – will take you past the housing development to which this community was designated and which they refer to as 'Rainbow Chicken' (because of the rows of small, cooped rooms) and 'Noddy Town' (in reference to the little, box-like painted homes). A tour through the Bluff township of Merewent will take you to 'Uncle Arthur's place'. Uncle Arthur entertains friends and visitors with tales from the past and the history of the area, and this is a good place to tuck into one of Durban's 'bunny chows' (half a loaf of bread hollowed out and filled with curry).

Wentworth Township was built as army barracks during World War II, but the buildings were later converted into homes and community centres. The former army prison is now a work centre for the disabled, the recreation hall is now the church, the army supply stores a shopping complex, and the parachute factory the local high school. One of the places of which the local community is particularly proud is Wentworth's Mandela Park, where a stone commemorates Nelson Mandela's strength and sensitivity, and his commitment to helping the people of Wentworth. The park was opened by President Mandela on 25 March 1995.

SHEBEENS AND TAVERNS

As African urban settlements began to grow around Durban after 1906, the shebeen became the place where people met to relax and share a drink. By 1907 there were over 100 shebeens, and today there are thousands throughout the townships – the better ones are even equipped with television so that patrons may watch sport on Saturday afternoons.

It is here that you will have the chance to talk to locals, who are invariably caught up in a lively discussion about anything from soccer and religion to politics and general social issues. There is also – inevitably – music in some form or other.

Shebeens that provide live music are generally referred to as taverns. Sibisi's Tavern in Lamontville, Bafuthi's Tavern in Chesterville and Thobile Tuck Shop in Isipingo all provide live music.

Contact the Tourist Junction (see page 185) for a list of tour operators who can accompany you to these and other shebeens or taverns.

Grace Ntombela

Grace has been running a shebeen from her small wood-and-iron house in Clermont since the early 1970s. Now an elderly single grandmother, Grace was born in the little house where she lives with her daughter and grandchildren. She has a regular clientele and loves visitors. On weekends, she braais meat which is served by her daughter. Her home is clean and quaint and has changed little since she was born. Grace's place is an example of a traditional shebeen and is highly recommended. Visit her shebeen with Hamba Kahle Tours. See page 185.

All in One

Also in Clermont, 'All in One' has a limited menu serving beers and spirits only (soft drinks may be bought from the shop next door). There is a television, clean toilet facilities and good security. See page 185.

Skhona's Tavern

Skhona's Tavern is a lively affair with pool tables, television and the normal range of beers, spirits and soft drinks. Traditional meals are cooked outside on braais. The tavern welcomes visitors. See page 185.

Nomalady's Tavern

Nomalady's Tavern is famous for having won the 1997 South African Breweries Competition as they had sold 14 000 more

15

cases of beer than any other tavern in Durban – some indication of the type of atmosphere you are likely to encounter. The tavern is well organised, catering is flexible and virtually anything can be arranged on order.

The inevitable television and sound system are provided, along with good toilet facilities. *See* page 185.

MUSIC AND DANCE

Isicathamiya

Durban's Beatrice Street YMCA, in the centre of town, is one of the best places in the country to see *isicathamiya* (pronounced iSi-Skat-a-mee-ya) – a fascinating dance form with roots in rural Zulu culture (*see also* box below). The performance

The origins of Isicathamiya

Isicathamiya developed during the apartheid years in response to the hostel conditions in which rural migrant workers found themselves living in Durban. It has spread throughout the country to regional and national competitions. Ladysmith Black Mambazo, the renowned South African band from KwaZulu-Natal who sang with Paul Simon, are perhaps the most famous exponents of *isicathamiya*.

When migrants first came to live in the cities, many lived in single-sex hostels where there were no recreational facilitates and little to do in the evenings.

People thus entertained themselves by singing, composing their own songs and dancing. The men practised in the small, cramped and overcrowded conditions of their hostel rooms, which prevented them from performing the traditional frenzied dances common to the rural areas. The term *isicathamiya* apparently refers to a chameleon; the nature of the performance is slow and controlled – like the deliberate movements of a chameleon. There is no musical accompaniment to *isicathamiya*,

not only because there was little space for musicians, but also because the hostel-dwellers were not allowed to make a noise. Historically, as women were not allowed in the hostels, the groups are all male. This situation is slowly beginning to change.

The odd performance hours originate in a time when Saturday night was the only night most people were free. Many of the migrants in the hostels worked during the day, even Saturdays, while others were occupied with soccer over the weekends. On Sundays, people attended church. Initially, hostel halls were hired for Saturday nights, the only time when the women – usually domestic workers – were able to attend the performances. In the early days, curfews banned black people from being out between 20h00 and the early hours of the morning. So the performers and patrons would arrive at the hall shortly before the curfew came into force, and they would simply sing and dance through the night. This tradition has continued, even though the curfew has long since been withdrawn.

begins late on a Saturday night – any time after 22h00 – and usually continues until 07h00 or 08h00, when the hall is needed for the Sunday church service.

An evening's performance is roughly divided into three sections, and it is advisable to arrive only after 02h00, which is when things really get going. The earlier part of the evening – from about 22h00 to 02h00 – is for the 'general' performances where between 10 and 18 groups perform two or three songs before moving off. Many members of the audience often nod off in their seats, only waking to listen to their favourite groups.

The main competition starts at about 02h30 – and don't be surprised if you find yourself appointed a judge. Normally the entrance fee for the general public is around R4,00, which is a little higher than some of the hostel performances because the performers need to cover the rental of the hall. You may not feel like watching all the groups perform but, if you drive down Beatrice Street on a Saturday night between 22h30 and midnight, you may see some groups out in the street practising their routines, with their fans.

All the isicathamiya song are original, composed by the groups themselves. It is quite expensive to participate and many of the groups undertake rigorous fundraising to pay for their uniforms (usually delightful renditions of 1950s' fashion) and travel expenses. Groups pay to perform and enter competitions, and entrance fees and some of the door takings are usually split between the prize winners. The group that can pay more usually has a better chance

of being allowed a good performance time. If the economy is good, and more people have employment, more groups are able to perform. When members of a group are unemployed, those who are working offer a helping hand. When this is not possible, groups only attend selected competitions or perform once a month.

One of the most entertaining aspects of a performance is the audience participation. Between songs, women from the audience, usually dressed in their best clothes, dance onto the stage and hand the men money – sometimes as much as R50,00 – beads or maybe a scarf, indicating who they think is the best performer. This is a variation of a rural custom whereby 'gifts' are given with the express intention of having them returned at the end of a performance, thus affording people a chance to meet.

Gumboot dancing

Another African dance form which is a delight to watch is the gumboot dance which apparently began on the docks of Durban harbour when workers discovered that the Wellington boots with which they were issued made a unique sound when slapped with a flat hand. Gumboot dancing spread to the mines where miners were also issued with gumboots as part of their uniform. Sometimes, some of Durban's hotels (but only some and only occasionally) offer gumboot dancing on an *ad hoc* basis during the holiday season, and the Bartle Arts Trust (BAT) Centre (*see page 185*) also has demonstrations of this foot-stomping, spine-tingling dance routine.

The Playhouse Company

Mainstream theatre and dance productions are performed at many of Durban's theatres, the largest of which is the Playhouse. Apart from its cultural purpose, it provides an educational function in both African and International dance forms. The company's Musical Theatre Department is well known for enthralling productions that portray South African life in a combination of vibrant dance, song and drama. Look out for performances by the rising stars of the Siwela Sonke dance group. Often described as 'challenging to watch', the troupe tackles controversial subjects such as rape, Aids and child abuse.

The Bartle Arts Trust (BAT) Hall

The BAT Hall at the Bartle Arts Trust (Bat) Centre (see pages 156 and 185) hosts musical events almost every Friday and Saturday night where you could catch anything from big-name Afro-jazz to kwaito.

The Folk Club

The Folk Club is another venue for live music and has been responsible for launching many of Durban's best bands. Monday night is folk club night, and the music usually starts after 19h30.

Jubes and the Nu Jazz Centre

These two music venues are connected to the University of Natal's jazz department. Jubes, which was established by local saxophonist Mfana Mlabo, boasts a host of talented local musicians. It is cosy, with plenty of atmosphere, and is a hot favourite among jazz lovers. Friday night features a band, while Saturday night is invariably a jam session.

The Nu Jazz Centre provides an excellent platform for established as well as visiting bands, and visitors to the centre can enjoy some original local music.

The Rainbow Restaurant

This club is an institution in Durban and one of the oldest Afro-jazz spots around. Although gigs usually happen on Sundays between 13h00 and 16h30, they are not always regular, so it is best to watch the press or contact The Rainbow to check it out (see page 185). It always has a great crowd and is guaranteed to offer you a slice of local life.

The Tree House

The Tree House is, in fact, the home of musician Steve Fataar, who is considered an institution in his own right. Here you can enjoy a meal while listening to anything from trance music to local and visiting bands. The evenings are fun and laid back but, like The Rainbow (see above), performances are irregular, so it is advisable to call beforehand (see page 185).

MUSEUMS AND GALLERIES

Apart from the KwaMuhle Museum (see page 148), Durban has a number of really good museums and art galleries where one can dip into the city's past.

The Campbell Collections

These rare and unique collections of archival resources are acknowledged throughout the world for their fine quality and the contributions to postgraduate research, and the fascinating museum is well worth visiting. The collections are housed in Muckleneuk, a graceful, Cape-Dutch inspired home built for sugar baron Marshall Campbell and his family. The Killie Campbell Africana Library has the world's best collection of books on South Africa, and a rich oral and photographic archive on the history of the country over the last two centuries. The William Campbell Picture Collections boast some of South Africa's finest works by black artists such as Jabulani Ntuli, S.M.T. Mnguni and Gerard Benghu. About 250 of Barbara Tyrell's paintings of African traditional life, Zulu society and customs add vitality to the collection. The highlight, though, is definitely the Mashu Museum of Ethnology which contains the region's finest collections of African cultural artefacts. Traditional utensils, weapons, carvings, masks, pottery and musical instruments are exhibited alongside a fine collection of traditional beadwork. The collections can only be viewed by appointment.

Time Warp Museum

This is a museum with a difference – and a little local flavour. Because Durban is a city of surfers, the museum offers a taste of coastal culture. The fun collection of surf boards dates from the 1930s to the present, and there is an assortment of surfing memorabilia from local surf clubs.

Durban Cultural and Documentation Centre

While the centre is directly concerned with the history, culture and development of South Africans of Indian origin, it also portrays their interaction with other cultures in the country. It serves not only as a place of learning and research, but also as a venue for the promotion of the visual and performing arts. The centre contains information about indentured Indians and the Mahatma Gandhi's stay in South Africa. There is a wonderfully exotic collection of Indian instruments, intricate jewellery, traditional costumes, religious icons, cutlery, farming implements, original Indian documents donated by members of the public, and a photographic exhibition depicting the lives of indentured labourers. Call in advance before visiting (see page 185).

KwaZulu-Natal Society of Arts (KNSA) and the Durban Centre for Photography (DCP)

This is one of Durban's trendiest visual arts venues. Its galleries host more than 20 temporary exhibitions every year (featuring a mix of local and international artists), the Durban Centre for Photography, a small but vibrant shop and a wonderful little restaurant, which offers stylishly presented, healthy food out under the trees and umbrellas. KNSA was founded in 1905, and is now situated in a specially commissioned gallery in the leafy suburb of Glenwood. The three galleries allow for work of established artists to be exhibited alongside student and community artists. The gallery shop sells a variety of artworks and collectibles.

The DCP is a non-profit organisation committed to promoting a better understanding of photography. This is achieved through educational programmes and workshops, and by hosting local and international exhibitions of all forms of photography from contemporary, historical, and documentary to commercial, student and art photography. There are also darkrooms for hire, which are specially equipped for the development of black-and-white film.

The African Art Centre

For those interested in indigenous African art, the African Art Centre has established itself as a stockist of quality and authentic items. The centre promotes and sells original works of art including beadwork, basketry, weaving, ceramics, carving and sculpture from the Zulu and Xhosa traditions, and encourages young as well as established artists in their pursuit of fine art. There is usually someone at the centre who can provide information about the artists, giving the works of art a more personal touch. Original works of high quality can be purchased at prices ranging from R3 to R3 000.

Andrew Walford's Shongweni Pottery Gallery

Andrew Walford's internationally acclaimed stoneware and porcelain is inspired by nature. A visit to his hilltop studio and gallery, beautifully situated overlooking vast tracts of indigenous bush above the Shongweni dam and nature reserve, is the perfect panacea to a hot, humid day of shopping in the city. Andrew holds open days – when a healthy lunch and herbal teas are served – but otherwise visits are by appointment only.

The Bartle Arts Trust (BAT) Centre

From across the bay, the BAT Centre does, in fact, resemble an enormous bat in flight. At any time of the day, and on most nights, the centre buzzes with activity as Durban's trendy set – artists, musicians, and other interesting people – meet for drinks upstairs on the veranda overlooking the bay, or downstairs in the coffee shop. There are always painters, sculptors, dancers or musicians at work in the various studios and galleries, so you can wander around and watch, and meet the artists face to face. There are also regular dance, art and music workshops and writing classes. At night, the BAT Centre comes alive with local theatre productions, African film or video festivals and live music. Also housed here are a number of galleries that showcase South African contemporary ceramics, hand-crafted jewellery, emerging local talent, and exhibitions of thought-provoking work. The Centre aims to encourage respect for local artists and supports the development of artistic endeavours that depict KwaZulu-Natal's rich cultural diversity. See page 185.

The Open Window Network (OWN) promotes developing community television and provides a production training resource facility for community organisations as well as for individuals who are interested in film and video.

PLACES OF WORSHIP

Spirituality has always played a significant role in the development of Durban's, and indeed South Africa's culture, informing as it often does, the values of a culture. In Durban there are any number of places of worship that cater for a vibrant diversity of spiritual practices. Mosques stand alongside Anglican churches, while Hindu temples and shrines adorn river banks. In the townships and on many street corners are *iSangomas* and *iziNyangas* (traditional healers) who can contact the ancestral spirits on your behalf, and there are many synagogues and cathedrals in the nearby suburbs. A visit to some of these fascinating places offers an extraordinary insight into the human values to which many locals aspire, and could enhance your understanding of the people you are likely to meet.

The Jumma Musjid Mosque

A distinctive feature of Durban is the call to prayer heard over the loud speakers from the city's mosques. The beautifully domed structure of the Jumma Musjid Mosque, often called the Grey Street Mosque, dates back to the late 1880s and is considered to be the largest and oldest mosque in South Africa. Tours around the recently refurbished mosque are fascinating, and visitors are told about the customs and beliefs of those who follow the Islamic faith. When visiting a mosque, women are required to cover their head and shoulders and preferably wear a long skirt that covers their legs – although a robe will be provided should you forget. Slip-on shoes are convenient because you will be required to leave them outside when entering the mosque.

Ebuhleni (Shembe Church)

One of the most fascinating and colourful aspects of Durban's spiritual life is the Shembe Church. The 400 000-strong followers of the Prophet Shembe combine a blend of Christian and traditional beliefs, and dance is the primary form of worship. The Shembe citadel sheltered the landless and dispossessed during the apartheid years, and the church – based on a strong, craft-based work ethic – is well known as a centre for black self-advancement.

Two great Shembe festivals are held every year. The first is on the first Sunday of the new year, when followers make a pilgrimage to the Holy Mountain – Nhlongakazi, near Ndwedwe – retracing the route taken by the Prophet Shembe. Setting out from Ebuhleni, Shembe's citadel overlooking the Inanda Dam, the 60-kilometre march, led by clergy and amakhosi (traditional chiefs), takes followers north to Ndwedwe, reaching the Holy Mountain late on the second day. Each pilgrim ascends the mountain and places a stone on the great Isivivane, a massive cairn alongside which the service is held. A second, month-long festival in July gives visitors an opportunity to experience the spectacular ceremonies where the faithful of the Holy Church of Nazareth Baptists (the name by which the Shembe followers are also known) – shield-waving warriors, young men in kilts and pith helmets, barebreasted maidens and traditional matrons – don their best, and dance in worship of God. The perfectly choreographed, if somewhat frenzied and up-tempo dancing, is usually accompanied by *imbomu* – long, deep-toned horns and pulsating drums. The extraordinary costumes and dance routines should not be missed.

If you are unable to attend either of the two main festivals, feel free to attend any of the regular Shembe ceremonies – members are very enthusiastic about receiving visitors – such as the baptisms where members of the church may be healed during rituals rich in symbolism.

Temple of Understanding

There are a number of small, elaborately painted Hindu temples in Durban, and many are very old – the spectacular Shree Amalvanar Alayam Second River Temple has been declared a national monument – but possibly one of the most magnificent is the Temple of Understanding in Chatsworth. The opulent architecture, with its golden steeples and tranquil moat, is unique in South Africa as the temple was designed and built by the International Society for Krishna Consciousness. The temple is renowned for its vegetarian lunches, so bear this in mind when planning the time you want to visit.

Mariannhill Monastery

Missions played an influential part in South Africa's history, and the Trappist monks were particularly active in the area that is now known as KwaZulu-Natal. Mariannhill Monastery, situated just outside Durban, is the centre from which sprang many other smaller missions throughout the province. It is quite simply – as one brochure describes it – 'a beautiful example of Trappist restraint and self-reliance.'

Self-reliance was one of the main tenets of the missionaries who, when building the monastery, used building materials – including the stained-glass windows – manufactured by the craftsmen-monks.

The monastery complex seems entirely self-sufficient, with its surrounding farmlands, herb garden, bakery, hand-made candle factory, schools, guesthouse accommodation and a chapel with a beautifully crafted wooden interior. It also includes the more elaborate St Joseph's Cathedral, which – boasting paintings, sculpture, and exceptional architecture – is considered by many to be a work of art in itself. In order to really appreciate the beauty of the cathedral, it is worthwhile attending a service, which gives one a more holistic and realistic appreciation of the monastic lifestyle and values.

MARKETS

Most South African cities have a plethora of outdoor flea markets and Durban is no exception. Some sell rather expensive goods, while others are flooded with cheap junk from Asia, China or the Philippines. A list of markets that are usually held only on Saturdays or Sundays in the parks and parking lots around Durban may be obtained from the Tourist Junction (*see* page 185). Two big permanent markets do exist, though, and should not be missed at all costs – more because of their novelty and vibrancy rather than because of what can be purchased there.

The Early-Morning Market, Victoria Street Market and Fish Market

The original Indian Market burnt down a number of years ago and was replaced by a more modern version that has now taken on a character of its own. Today, the market is as busy and interesting as its predecessor, and vendors and shopkeepers still try to entice you into their establishments to buy. Just about everything is offered for sale: from oriental brassware, to African baskets, Hindu flame lamps, sacks of lentils and split peas. The exotic aromas of soaps and sweet-smelling incense mingle with the curries and spices. The smell of the next-door Fish Market can be overpowering, but the market itself is quite exotic and if you can stand the odours of the fish, crabs, squid and prawns that arrive fresh from the coast every day, it is really a fascinating place to visit. The fishmongers are as colourful and cajoling as their colleagues in the market next door.

Warwick Street Triangle and Muti Market

For years the pavements around the Warwick Street Triangle were crammed with informal traders and traditional healers selling exotic collections and mixtures of indigenous herbs, plants, bark, snake skins, birds wings, crocodile teeth, dolphin skulls and monkey paws. But the area has been upgraded and the traders are now housed under more sanitary conditions. This is truly a fascinating market because, not only is it the biggest of its kind in the southern hemisphere, it offers a real

insight into many traditional beliefs and customs. There is every possibility of finding an *iSangoma* (spiritual healer) willing to 'throw the bones' for you. You may, however, need an interpreter because many of the people plying their trade here are from deep rural areas and have come to the city to help their people cope with the stresses and strains of urban life and often do not speak English well. Some of the concoctions they make may look quite horrifying to a Westerner, but, before condemning any of the practices, remember that many of these healers have a holistic approach to life that may differ from yours. They also have vast botanical and zoological knowledge in which many Western pharmaceutical companies are becoming increasingly interested.

Dalton Road Traditional Market

From the outside, the market on Dalton Road can look rather daunting, stuck as it is in a run-down industrial area behind a busy bus rank. Visitors should consider taking a Zulu-speaking guide, mainly because there is every chance of not finding a single person who speaks passable English. The Dalton Road market is one of Durban's main suppliers of traditional costumes and accessories, such as drums, shields, cowhide skirts and the elaborate head-dresses worn by Zulu dancers in traditional ceremonies. Many of the craftsmen are from rural backgrounds, and while they may have lived in Durban for some time, they retain many of their traditions and customs, and few have mastered much

15

English. The market is patronised largely by Zulu people, so this is a good opportunity to buy authentic crafts and 'curios' (authentic goods made for Zulu people, but often snatched up by tourists) at a much lower price than you may find anywhere else – other than in the rural areas. However, unlike their Indian counterparts, traders are unlikely to bargain much because prices are often already exceptionally low in order to make the items accessible to everyone. Dalton Road is also one of the few places where you can buy recycled tyre shoes, or have them made to fit.

The beachfront beadwork and basket sellers

Durban beachfront would not be the same without the many women selling crafts along the pavements. They have become an institution in Durban and it is a treat to watch them weaving, crocheting and threading their intricate bead designs. Apparently, many of these women belong to the Shembe Church, whose leader was a great advocate of self-employment. This is also a good place to find reasonably priced baskets, mats and sun hats woven from natural products such as grasses, palms and bark. The quality of the craftwork varies, however, and, sadly, there are a number of cheap 'curios' imported from the East – often mistaken by foreigners for indigenous crafts. If you want something truly African, look at what the women are making, or ask if the craftwork is of South African origin. By supporting the women, you are also contributing to keeping traditional crafts and skills alive.

PIETERMARITZBURG & THE MIDLANDS

For many years, the province previously known as Natal (now KwaZulu-Natal) was euphemistically referred to as the 'last outpost' because of its close ties to the British colonialists. Although the town of Pietermaritzburg, the original provincial capital, was established as a small Boer outpost, it was quickly enveloped within the colonial English fold. The dozens of redbrick buildings still attest to this heritage, and Pietermaritzburg is a good place for historic walkabouts. It is a university town and many of KwaZulu-Natal's more affluent private schools are situated in or near the city.

The rolling hills of the rural farming districts just north of Pietermaritzburg – an area called the KwaZulu-Natal Midlands – are reminiscent of pastoral Europe, with its

The Midlands Meander

A good way to meet the locals, particularly artists and crafters, of the rural communities north of Pietermaritzburg is to tour the Midlands Meander, and visit the weavers, painters, potters, cobblers and other craftspeople of the region. The signposted route – numbered maps are readily available – takes you through the small towns and farmlands of the Midlands, and stops at the area's many craft shops, studios, galleries, coffee shops, tea gardens and restaurants.

warm summers and frosty winters. But this is only half the story because, as with every city in South Africa, Pietermaritzburg is surrounded by sprawling townships.

The townships of Edendale and Mbali were once scenes of violence and upheaval, but are today once again peaceful and settled. Visits into these areas are not formally organised, although plans are afoot and enquiries may be made at Pietermaritzburg Tourism (see page 186).

MUSEUMS AND GALLERIES

Tatham Art Gallery

The Tatham Art Gallery is situated in the old Supreme Court buildings, another of Pietermaritzburg's fine redbrick structures. The Gallery is worth visiting for its fine collection of works by black and white South African artists, as well as traditional crafts such as baskets, beadwork, and ear plugs once worn in the ear lobes by some Zulu groups (although this is not a custom seen much nowadays, except in really rural areas of the province). There is an active emphasis on education and a variety of short courses, talks and workshops are held on a regular basis. There is also a good restaurant-cum-coffee shop upstairs.

Voortrekker Museum

This small museum is of immense importance to many Afrikaans-speaking South Africans because it is situated in the original Church of the Vow, which has been renovated over the years. Prior to what was later to become known as the Battle of Blood River, a Boer commando under the leadership of Andries Pretorius vowed that, should God grant the Boers victory against the Zulu, they would commemorate the day by building a church. About 3 000 Zulu warriors died in the battle, while the Boers suffered no casualties.

Today, the museum houses a variety of interesting Voortrekker artefacts, including Piet Retief's prayerbook, an old wagon, and flintlock rifles. Next door to the museum is Andries Pretorius's thatch-roofed cottage, also open to the public.

Natal Museum

One of the country's five national museums, the Natal Museum has a little of everything, the most interesting of which is the exhibit on sub-Saharan cultures, which highlights religious, ceremonial, military and household artefacts from across the continent. Other displays include a natural science hall featuring displays of massive dinosaurs, birds, marine life and African animals. There is also a recreation of a Pietermaritzburg street scene of the 1880s – complete with shops, a pharmacy and smithy, and a settlers' cottage.

CULTURAL VILLAGES

Ecabazini Zulu Cultural Homestead

This small Zulu homestead and farm just outside Pietermaritzburg overlooks the Albert Falls Dam and the distant Karkloof mountains. Here you can meet Cedric Hood or 'CJ' as he is called, the 'white Zulu' who has adopted Zulu customs.

16

Visitors' accommodation is in authentic beehive homes, or rondavels, and the emphasis is on preserving the authentic Zulu way of life. There is no electricity and food is prepared over an open fire. A fascinating tour takes visitors into the farmlands to see how traditional crops such as *imfe* (sorghum), *amadumbi* (a yam-like potato) and *amabeca* (melons) are grown.

MARKETS

Alexander Park

Alexander Park hosts two good markets on the first and last Sunday of the month. These markets are not 'flea markets' in the traditional sense, where old, secondhand goods are sold for a song, but rather a selection of handcrafted goods, clothes, leatherwork, woodwork and similar items is on sale – and there are few 'bargains' to be had. Although there is plenty of the rather predictable fast foods on offer, there are also wonderful home-baked goodies.

Victoria Street Farmers' Market

Another fun market is the early-morning farmers' market, which takes place behind the Clover Dairy in Victoria Street on Saturday mornings. Farmers from the surrounding areas bring their produce to town and you can buy fresh eggs, herbs, honey and a variety of fruit and vegetables. The market usually closes by 09h00.

Art in the Park

The Gordon Verhoef & Krause Art in the Park exhibition is one of Pietermaritzburg's premier 'cultural' events. Every year, for five days during autumn (May), 60 of South Africa's top artists gather in Alexander Park to display their work under the trees. There is a tea garden and wine tasting events and, throughout the five days, there are a number of musical performances. Art in the Park is South Africa's largest outdoor art exhibition and a wonderful opportunity to meet and chat to artists and other South Africans.

MEET THE PEOPLE

Nottingham Road Hotel & Pub

The Nottingham Road Hotel is an institution in the area and a favourite for locals and visitors alike. The hotel is especially popular during the winter, when a huge fire is lit in the hearth and the pub is filled with farmers and students from the nearby town of Pietermaritzburg.

Ixopo Buddhist Retreat

Although South Africa has a surprisingly large community of Buddhists, you do not have to be a Buddhist to spend time at the retreat. Visitors are welcome to attend the various courses run throughout the year – from weekend courses in basic Buddhism, to birdwatching, relationships, ecology and month-long retreats. Walks through the magnificent setting of grasslands and wooded areas are very peaceful, and a beautiful white stupa – a domed structure around which people walk in meditation – overlooks the rolling foothills. Days begin early with meditation and there is usually a period of silence on most mornings. For an insight into Buddhism in South Africa – or even just a place to rest and enjoy the natural environment – the Ixopo Buddhist Retreat is a truly wonderful place to visit.

DRAKENSBERG

The Drakensberg area is a vast and majestic wilderness of massive mountains that form the Great Escarpment, part of which is the natural barrier between KwaZulu-Natal and the mountain kingdom of Lesotho. One of the earliest people to inhabit the areas surrounding the Drakensberg were the San (Bushmen), who left immense art galleries on the walls of caves and rock faces in the foothills. Since then, groups of Nguni people, many fleeing Shaka's battlefields, either settled in the area – their descendants are still there – or passed through en route to safer havens. Farmers of Dutch and English descent settled on the fertile lands to farm, assisted in some instances by Indian indentured labourers. More recently, many displaced Zulu speakers were moved from other parts of the province to the remote rural areas at the foot of the Drakensberg during the apartheid government's forced removals. Finally came the artists and craftsmen, drawn to the beauty of the area and the growing tourist trade. There is an interesting mix of cultures in this friendly, if somewhat conservative, farming district.

Winterton Museum

If you want some background to the Drakensberg, its history is alive and well and sharing a house with a library in the picturesque town of Winterton in the central Drakensberg area. This little museum is certainly worth a visit, representing as it does the living history of the people in the area, past and present: people from the Stone Age and Iron Age, the groups who fled Shaka's invading armies during the Difaqane ('the crushing'), and the first white settlers – Voortrekkers and British. The wedding gear and photographs on display belonged to the grandparents and great-grandparents of the present-day Stockils who own Mambasa Hutted Camp (see page 164).

Using materials which they collected in the same way their ancestors did, the local Ngwane people have built authentic grass homes alongside the museum, while farmers in the district donated old farm implements and other tools used by their pioneering forefathers. If you are planning a hike into the mountains to see any of the San paintings, first take a look at the San Art Gallery consisting of 10 panels of 180 photographs. The last San were seen in the Drakensberg mountains in the 1870s.

Bringing the exhibit into the present is a small but poignant display of one of the actual voting booths, UV detectors and banners used by the Winterton community during South Africa's historic first democratic elections in 1994. There are even a few photographs taken by a local amateur of the locals queuing to vote.

The museum also houses an outstanding collection of books on the Anglo-Boer War and, if you're planning a visit to the battlefields (see page 171), make use of the little reading room to brush up on some facts.

163

Outside there is an odd but amazing wooden 'caravan', built in 1918 by an eccentric local, Maximillian John Ludwig Weston – more commonly known as Admiral John Weston – in which he drove his family right the way across Africa to tour Europe, returning to settle in the Bergville district in 1933.

Mambasa Hutted Camp

Mambasa is a cultural village with a difference. This is certainly not a big commercial venture where the Zulu are out in full force, dressed in traditional outfits and performing at set times for tourists. It is run by a local farming family and some of their farm labourers, and tourists are able to stay in the camp, which is a replica of an old-fashioned traditional village, but with some additional conveniences. The camp is used predominantly by school groups who want to combine a cultural experience with historical and environmental education. Mambasa is ideally suited to larger tour groups, although smaller groups and individuals are easily and often accommodated.

The camp of traditional beehive dwellings, made by local rural Zulu women, is situated on the banks of the mighty Tugela River and has an evocative atmosphere – particularly at night when the coals are glowing in the fire and the jackals are calling from the surrounding hills. The entire area is also steeped in human history: there are ancient Stone and Iron Age sites, and you can sometimes find weathered and well-worn grindstones and other stone implements dating back thousands of years (which should not be moved

or removed under any circumstances). Across the river valley is Vaalkrans, where Boer and Briton dragged their cannons across the veld in order to do battle against each other – and the hills still seem alive with the sounds of the various battles fought there. Legend also has it that clay pots of gold are buried nearby, and local Zulu residents say that city folk still come at night to dig for it – and evidence of the excavations scar the hillsides.

Mambasa is owned by the Stockil family, local farmers whose ancestors arrived in the district in 1876. Renée Stockil runs Mambasa with the help of a Zulu couple, and they provide a unique cultural experience. Try your hand at beadwork or sculpting clay pots, and see the beer-making demonstration (and share a drink of authentic, traditional Zulu beer afterwards).

San (Bushmen) Paintings

There are litrally hundreds of sites in the Drakensberg where you can find San paintings but, perhaps wisely, most are not

The Drakensberg Meander

A meander through the Champagne Valley of the central 'Berg will take you to any number of artists' studios, craft shops, herb gardens, tea gardens and restaurants, and is a good way to meet people and chat to the locals. For maps of the route and more information, contact the Drakensberg Tourism Association, (see page 186).

open to the general public – mainly because many of them have been defaced or vandalised by thoughtless visitors who have thereby destroyed some of the last reminders of the presence of hunter-gatherers in the area during the latter half of the Stone Age. However, there are still a number of inspiring sites which are open and may be viewed.

Main Caves

Main Caves in the Giant's Castle Game Reserve in the central Drakensberg region is one of the most important San painting sites. More than 500 paintings, some now barely discernable, can be viewed on two massive rock overhangs, and many depict the eland – large antelope still found in the Drakensberg region, and of special spiritual significance to the San – most notably in the Northern Cave.

Guided tours of the Main Caves site, only 30 minutes' walk from the Giant's Castle camp site, may be arranged.

Injasuti

Injasuti is also in the Giant's Castle Game Reserve. Battle Cave, in the Injasuti Valley, holds approximately 750 paintings on the rock walls, but it is the content of the paintings that is most interesting: one vignette depicts a red monochrome scene of two feuding San groups, from which the cave derives its name. There is also one of the few paintings of a lion to be found in the Drakensberg.

The word injasuti is the anglicized spelling of the Zulu noun, *enjesuthi*, which means 'the well-fed dog' – referring to the fact that there was once so much game in this area that the hunting dogs of the early Nguni hunters never went hungry.

Cannibal Caves

The paintings in Cannibal Caves in the south/central 'Berg, are faint and not of as great interest as some of the others, but the cave itself has a lively history. During the mid-nineteenth century, a group of cannibals (not of San origin) lived in the caves, roaming the area of present-day Lesotho. They marauded and attacked lone travellers or small groups escaping the Difaqane (*see* page 163). Their victims were apparently strung up in the cave to keep them fresh for eating. Rumour has it that when 'food' was in short supply, the cannibals bartered and ate their own wives and children.

Drakensberg Boys' Choir

It may seem odd to find one of the world's foremost choir schools tucked away in a small rural community miles from any-where, but here it is, nestled at the foot of the central Drakensberg mountain range – no doubt drawing inspiration from the majestic peaks of Champagne Castle and Cathkin Peak. This choir is often men-tioned in the same breath as the Vienna and the Harlem boys' choirs, and their con-certs are not to be missed. International concert tours are undertaken annually, and the choir regularly also goes on local tours, so look out for them in other parts of the country.

In recent years, a beautiful theatre was built at the school and every Wednesday

16.

afternoon, during term time, there is a performance to which members of the public are invited. There are also other scheduled evening performances – details may be obtained from the school – and throughout the year, the programme covers 'themes' such as the magnificent Christmas concerts. Choirs may not normally be your thing, but, if you enjoy or would like to hear foot-stomping, spirit-rousing and sometimes lump-in-the-throat African music, look out for concerts where the boys sing indigenous music. You won't regret it – nor forget it. Also look out for the Music in the Mountains festival during April/May every year.

Splashy Fen Music Festival

Originally a small gathering of musicians for a few days of 'jamming' on a farm in the Drakensberg foothills, Splashy Fen has grown into a Woodstock-like festival of contemporary music featuring the cream of South African folk and acoustics musicians – and the occasional top-name overseas artist. Every year during April/May, performances take place on a folk-club free stage (where 'performers' are free to get up and 'jam'), a marquee, and an open-air 'amphitheatre' – and there is the ever-popular craft market.

Although accommodation is available at guesthouses and B&Bs in the area, most people bring their families and camp at the river or on the surrounding hillsides. A classical festival – 'Seriously Splashy' – also takes place in September and features philharmonic orchestras, string quartets and other classical performers.

Ardmore Ceramic Art Studio and Guesthouse

This rustic rural studio and gallery, built in the old stone stables on a farm in the foothills of the Drakensberg mountains, is probably one of the most unusual and interesting ceramics studios in the country. Ardmore farm was once the home of internationally acclaimed ceramic artist Fée Halsted-Berning and her protégée Bonnie Ntshalintshali. Although Fee and her family no longer live there, she still operates the Ardmore studio and her home is now a guesthouse.

Few of the mostly women artists from the surrounding rural farmlands – employment is scarce and poverty common – have any formal education or training in art, yet their work is sought after throughout the world. In this lush meadow in the Champagne Valley, you can watch the women create their often fun, sometimes functional pieces – from domestic ware through to sculptural art – which reflect their uniquely naive perspective of the world. There are any number of artists working in the studio and there is always someone there to show you around the converted stable studio and shop.

The work of these rural women is highly original and colourful and, while it is in no way 'traditional', it is unmistakably African, often with mythological or biblical references. Zebras race around the lip of a teapot, lizards scamper across tureens and butterflies flutter over dinner plates, and black saints, arms outstretched, proclaim words of wisdom, while a giraffe festooned with birds provides the handles of cups and jugs. The artists work together in the true communal fashion of Africa, some working the clay, others painting, while another glazes, and it is a delight to wander around while the women work in the studio or sit outside in the sun painting, singing and gossiping, with the radio blaring Zulu programmes in the background.

Their unique work has received international acclaim and is exhibited in galleries around the world, but to see it being created in these lovely surroundings makes it all the more special. For day visitors to Ardmore, the guesthouse provides tea and scones under the trees, with the Drakensberg mountain range as a backdrop.

Punch and his aeroplanes

A young man in his late teens, with little formal education, who has lived his entire life in a small village at the foot of the mountains in the northern Drakensberg area, has become famous for his aeroplanes. Punch makes his aeroplanes out of old tin cans and virtually anything he can lay his hands on. As a child, he was fascinated by the 'planes he saw passing overhead, and began building aeroplanes and helicopters of all shapes and sizes. He is a prolific worker and his magnificent pieces can be seen whirring around on tall poles outside shops and village houses along the road towards Mont-aux-Sources. He was 'discovered' a few years ago and has since exhibited in galleries throughout the country. He still works in his mother's little rural homestead, where he has built an enormous aeroplane in the garden in which he lives. Ask for directions from the hotels (most of the staff will know) or at any of the trading stores or shops along the route – or wherever you see one of his enchanting aeroplanes.

KwaZamokhule

KwaZamokhule, a school for physically disabled children, is located on the route to the central Drakensberg resorts. In the Zulu language, *KwaZamokhule* roughly means 'try your best', and, in the over-crowded lands surrounding Loskop in the Drakensberg foothills, this can make a significant difference. During the apartheid years, few facilities were provided for black people in rural areas, with the result that churches sometimes stepped in to fill the gap. In this case, the Lutheran Church established a facility for physically handicapped children, and today the little school caters for approximately 90 pupils, ranging in age from pre-school to Grade Seven (children of about 12 years of age).

Rather than tuck the children away in institutions because of their physical handicaps, the dedicated staff are determined to include the children in as much of the real world as possible, and visitors thus make a valuable contribution to the children's lives. It is a rare opportunity to talk to South African children and, at the same time, know you are making a difference. The staff are all locals, so they can give an informed and personal history of the area and talk about the challenges faced by rural families of disabled children. The children learn a number of crafts such as pottery, beadwork, and leatherwork, and some of their work is on sale.

The Dioconic Handcraft Centre

The centre – affiliated to KwaZamokhule and just across the way – runs a handicraft centre for women from the Loskop and Bergville areas. Although some work on the premises, most of the women produce their grasswork, baskets and beadwork at home and then bring the finished items to the centre, from where they are sold or exported. The centre also produces communion wafers for export, and many of the church vestments they make – gowns, stoles, albs and altar clothes – are also sold all over the world. A small medical clinic is open for visits on Tuesdays, and there is a small guesthouse on the premises.

ZULULAND

Most tourists tend to visit Zululand because of its associations with the Anglo-Boer and Anglo-Zulu wars, but even if you have no interest in wars, this is where – despite the modernisation of much of traditional Zulu life – many Zulu still loyally adhere to their customs, rituals and ceremonies, and there are a number of sites of cultural significance to the Zulu nation. In the past, many of these sites were considered by the previous government to be neither interesting nor important and, as a result, some are little more than a small plaque on a tree in some remote valley. More recently, however, the graves of the Zulu kings and influential members of the royal household, and the great royal Zulu homesteads that were once razed to the ground by the British Imperial forces are being restored, developed and made more accessible by the KwaZulu Monuments Council and Heritage Trust.

HISTORICAL & ARCHAEOLOGICAL SITES

Stanger/Dukuza

Few visitors to South Africa have not heard of Shaka Zulu, the warrior king who is credited with building the mighty Zulu nation. kwaDukuza, the site upon which the town of Stanger was built, was Shaka's last great capital. An old mahogany tree still grows in the grounds of the municipal offices and it was here, according to legend, that Shaka was assassinated by his half-brothers, Dingane and Mhlangana. Today there is also an interpretative centre with more information about the great warrior kings. Other sites of cultural interest nearby are Shaka's Spring (from where unpolluted water for the king was fetched), Shaka's swimming and bathing place on the Imbozamo River, Shaka's Cave (a shelf above the pool where Shaka would rest) and The Execution Cliff (where executions took place).

Emakhosini

Emakhosini, or Valley of the Kings, is a microcosm of the history of southeastern Africa. Evidence of human habitation includes the Stone Age San, Iron Age farmers, through the 15th-century settlements associated with the Buthelezi and Khumalo groups – who would later play a significant role in the formation of the

Zulu Kingdom – and on to present day. The great Zulu warrior king Shaka was born in the Emakhosini in about 1785 and it is here that his forebears, *amaKhosi* Zulu (nKosinkulu), Phunga, Mageba, Ndaba, Jama, Senzangakhona and Dinizulu lie buried.

Today, the Emakhosini is divided up into cattle farms and is largely under private ownership. But because many Zulu royalists and traditionalists believe the valley to be sacred, steps are currently being taken to purchase land and preserve a culture and history that has left an indelible mark on the stage of the world, and South Africa in particular. The sites of these old graves have not been developed as tourist attractions, but they may indeed be visited. At certain times of the day, the atmosphere at some of these lonely graves evokes the spirit of an ancient Africa.

The sites are not easy to find though, and until they are properly signposted it is advisable to contact the KwaZulu Monuments Council and Heritage Trust (*see* page 187) before setting out.

Mgungundlovu

Mgungundlovu, which is situated in the Emakhosini valley, was the royal capital of Zululand during the reign of Dingane, who was instrumental in the murder of his half-brother Shaka and succeeded him as king. The name Mgungundlovu roughly translates into 'the secret conclave of the elephant' or 'the place of the elephant' (*indlovu* means 'elephant', which is traditionally a metaphorical reference to the stature of the king).

Archaeological excavations here have uncovered the charcoal remains of the outer palisade that enclosed this massive homestead, which housed up to 7 000 residents, and a section of the royal area has been reconstructed. Also exposed are a number of the original floors, which were baked hard like pottery when Dingane ordered Mgungundlovu to be burnt down in 1838. One of the most exciting archaeological finds has been the floor of the king's residence. It has a diameter of approximately 10 metres, probably the largest ever to be built in the traditional Zulu manner. Charcoal remains of the 22 supporting posts – mentioned in reports by those who visited the king in his dwelling – and the unique six-pointed hearth is not found in any other homes, verify that this was indeed Dingane's dwelling. There are also excavations of a copper smithing site, grain pits and other areas of importance. Many other permanent structures are to be re-erected as authentically as possible and there are plans for further conservation of this historical site. A guide is sometimes on hand to take you around the homestead, but if not, a very informative leaflet is available at the entrance.

Ondini

Ondini, which means 'high place', was the military capital of King Cetshwayo, and the Ondini Museum includes an interpretative centre, a statue of the king, and a partial reconstruction of the great homestead. There is always someone to take you around to view the magnificent beadwork collection, the exhibits on the various

70

sub-cultures of the Zulu, children's arts and crafts, an explanation of the rites of passage or 'life cycle' of the Zulu from birth to death, and a number of other displays portraying a culture in transition. Also on display is a silver mug – presented to Cetshwayo by Queen Victoria – that was lost and has only recently been found, and a poignant letter written by a British soldier the day after the Battle of Ondini.

The site of the homestead has been partially reconstructed, and the ruins of an unusual four-cornered Western-style house built in the homestead with the assistance of a Norwegian missionary, is still to be restored. There is also the large rock upon which Cetshwayo used to sit when he bathed, and from which he could see across the hills.

Ondini was destroyed by fire in 1879 following the Zulu's defeat by the British and, true to Zulu tradition which restricts the reuse of royal land, little of the site – apart from some archaeological exploration – has been disturbed since it's destruction.

It is possible to stay overnight in a traditional Zulu homestead – with modern amenities laid on – just a stone's throw from Ondini. Grazing nearby are herds of the white Nguni cattle so highly prized by the warrior kings.

Ulundi and Surrounds

There are a number of other sites of historical and cultural interest in and around Ulundi and the Emakhosini.

- The Ulundi Battle Monument marks the site of the last battle of the Anglo-Zulu War of 1879.

- Nodwengu was the Zulu capital during the reign of Mpande, the father of Cetshwayo. A site museum has been erected next to Mpande's grave in the developing centre of Ulundi.
- At KwaMatiwane lies the grave of the Voortrekker leader, Piet Retief, who, while visiting Dingane in his homestead, was clubbed to death and impaled along with 70 of his compatriots on the orders of Dingane in 1838.
- KwaGqokli Hill is the site of Shaka's first military success against the powerful Ndwandwe people in 1818. The original site may be seen from a lay-by on the new road (as yet unnamed).
- Siklebheni is the home and grave site of Senzangakhona, father of the three successive Zulu kings, Shaka, Dingane and Mpande.
- Nobamba was the homestead of kings Jama and Dinizulu, and is still considered to be one of the most sacred sites in the Emakhosini.
- Fort Nolela is where the British, under Lord Chelmsford, camped before crossing the river to engage with the Zulu in the final battle of the Anglo-Zulu War.
- kwaBulawayo was Shaka's first capital, and dates to about 1816.
- The Mthonjaneni spring was apparently Dingane's personal water source and is now a national monument – as is the nearby British fort.
- The Biyela ancestral site is a memorial to the founders of the Biyela group and the ancestral site of both the Biyela and Buthelezi groups who have played a significant role in Zulu history and politics.

• The Witvoloos Furnace Site is best known for the work of French Angus, a famous painter during Mpande's reign. Angus depicted scenes of Zululand – the most famous of which is of a blacksmith's furnace, which many historians believe to be the Witvoloos Furnace.

BATTLEFIELDS

There are any number of ways to go about touring the battlefields for which Zululand is famous. Either you can drive yourself to each site, or you can go to some of the battlefields by horse-back – which invokes a wonderfully authentic feel – or there are a number of excellent and experienced battlefields tour guides who will accompany you. Unless you have a fairly good understanding of the historical significance of the area, start with a basic tour. The events that took place on those battlefields approximately 120 years ago changed the course of South African history. On paper they are terribly thrilling, but many of the battlefields are little more than open grassland dotted with sad memorials, and, in order to make them come alive, you need a good guide who can conjure up the events in your imagination.

Rorke's Drift and Isandlwana

These two battle sites near Dundee need a knowledgeable historian or a good guide to really make them come alive – although it must be said that, at certain times of the day, a strange, rather sad feeling hangs over them and one can imagine the bloody aftermath of the ferocious fighting that took place here more than 120 years ago.

On 17 January 1879, the assembled Zulu army of about 20 000 warriors marched from Cetshwayo's capital at Ondini to confront the British army camped at Isandlwana. The British were overcome and the Zulu then moved on to attack the supply depot at Rorke's Drift. The British, however, had been warned by survivors from Isandlwana, and barricaded themselves in. Despite the fact that approximately 4 000 Zulu warriors continued to assault Rorke's Drift from mid-afternoon until after midnight, they could not dislodge the British soldiers, and the attack was finally called off.

There are any number of written accounts of these famous and decisive battles, but more immediately accessible are the model and audio-visual recreations of the various battles at the Rorke's Drift Museum. There is also a self-guided trail; for particulars, consult the information leaflet available from the museum. The original, thatched mission house at Rorke's Drift, which was used as a hospital during the battle, was rebuilt a few years later and now houses part of the Evangelical Lutheran Mission. The nearby Rorke's Drift Arts and Crafts Centre, started by the mission, has become very well known and you can buy a variety of excellent locally made crafts.

Rorke's View Guest House

If ghosts, horse trails through the battlefields, and Nguni cattle interest you, the Nebbes will be able to help. This young couple are farmers, who have started a horse trail through the Rorke's Drift and

17

Isandlwana battlefields. You do not need to know how to ride – Mark is a qualified riding instructor and his horses are accustomed to inexperienced riders – and seeing the battlefields by horseback is truly a unique experience. But, if that does not appeal, there are great walks around the farm, too. Mark and his father keep a herd of traditional Zulu Nguni cattle – there are also haunted caves on the farm (Zulu labourers are careful to avoid them at all costs). During the cold winter months the Nebbes light a fire in their small homely pub, and can keep you engrossed for hours with stories and anecdotes about the area and its people.

Easby Guest House

Easby is owned by Chris and Grietjie van Schalkwyk. It is not a home-stay in the traditional sense of the word but rather a B&B, but they are warm, welcoming and very knowledgeable about the area. The guesthouse is a charming, old house, which was occupied by General Louis Botha during the Anglo-Boer war in 1900. It was originally built by the Coventry family in 1897 and has had many owners since then, some of whom made rather odd alterations to this otherwise beautiful country home. Much of the home remains as it was at the time of General Louis Botha's occupation and, over a home-cooked South African meal, Chris can fill you in on all the details of both the house and the surrounding district – past and present – where he has spent much of his life. The house is conveniently situated between the battlefields and the Drakensberg mountains.

CULTURAL VILLAGES

In order to make some sense of Zulu history and provide some sort of context for your visit to Zululand, make a point of visiting one of the many cultural villages situated here.

The most reliable way to meet traditional people is via the staff of the cultural villages and, if you let them know beforehand, they may be able to arrange for someone to accompany you to one of the celebrations. The best times for traditional festivities are usually long weekends and holiday periods such as Easter and Christmas when the young men are home from the cities. It is at these times – before the men have to go back to work – that many people plan weddings and other ceremonies.

First prize in cultural experiences is a coming-of-age ceremony, wedding or traditional stick-fighting bout, but the areas in which most of the authentic ceremonies and celebrations take place are rather inaccessible to outsiders – it is not simply a matter of driving around until you find something. The dirt roads are often in poor condition, and the people – while hospitable and friendly – speak little English. An authentic experience may take some planning and, being in Africa, a little time.

Shakaland

Shakaland, originally the film set of the internationally acclaimed *Shaka Zulu*, is one of the better-known cultural villages. The tours – one in the morning and another in the late afternoon – usually start with an explanation of the layout of a traditional

Zulu homestead (or a kraal). These days, few people are likely to see people living in beehive homes, but the contemporary homesteads you see when driving around remain much the same in design. Shakaland also offers demonstrations of beadwork and pottery, and the chance to taste traditional beer and see how it is made. Today, most traditional communities use modern plastic or enamel containers rather than handmade clay pots, so it is largely the tourist trade that has helped prevent these skills from being lost.

Also seen here are the traditional ways of making spears and shields, skills which are, to a large extent, slowly disappearing and, here too is one of the few men still able to make the broad stabbing spear introduced by Shaka. The spear-throwing – remnants of warfare prior to Shaka's introduction of the stabbing spear – and stick-fighting demonstrations are elements seldom witnessed beyond the context of a rural wedding ceremony. Visitors are also given the chance to test their own spear-throwing skills.

iSangomas, who live in their own section of the village may 'throw the bones' for you, but remember there may be other opportunities to meet traditional healers in more authentic settings in other parts of the country. The highlight of a visit is, without a doubt, the foot-stomping, ground-shaking demonstrations of traditional dance forms which, although contrived for the tourists, provide an outstanding display and are thoroughly enjoyable entertainment.

The beehive homes – part of the original set for Shaka Zulu – have been renovated and today provide semi-ethnic overnight facilitates. The restaurant provides a selection of Western-style dishes as well Zulu specialities such as samp, beans, pumpkin, *mfenu* (a spinach-like dish) and *amaDumbe* (sweet potatoes).

Simunye

Simunye offers much the same programme as Shakaland, but the venue is smaller and more intimate. The setting, however, is quite breathtaking and the accommodation is an African fantasy. In some ways, Simunye feels more authentic but, at times, you may feel part of a magnificent African movie production. One of the highlights of the visit is a ride into the valley on horseback or by ox-wagon. On arrival at Simunye, a Zulu *impi* (battalion of warriors) baring flaming torches meets you at the entrance to the village. Light in the village is provided by hurricane lamps or candles as there is no electricity.

If you enquire beforehand and there are traditional celebrations happening in the area beyond the village, the staff – most of whom were born and raised in the surrounding region – will take you along to experience the real thing. Most staff members here are of the Biyela group, who have been closely associated with Zulu royalty since the times of the great warrior kings. The elders of the Biyela lineage are also perhaps one of the last repositories of Zulu oral history, and some of Simunye's staff are the grandchildren, great-grandchildren or at least distant relatives of famous Zulu warriors who participated in the fierce Anglo-Zulu wars.

17

DumaZulu

DumaZulu offers much the same experiences as Shakaland and Simunye in that it is a living museum where you are able to see how many traditional Zulu people live their daily lives, cooking, making beer, doing craftwork and dancing. There is also an indigenous snake pit and crocodile park which one would not normally find in any Zulu village. Both the snake pit and the crocodile park are fascinating and visitors have the chance to see animals they would probably not see in the wild. World-renowned anthropologist Graham Stewart and his team also conduct daily tours that try to capture the life and times of the Zulu nation during the reign of Shaka.

The accommodation represents different ethnic groups in southern Africa, including Zulu, Swazi, North Sotho, South Sotho, Xhosa, Venda, Tsonga, Ndebele and Tswana, and the decor reflects the handcrafts made by each of the different cultures. Some of the dwellings are modern versions of traditional homesteads, while others are painted in the traditional style of the group; all of them are comfortable and welcoming.

Isibindi Lodge

Although the up-market iSibindi Lodge is not a cultural village at all, it does provide an exciting and professional cultural experience. Just a stone's throw away from the lodge is a Zulu village where you can learn about the courageous struggle of the Zulu people to hold onto their culture and beliefs. Not only can guests participate in daily family activities – such as Zulu dancing and a traditional meal – but there is also the opportunity to tour the battlefields with an outstanding guide provided by the lodge.

HLUHLUWE-UMFOLOZI AREA

ARTS AND CRAFTS

There are plenty of places to buy craftwork throughout the province, but it is usually cheaper to buy from the source and, more often than not, that source is rural Zululand. There are many roadside craft stalls, but the quality of work is variable. When travelling north from Durban along the N2 – and especially when near the Mtubatuba area – look out for the roadside vendors with their woodcarvings, basketry and pottery.

Other informal, but slightly more organised, markets may be found at the entrances to many of the province's game reserves. As part of the neighbour relations programme of the KwaZulu-Natal Conservation Services, the organisation has been assisting women – and some men – to develop, not only their crafting skills, but, in some cases, also their business skills. Many of these projects have greatly empowered the impoverished rural Zulu women living near the game reserves, of whom many are the sole bread-winners for large families. The women, once disadvantaged and excluded from conservation and tourism, are now beginning to participate in these activities in a more meaningful manner.

Projects such as these also support and encourage the continued use of traditional skills. Items available from craft centres at the reserves' gates are usually considerably cheaper than those on sale at curio shops within the reserves or in towns that cater largely for the tourist market. Although most of the products sold at any of the craft centres are made by the women themselves or obtained locally, items from other areas – even other African countries – may also be purchased. If, however, you particularly want to support the locals, ask where the item was made – many pieces are inscribed with the crafter's name. Most of the craft centres carry similar ranges of products, but some places are better known for certain items. If you are looking for something specific and are travelling near any of the game reserves, consider the following:

- Mdletsheni Curios at Hluhluwe's Memorial Gate specialises in beadwork.
- Sodwana is well known for the beautiful coloured baskets woven by the locals.
- The people of St Lucia make exceptional Zulu beadwork and decorative mats.
- At Mkuze's Kwa-Jobe Village, you can get wooden platters and baskets.
- For sale at the Mambeni Gate at the Umfolozi section of the Hluhluwe-Umfolozi Park is the *amaQutha*, the beer baskets for which the women from the Hlabisa district have become world famous. They also sell fine embroidery.

The craft centres located outside the game reserves to the northwest specialise in other products:

- Weenen is well known for its clay pots.

- At Wagendrift you can buy traditional Zulu attire and wooden platters.
- Cathedral Peak in the Drakensberg is best known for baskets – as are Giant's Castle and Royal Natal (which also has some good beadwork).

There are no 'middle men' at these centres so profits go directly into the pocket of the individual artists, many of whom are supporting up to 15 people in their extended families. By supporting the centres, not only can you obtain some exquisite traditional Zulu arts and crafts at competitive prices, but you are also contributing to the previously disadvantaged communities.

Ilala Weavers

At the time that Ilala Weavers was established some 20 years ago, the traditions of Zulu women's handicrafts were in danger of dying out. Ilala Weavers has helped, and continues to help, rural Zulu women – and men – to utilise their skills to attain some level of self-sufficiency. The crafters all work from home and take their products to Ilala Weavers from where it is marketed, both locally and internationally. As well as continuing to make many traditional items, the women also craft modern products, such as woven lampshades, salad servers, key rings, pencil dolls and a wide range of fashion accessories, such as hats and scarves. In an adaptation of the traditional grass *imbenge* – a small, saucer-shaped bowl used to cover the clay beer pots – brightly coloured telephone wire is used, producing striking colour and pattern combinations. Ilala Weavers is packed with craftwork of immense skill and beauty, and there is always someone on hand to give you an explanation of what the items are and, if it is traditional, what it would be used for in a Zulu home. The items are sometimes quite a bit more expensive than they may be elsewhere, but the quality is outstanding. Attached to the shop is a great restaurant overlooking a garden of big, shady trees.

Mcunu B&B

The Mcunu household is the real thing – a polygynous Zulu home, and one of the most traditional you are likely to find. Initially assisted by a non-government organisation, but now operating alone, the two wives and their almost entirely female household (the husband is away most of the time, working on the mines), provide one of the most authentic rural home-stays in Zululand. The family is not native to the area, but were displaced from the Tugela Ferry district by faction fighting some time ago. Tugela Ferry is one of the real bastions of old Zulu culture, and the two women still adhere loyally to those traditions. To a large extent, they still even dress in the traditional fashion. On arrival at the small traditional homestead, visitors are usually met by the second wife and one of the teenage daughters. Few members of the family speak English, so the young school-going daughters – although very shy, in the traditional manner of Zulu women – act as translators. Guests are accommodated in a separate rondavel and, as a concession to Westerners, a small ablution block has recently been built. Family members will take you with them as they go about the daily chores, so you can milk the cows, feed chickens and even try your hand at ploughing behind the oxen. Visitors eat with the family, and attempts at communication are an entertainment in themselves. Breakfast is laid on and lunch or dinner may be provided – although the women need prior notice – and the food is the traditional fare the family would usually eat. You may not want to spend more than one night, but it provides a great excursion from the nearby Hluhluwe-Umfolozi Park.

The Shezi Homestead

Mrs Shezi is a widow who has opened her home to visitors. Both the Mcunus (see above) and the Shezis have kept their traditions and have been little influenced by the outside world. Living in such remote areas, the roads are bad and there are few services such as running water or electricity. Guests may visit the homestead for a traditional meal and a 'cultural programme' that includes a visit to a local school, dancing and meeting local people. Even though they may not speak English very well, they are extremely friendly and hospitable, and there is always someone on hand to translate. By visiting the Shezi family, you know you are sharing and contributing to the conservation of this warm and hospitable culture.

Songs of Zululand

Much of what tourists see of the Zulu people is presented in its historic context, but the unique and innovative Songs of Zululand project, undertaken by schools in the Mtubatuba region, gives visitors an opportunity to meet young, contemporary rural South Africans. Each day of the week, pupils from schools located along the road between the Hluhluwe-Umfolozi Park game reserve and the town of Mtubatuba, perform the songs and dances of Zululand at their schools.

The youngsters perform adaptations of songs and dances that once told stories of great warriors or preparations for battle, but nowadays – reflecting the transitions within traditional culture – tend to be about studying for exams and going to the city. The songs and dances they perform are the ones they would use in their day-to-day life, at weddings, church and other celebrations and festivities. These include *isicathamiya* (*see* page 152), Afro-gospel, *imbohohlo* (wedding songs), *izinyoni ezimhlope* (meaning 'white birds', and a modern form of music fusing old with new), *ingoma* (performed by boys and girls together), gumboot dancing (a modern form of *ingoma* developed on the Durban docks and transported to the mines; *see* page 153), and *indlamu* (a traditional dance, with drums and full traditional attire, most commonly associated with Zulu culture), and all are accompanied by explanations of their significance.

The project began in response to the request by school children to meet tourists. The schools are all well signposted and it is simply a matter of driving a short way off the main road to participate in the performances. The performances take place at a different school every day and usually begin at about 12h30. On arrival, visitors are met by the teachers, who are often willing to discuss life in the rural areas: what it is like to live without electricity, to be away from their own children who often live with grandparents in the city or elsewhere, where they studied and why they became teachers.

A reminder: Do not give money to the children. There is no charge for the shows, but donations are encouraged and donation boxes are located at each school. The money is administered by the Mtubatuba Publicity Association (*see* page 187) and goes towards school projects. In this way, both tourists and the pupils – and, therefore, the community – benefit.

ESTCOURT

Ikukhanya Kwelanga Village

Sandile Ndlovu, a traditional healer, runs this 'village' outside Estcourt, and has done much to promote and enhance the status of traditional healers in Zululand. He is head of the Zizamele Trust, an organisation of traditional healers with more 100 members and satellite committees in areas as far away as Bergville. Sandile has converted his homestead in one of the townships outside Estcourt into a 'cultural village', but – unlike most others – Ikukhanya Kwelanga is owned and run entirely by a Zulu. Together with a group of traditional healers, Sandile – who is extremely knowledgeable about indigenous flora – has planted a nursery growing medicinal plants that are fast becoming difficult to find in the wild, and visitors are welcome to tour the small nursery with him. He also works with the youth in the area and has put together a dance troupe to entertain his guests, who are accommodated either in authentic Zulu dwellings or in a more Western and urban version of a traditional homestead. There is also the chance to visit a local tavern, milk a cow, meet other traditional healers, meet the family, meet the neighbours (they may teach you a few Zulu words) and, in fact, meet just about everyone else in the small farming town of Estcourt. Sandile, it seems, knows everyone and everything.

DUNDEE

Blood River Monument

This is one of those many places scattered across the grasslands of Zululand between Dundee and Vryheid that echo with voices of ghosts from the past. The 64 great bronze ox-wagons marking the Blood River battlefield are arranged in the precise laager formation used by the Voortrekkers in 1838 when the massed impis of Dingane advanced, and were slaughtered in their thousands. The day, 16 December which used to be called 'The Day of the Vow' or 'Dingaan's Day', is still a public holiday in South Africa, but it is now more appropriately observed as the Day of Reconciliation. See also Voortrekker Museum on page 161.

Talana Museum and Miner's Rest tea shop

The Talana Museum, on the outskirts of Dundee, stands on the site of the Battle of Talana, the opening battle of the Anglo-Boer War. The museum consists of nine separate buildings with fascinating exhibits covering the early San hunter-gatherers through to the rise of the Zulu nation. During the great Zulu wars, many indigenous groups throughout southern Africa resorted to cannibalism during times of need and insecurity. Among the displays are exhibits of the extermination of the cannibals who lived at Biggarsberg, as well as Africana on the Boer War. Two of the museum buildings were used by the victorious British as dressing rooms during the Battle of Talana. Part of the complex is a restored miner's cottage, which has been turned into a charming tea shop where you can rest and order refreshments after a day under the African sun.

San Sites

The San lived in this area between 2 000 and 4 000 years ago and left behind reminders of their existence, in the form of art on the walls of rock shelters and caves. Since most of the rock art – and the Iron Age smelting sites – are unmarked, the Dundee Publicity Association (see page 187) can provide a guide who will take you to see them.

Valley of the Cannibals

In the early 1800s, in the scenic valleys around Rorke's Drift and Helpmekaar, lived the people who had fled from the ravages of the growing Zulu nation. They took refuge in the hills and turned to cannibalism to survive. Large groups, under the leadership of Hlupane, settled in the valleys and hills of this region. Nowadays, guided tours from the tourism office in Dundee take visitors to the Cannibal Caves, the Cannibal Rock and The Pantry.

LADYSMITH

Ladysmith Cultural Centre and Museum

Both the cultural centre and museum are housed in a restored Victorian home. There are a number of fascinating exhibits – including one devoted to the town's most acclaimed sons. The Ladysmith Black Mambazo Hall is dedicated to the choir that went on to become world famous. Life-size cut-outs of the group's members fill a mock stage and, as you enter, the music begins to play. There is a photographic record of their history and achievements, including pictures with American musician Paul Simon, and some of their major music awards are also on display. At the entrance to the centre is a Walk of Fame where all the members of the group have had their footprints set in cement for posterity.

Another room is set aside for Ladysmith's other great achievers, among them Sugarboy Malinga (once WBA boxing champion), Lallitha Jawahirilal (world-famous artist) and Veronica Abrahamse (Springbok athlete). There is also a small gallery where people from the area display their arts and crafts for sale, and a cultural depiction of people of the region at various times throughout history. The little centre has an enchanting community feeling and reflects the sense of pride of the people in the area.

Maria Ratschitz Mission Farm

Maria Ratschitz Mission has a rich, although somewhat sad, history and has seen some difficult and traumatic times. Currently owned by the Catholic Church, the mission was established in 1889 by two Trappist monks in a beautiful rural setting at the base of the Hlatikulu Mountain. Once a vibrant and active centre which survived the turbulent introduction of the 1913 Land Act that formed the basis of separating black and white South Africans, the mission fell into disrepair when the community it had served for so many years began to suffer under the apartheid laws. The biggest contributing factor was the forced removals in the late 1960s and early 1970s, when hundreds of people involved with the mission were compelled to leave the area. After 1975, without a viable community to serve, there was no longer a resident priest and the mission fell into decline. After 1991, however, political changes within the country meant that the centre could be redeveloped and, once again, play a significant role in the community. Today, the cathedral has been restored by dedicated craftsmen, and the buildings are being returned to their former glory. Services are held every Sunday, but the most stirring are those held during Easter and Christmas.

TOWNSHIP TOURS

For many years, people living in townships were excluded from the main activities of their nearby towns, but the town of Ladysmith is attempting to rectify this by organising tours through Ezakheni, Steadville, Umbulwana, Tsakane and Shayamoya townships.

Situated next to a large rural town, these townships differ considerably from those outside the big urban centres and have an atmosphere that is both rural and urban. During a tour to the rural townships, visitors may be invited to enter the homes, meet the people, eat a traditional home-cooked meal, drink Zulu beer, attend traditional ceremonies and even stay overnight with a township family. Organised tours usually start on Umbulwana Mountain where a guide will point out the indigenous trees and plants that are used by traditional healers.

In the past, Ezakheni, like many other townships, experienced much violence, but today it is peaceful and a fascinating place to visit. It is probably the only township in the country where a visitor can see, firsthand, the results of the freedom struggle and the political wars that rocked the region. In most other townships decimated by violence, houses have been rebuilt and re-occupied, but some of the houses in Ezakheni have been left as they were when the occupants fled in terror or after they were burnt to the ground. The people of Ezakheni say they want these ruined houses to be kept as a reminder of what they have been through – and of what they never want to go through again.

Be sure to ask the townsfolk about the area's flood disasters. Generally, it is the poorer communities who settle on the low-lying areas who are most affected by the terrible flash floods that periodically ravage areas of southern Africa. There is still some evidence of the most recent floods, and people here will tell you their heart-breaking stories.

BABANANGO

Stan's Pub

If you would like to meet local farmers, or even simply passers-by, Stan's Pub in Babanango is the place to stop for a beer and wholesome 'pub grub'. Apart from Stan – a colourful character himself – the pub is quite unusual. Attached to the small, five-roomed Babanango Hotel, it is crammed with bits and pieces – some interesting, some funny, some historic and some rather rude, but all colourful and reflecting, in some way, the character and culture of the people of the district.

MAPUTALAND

Maputaland is the northeastern region of KwaZulu-Natal. Its northernmost point is a magnificent chain of lakes, known as Kosi Bay, which border Mozambique, and in the west it is bound by the Lebombo mountains. To the east lies the warm Indian Ocean and, in the south, Lake St Lucia's estuary.

Although many people tend to include Maputaland with the rest of Zululand, the people living in the region come from different backgrounds and often consider themselves as quite separate. Today Maputaland is inhabited by an interesting mix of Thonga, Zulu, Swazi and a few white South Africans living at the interface between Old and New World cultures.

Their close proximity to both Swaziland and Mozambique makes the customs of the local inhabitants all the more interesting and colourful. In this rich mixture of peoples and cultural influences, it is not unusual to hear three or four different languages being spoken at a gathering.

In many areas, traditional customs and crafts are still practised, but the tarring of roads, infrastructural developments and modern technology have begun to have a profound (and inevitable) effect on some of the older cultural practices and traditions. Here you will find a microcosm of Africa's problems: a rapid increase in population numbers, emigration of labour, a lack of firewood, and a decrease in the quality of the grasslands. Maputaland is, however, still one of the most beautiful areas and, in terms of traditional African culture, it certainly rates as one of the most interesting.

For hundreds of years, people have harvested marine life along the beautiful stretches of beach that are also the ancient breeding grounds for leatherback and loggerhead turtles, and the coral reefs have provided an amazing variety of fish. Giant raffia palms, reeds growing around the numerous lakes and pans, and the lush dune forests have all provided natural resources on which local people have depended for centuries for food, building materials and medicine.

Although this is now slowly changing in the face of the onslaught of Western culture, Maputaland still offers unique opportunities for visitors to experience how the local people interface with their natural environment.

The Fonya (Fish Drive)

One of the most fascinating features of the area is the traditional *fonya* or fish drive. There are a number of pans in the region, some of which dry up completely during the drier winter months, but fill up again during the summer rains. In the old days – in winter or when the water levels were low – the men would gather and, armed with spears and the distinctive *fonya* baskets, head for the pans. A group of men would wade, waist-deep, into one end of the pan in a long row and 'beat' the water, driving the fish across the pan. When a shoal of fish was isolated, the men would use their baskets to trap them. The hole at the top of the *fonya* basket allowed the fishermen to grab, or sometimes stab, the fish while it was still in the water. These days, with the absence of men due to migrant labour, it is more often the women who organise a fish drive. But it is always a noisy and happy occasion, with the entire community taking part. *Fonyas* are seasonal and, because of this, they are not held on prescribed days or dates, so when you are in the area be sure to ask whether one is about to take place. If you are lucky enough to be there at the time, you won't be disappointed. The beautiful *fonya* baskets have become very popular with tourists and may be bought at some of the roadside craft 'stalls'.

Ilala Palm Wine

Apart from the majestic and massive raffia palms that once provided one of the prime sources of roofing materials – before the introduction of corrugated iron – another

177

useful palm growing in the area is the ilala, which is used for domestic handicrafts and from which is made the ilala palm wine for which the region is fast becoming famous.

Tapping *ubusulu*, or ilala palm wine, was the business of men, although, once again, in their absence, women have now become more involved. Tapping is extremely labour intensive. A healthy clump of ilala plants is selected, burnt and, some time later, the stems are trimmed. A funnel-shaped leaf is inserted into each stem, and the sap drips down into a calabash, tin or bottle. The plant is trimmed about three times a day over a period of five to seven weeks and, to protect the sap from insects, sun and rain, a little woven cover made from the ilala, called a *isiskhabakela*, is used. The sap does not need time to ferment, as it is alcoholic right away – but it does become stronger the longer it is left. It is a good source of vitamins and has played an important part in the diet of the locals. You will most likely be offered palm wine when visiting any of the Thonga people, but be warned – it may look like litchi juice and taste sweet and refreshing, but it should be approached with caution. Some of the local hotels and lodges offer tours or are able to arrange for you to visit some of the wine tappers (*see* Rocktail Bay Lodge and Kosi Forest Lodge on page 183).

Ancient Fish Kraals or Traps

The Zulu are very often associated with their Nguni cattle and are not well known as fishermen. The Thonga people of Maputaland, however, are highly regarded as skilled fishermen, and their fish kraals and traps could well date back to prehistoric times.

Almost sculptural in their simple beauty, the fish kraals built in the clear waters of Kosi Bay consist of a fence of thin poles and woven reeds placed in the water in such a way that fish are guided into the circular 'kraal' and trapped there. The fishermen check their traps at particular times of the day and spear any fish caught inside.

There are very few new fish kraals, as most have been handed down and maintained by a single family for generations. Most are still is use on a daily basis, and visitors may even be lucky enough to see a fisherman knee deep in the water clearing his traps. As with the ilala wine tappers, some of the local hotels and lodges will take visitors by boat to see the fish traps.

ARCHAEOLOGY

Although there is ample evidence of Maputaland's early inhabitants – perhaps even pre-dating the early Stone Age – until recently, not much has been done about preserving sites of archaeological importance. The result is that although there are sites of great interest, not many are accessible to the general public. However, if you are interested in visiting some of the places off the beaten track, ask one of the conservation officers from the KwaZulu-Natal Conservation Services' game reserves or the staff of the local museums at Eshowe, Stanger and Ulundi who will point you in the right direction. Alternatively, visit places such as the shell middens containing early Stone Age pottery south of the

Enkwazini in St Lucia Bay or Border Cave, but remember that if you are fortunate enough to have the opportunity to visit any of these places, it is a crime to touch or remove any of the artefacts.

MEETING THE PEOPLE

It is not always easy to meet rural communities or get to know the people and their traditions. One of the best ways is to stay at least one night at one of the few lodges in the area, where staff know the nearby local inhabitants and can take you to meet them. Some of the lodges have made a point of supporting their rural neighbours and including them in tourist activities.

Rocktail Bay Lodge

Situated south of Kosi Bay, Rocktail Bay Lodge – magnificently located near Rocktail Bay beach – offers its guests opportunities to meet the rural locals. Andy Coetzee, who runs the lodge, has a very firm opinion on cultural tourism and is sensitive to the many problems that can arise. Andy or one of his staff members will drive you through the nearby homesteads, and will point out the effects that Western culture, the migrant labour system, and formal conservation are having on the rural communities. You may also have the chance to visit the home of a traditional healer, and stop at a rural spaza shop, where there are seldom more than 10 items from which to choose – although one will inevitably be an ice-cold beer (one of the great phenomena of Maputaland is that you can always find a cold beer). You

will see ilala palm wine tappers (see page 182) and possibly be able to taste some wine. In the pans near Rocktail Bay Lodge, local fishermen build the *isilulu*, a smaller and rather different version of the Kosi Bay fish traps (see page 182), made from natural reeds harvested in the area and used to catch tiny barbel and other indigenous fish. Near to Rocktail Bay Lodge is a swampy area, where visitors can sometimes spot the odd hippo.

Because turtles were fast becoming endangered, local people are no longer allowed to harvest turtles or their eggs along this stretch of coast, and a very successful research programme has been in place for about 20 years. Rocktail Bay has been supporting the monitoring programme and, during turtle breeding season, visitors to the lodge may be taken along when Rocktail Bay staff go on their nightly monitoring drives and actually witness the ancient ritual of turtles coming up the beach to lay their eggs in the dunes.

Kosi Forest Lodge

Kosi Forest Lodge also offers access to local customs. Although it is not close to the beach, a short drive and a walk past a magnificent stand of giant raffia palms – still harvested by the locals – will take you right to Kosi Lake. Staff will ferry you in a small motorised boat to see the ancient fish traps at the estuary and there are also 'palm wine tours' to visit a local 'tapper' – more than likely, a charming old gentleman who has been tapping ilala palm wine for years. Although his English is rather limited, he has a wonderful repertoire of stories which are translated by the staff. If he is not available, the lodge staff – all are from the area – will take you to meet someone equally interesting and you will be able to taste the ilala palm wine (see page 182).

Kosi Bay Community Camp

This small camp was established by the local black communities living on the peninsula that divides the Kosi Lake system from the sea. The camp is centred around the shack used by the late David Webster, an anthropologist activist who was murdered at his home in Johannesburg by members of the notorious apartheid hit squads in the late 1980s. The communities here played an important role in the struggle against oppression when they fiercely resisted attempts to remove them from the land their forefathers had inhabited for more than 700 years. The original idea was that the villagers would establish and eventually run a tourist camp themselves – and would thus not be removed. Not only is the camp situated in one of the country's most beautiful, unspoilt natural areas, but it also provides the opportunity to talk to many of the locals who knew or worked with David Webster and who were involved in the resistance campaigns. Community members have been trained as turtle tour guides and many of the families who own the ancient fish traps of Kosi Bay live on the peninsula. You can arrange to visit one of the villages – have a meal, drink ilala wine, and hear the stories of the struggle.

KWAZULU-NATAL DIRECTORY

KWAZULU-NATAL
GENERAL

Tourist Junction (Durban Tourism Office), First Floor, Old Station Building, 160 Pine Street, Durban; tel: (031) 304-4934, fax: (031) 304-6196, e-mail: funinsun@iafrica.com

DURBAN
TOWNSHIP TOURS

KwaMuhle Museum (see Museums and Galleries on this page)

The Gandhi Settlement (see Tourist Junction above)

The Ohlanga Institute and Rev John Dube's Grave (see Tourist Junction above)

Hamba Kahle Tours (see Tourist Junction above); tel: (031) 305-5586

Basil Xaba, cell: 083 439 3194

Tekweni EcoTours, 169 9th Avenue, Florida Road, Morningside, 4000; tel: (031) 303-1199

SHEBEENS AND TAVERNS

Grace Ntombela, contact Basil Xaba or Hamba Kahle Tours (see Township Tours above)

All in One, contact Hamilton or Dakie Mchunu; tel: (031) 707-3202

Skhona's Tavern, tel: (031) 906-2238 (see also Tourist Junction above)

Nomalady's Tavern, contact Mrs Mokwe; tel: (031) 400-0993

Sibisi's Tavern (see Tourist Junction above)

Bafuthi's Tavern (see Tourist Junction above)

Thobile Tuck Shop (see Tourist Junction above)

MUSIC AND DANCE

Isicathamiya, YMCA, Beatrice Street, Durban; tel: (031) 309-3857

Gumboot Dancing (see Tourist Junction above)

The Playhouse Company, 231 Smith Street, Durban; tel: (031) 369-9555

The Bartle Arts Trust (BAT) Hall (see Bartle Arts Trust (BAT) Centre below)

The Folk Club, The Tusk Inn, Sarnia Road, Seaview; tel: (031) 567-0326

Jubes, contact Mfana Mlabo, cell: 083 779 3777

Nu Jazz Centre, Jazz Department, University of Natal, Durban; tel: (031) 260-3385

The Rainbow Restaurant, contact Ben Pretorius; tel: (031) 702-9161

The Tree House, contact Steve Fataar; tel: (031) 44-1195

MUSEUMS AND GALLERIES

KwaMuhle Museum, 130 Ordinance Road, Durban; tel: (031) 300-6310

The Campbell Collections, 22 Marriot Road, Berea; tel: (031) 207-3432, fax: (031) 207-3711

Time Warp Museum, Ocean Sports Centre, 190 Lower Marine Parade, Durban; tel: (031) 368-5842

Durban Cultural and Documentation Centre, corner Epsom Road and Derby Street, Greyville; tel: (031) 309-7559, fax: (031) 309-7088

KwaZulu-Natal Society of Arts (KNSA) and the Durban Centre for Photography (DCP), 166 Bulwer Road, Glenwood; tel: (031) 202-2293

The African Art Centre (see Tourist Junction on this page); tel: (031) 304-7915

Andrew Walford's Shongweni Pottery Gallery, contact Andrew Walford; tel: (031) 769-1363

The Bartle Arts Trust (BAT) Centre (and BAT Hall), contact Neil Comfort; tel: (031) 332-0468/0451 (BAT Centre), tel: (031) 337-8451 (BAT Hall)

PLACES OF WORSHIP

Jumma Musjid Mosque (Grey Street Mosque), corner Grey and Queen streets, Durban; tel: (031) 307-4786

Ebuhleni (Shembe Church), (see Tourist Junction on this page); tel: (031) 507-3599

18

Holy Church of Nazareth Baptists (Shembe Church) (see Tourist Junction on page 185)
Temple of Understanding, Bhaktieedanta Sami Road, Chatsworth; tel: (031) 403-3367/3328
Shree Amalvanar Alayam Second River Temple, Bellair Road, Bellair, Durban.
Mariannhill Monastery and Guest House, take Exit 23 off the N3 to Pinetown and Mariannhill, and follow the signs; tel: (031) 700-4288 (monastery), tel: (031) 700-2059 (guesthouse)

MARKETS

The Early Morning Market, Victoria Street Market, Fish Market, Warwick Street Triangle and **Muti Market** are all in the Warwick Street/ Victoria Street area and within walking distance of each other.
Dalton Road Traditional Market, Dalton Road, Umbilo

PIETERMARITZBURG & THE MIDLANDS
GENERAL

Pietermaritzburg Tourism, 177 Commercial Road, Pietermaritzburg; tel: (0331) 45-1348, fax: (0331) 94-3535, e-mail: ppa@futurenet.co.za
Tour Guide Association, contact chairman Evan Jones for information on local guides; tel/fax: (0331) 44-3260
The Midlands Meander, (see Pietermaritzburg Tourism above)

MUSEUMS AND GALLERIES

Tatham Art Gallery, Commercial Street; tel: (0331) 42-1804
Voortrekker Museum, cnr. Longmarket and Boshoff streets; tel: (0331) 94-6834
Natal Museum, 237 Loop Street; tel: (0331) 45-1404

CULTURAL VILLAGES

Ecabazini Zulu Cultural Homestead, PO Box 13351, Cascades, Pietermaritzburg 3202; tel/fax: (0331) 42-1928, 082 955 1404 (cell)

MARKETS

Alexander Park markets, contact Monica Ash, tel: (0331) 6-5055, or see Pietermaritzburg Tourism on this page
Victoria Street Farmers' Market (see Pietermaritzburg Tourism on this page)
Art in the Park (see Pietermaritzburg Tourism on this page)

MEET THE PEOPLE

Nottingham Road Hotel and Pub, PO Box 26, Nottingham Road 3280; tel: (0333) 3-6151
Ixopo Buddhist Retreat, PO Box 131, Ixopo 3276; tel: (0336) 34-1863

DRAKENSBERG

Drakensberg Tourism Association, tel: (036) 448-1557
Winterton Museum, Church Street, Winterton, 3340; tel: (036) 488-1620
Mambasa Hutted Camp, contact Renée Stockil, tel: (036) 488-1003, fax: (036) 488-1116
The Drakensberg Meander (see Drakensberg Tourism Association above)
KwaZulu-Natal Conservation Services, Reservations Office (San paintings), PO Box 13069, Cascades, Pietermaritzburg 3202; tel/fax: (0331) 845-1000
Natal Museum, Archaeological Service (in-depth archaeological information), 237 Loop Street, Pietermaritzburg; tel: (0331) 45-1404, fax: (0331) 45-0561
Drakensberg Boys' Choir, The Rector, Private Bag X20, Winterton 3340; tel: (036) 468-1012/3/4, fax: (036) 468-1709

Splashy Fen Music Festival, tel: (031) 23-9812, fax: (031) 23-1605

Ardmore Ceramic Art Studio and Guesthouse, PO Box 1005, Winterton 3340; tel/fax: (036) 468-1314

KwaZamokhule, Private Bag X7008, Estcourt 3310; tel/fax: (0363) 33-5519

Dioconic Handcraft Centre, PO Box 108, Estcourt 3310; tel/fax: (0363) 2-4752

ZULULAND
GENERAL

Dundee Publicity Association, Civic Gardens, Victoria Street, Dundee; tel: (0341) 2-2121, fax: (0341) 2-3856

Ladysmith Tourism Information, PO Box 29, Ladysmith 3370; contact Thami Cele, tel/fax: (0361) 2-2992

KwaZulu-Natal Conservation Services, PO Box 1602, Mtubatuba 3935; tel/fax: (035) 550-0569; or PO Box 13069, Cascades, Pietermaritzburg 3202; tel: (0331) 845-1999

African Sky Tours, PO Box 521, Estcourt 3310; tel/fax: (0363) 24688

KwaZulu Monuments Council, contact Barry Marshall, The Director, PO Box 523, Ulundi 3838; tel: (0358) 70-2050/1/2/5, fax: (0358) 70-2054

Heritage Trust (see KwaZulu Monuments Council above)

HISTORICAL AND ARCHAEOLOGICAL SITES

For information on the historical and archaeological sites in Stanger/Dukuza, Emakhosini, uMgungundlovu, Ondini, the Valley of the Cannibals and Ulundi and surrounds, contact the KwaZulu Monuments Council or the Heritage Trust (see Zululand, General above).

BATTLEFIELDS

Rorke's Drift Museum, PO Rorke's Drift 3016; tel: (034) 642-1687

Rorke's Drift Arts and Crafts Centre, PO Rorke's Drift 3016, tel: (034) 642-1687

There are a number of accredited tour guides who conduct tours to Rorke's Drift, Isandlwana and other battlefields, and a list can be obtained from the tourist bureau in each centre. For additional information, contact **David Rattray** (considered to be one of the best guides), tel: (013) 752-6259, fax: (013) 752-8146; **Evan Jones**, tel/fax: (0331) 44-3260; **Dudu Manyathi**, tel: (034) 271-1900 (ext. 2277) or (034) 271-9710; **Kenneth Buthelezi**, tel: (034) 271-0634

Rorke's View Guest House (battlefields and horse trails), PO Box 683, Dundee 3000; contact Mark Nebbe, tel: (034) 642-1741, fax: (034) 642-1654

Easby Guest House, PO Box 465, Bergville 3350; contact Chris and Grietjie van Schalkwyk, tel/fax: (036) 448-1128

CULTURAL VILLAGES

Shakaland, PO Box 103, Eshowe 3815; tel: (03546) 912, fax: (03546) 824

Simunye (see Shakaland above)

DumaZulu, PO Box 79, Hluhluwe 3960; tel: (035) 562-0144, fax: (035) 562-0205

iSibindi Lodge, contact the iSibindi Eco Reserve, PO Box 124, Dundee 3000; tel/fax: (034) 642-1620

HLUHLUWE-UMFOLOZI AREA
ARTS AND CRAFTS

For information on the craft centres associated with the game reserves, contact Paula Morrison, Community Conservation Co-ordinator: Zululand (see KwaZulu-Natal Conservation Services on this page)

Ilala Weavers, PO Box 195, Hluhluwe 3960; tel:
(035) 562-0630/1, fax: (035) 562-0361
Mcunu B&B, contact Paula Morrison, Community
Conservation Co-ordinator: Zululand (see KwaZulu-
Natal Conservation Services on page 187)
The Shezi Homestead, contact Paula Morrison,
Community Conservation Co-ordinator: Zululand
(see KwaZulu-Natal Conservation Services on
page 187)
Mtubatuba Publicity Association (Songs of
Zululand), PO Box 81, Mtubatuba 3935; tel:
(035) 550-0781, fax: (035) 550-0721

ESTCOURT

Ikukhanya Kwelanga, contact Sandile Ndlovu,
cell: 083 475 0557 (see also African Sky Tours
on page 187)

DUNDEE

See Dundee Publicity Association on page 187
Blood River Monument, tel: (0346321) 695
Talana Museum, tel: (0341) 22654, fax: (0341)
2-2376
San Sites, see Dundee Publicity Association on
page 187

LADYSMITH

See Ladysmith Tourism Information on page 187
Ladysmith Cultural Centre and Museum, The
Curator, PO Box 29, Ladysmith, 3370; tel: (0361)
2-2231, fax: (0361) 2-2992
Maria Ratschitz Mission, tel: (0361) 32-3074

BABANANGO

Stan's Pub, 16 Justice Street, Babanango 3850; tel:
(0358) 35-0027

MAPUTALAND
GENERAL

Hluhluwe Tourism Association, PO Box 399,
Hluhluwe 3960; tel: (035) 562-0353

ARCHAEOLOGY

KwaZulu Monuments Council and Heritage
Trust, contact Barry Marshall; The Director, PO Box
523, Ulundi 3838; tel: (0358) 70-2050/1/2/5, fax:
(0358) 70-2054
KwaZulu-Natal Conservation Service, PO Box
13069, Cascades, Pietermaritzburg 3200; tel/fax:
(0331) 845-1000
Natal Museum, Archaeological Service (in-depth
archaeological information), 237 Loop Street,
Pietermaritzburg; tel: (0331) 45-1404, fax: (0331)
45-0561

MEETING THE PEOPLE

Rocktail Bay Lodge, PO Box 5219, Rivonia 2128;
tel: (011) 807-1800, fax: (011) 807-210, e-mail:
enquiry@wilderness.co.za
Kosi Forest Lodge, PO Box 275, Umhlali 4390; tel:
(0322) 947-1538 (bookings), tel: (035592) 92197
(lodge)
Kosi Bay Community Camp, tel: (031) 791-0178
(bookings), tel: (031) 21-3126 (The Wildlife Society,
which takes bookings on behalf of the community)

INDEX